THE EMERGENCE OF MODERN MARKETING

D0306283

Editors

ROY CHURCH
ANDREW GODLEY

FRANK CASS
LONDON • PORTLAND, OR

First published in 2003 in Great Britain by
FRANK CASS AND COMPANY LIMITED
Crown House, 47 Chase Side,
Southgate, London N14 5BP, England

and in the United States of America by
FRANK CASS
c/o International Specialized Book Services, Inc.
5824 N.E. Hassalo Street, Portland, Oregon 97213-3644

Website: www.frankcass.com

British Library Cataloguing in Publication Data

The emergence of modern marketing
1. Marketing – History – 19th century 2. Marketing – History
– 20th century
I. Church, R.A. (Roy Anthony), 1935– II. Godley, Andrew
658.8'009034

ISBN 0 7146 5390 X (cloth)
ISBN 0 7146 8326 4 (paper)

Library of Congress Cataloging-in-Publication Data

The emergence of modern marketing / editors, Roy Church, Andrew Godley.
    p. cm.
Includes bibliographical references (p.) and index.
    ISBN 0-7146-5390-X (cloth) – ISBN 0-7146-8326-4 (paper)
    1. Marketing–History. I. Church, Roy A. II. Godley, Andrew, 1963–
    HF5415 .E614 2003
    380.1'09–dc21   2002151434

This group of studies first appeared in a Special Issue of *Business History*
(ISSN 0007-6791), Vol.45, No.1 (January 2003) [*The Emergence of Modern Marketing*].

Printed in Great Britain by
MPG Books Limited, Bodmin, Cornwall

Contents

The Emergence of Modern Marketing: International Dimensions

ROY CHURCH and ANDREW GODLEY

University of East Anglia
University of Reading

In entitling this collection of essays 'The Emergence of Modern Marketing' we are referring to the characteristics of *persistent, systematic, and increasingly widespread* marketing methods adopted by businesses from the nineteenth century onwards. In addition to selling, therefore, the term includes advertising, branding, pricing, promotion, market research, and product planning and development, all of which figure in the articles that follow. 'Modern marketing' also encompasses increasingly complex distribution systems, another major theme developed by several authors in this collection. In the history of modern business, historians have paid much greater attention to the emergence of the modern corporate form and managerial structures, technological innovation, and business finance, than to marketing. To a large extent this reflects the ambivalence of economists in treating the subject of marketing, tending to emphasise causal relationships with industrial concentration and therefore its anti-competitive aspect, though the degree has varied, even in recent times, between industries, market segments, and countries. But even if advertising expenditures are interpreted as barriers to market entry, they may be regarded in the same light as other fixed costs.[1] Historically, certainly before World War II, firms which succeeded in clearing the barrier, especially when in conjunction with the introduction of a new product or brand, have become competitors, in many cases replacing existing market leaders.

Theorists of international business have adapted the transaction costs framework to emphasise that contractual relations dealing with firm-specific assets, such as product brands and reputation, show that transferring such assets between countries is costly. Given that a firm's reputation, or added value incorporated in its brand, represents tangible assets, effective pricing becomes hazardous and increases the risk of opportunistic behaviour among contracting parties. Transaction costs theory strongly suggests that much multinational activity in the past has been led by marketing rather than by technology.[2] This is the framework in which Kim has offered a reinterpretation of the rise of the corporate form in the USA. Using census data, Kim's analysis is the first systematic attempt to understand why some firms in some industries possessing many plants and employing a majority of the workforce grew to dominate the American economy. His conclusion challenges the Chandlerian emphasis on the technical economies of scale and scope. He concludes that when looking at nation-wide statistics (rather than selected case studies of a few of the very largest enterprises), economies in marketing emerge as the most important determinant in explaining the emergence of the modern multi-unit business enterprise.[3] This seminal reinterpretation of the rise of big business underlines the importance for historians of seeking a deeper understanding of the determinants and impact of modern advertising, and of the links historically between the various dimensions of marketing activity relating production, product development, branding, advertising, distribution, and other strategies. It is therefore timely to reconsider the role of marketing in the emergence of the modern enterprise.

This collection of essays begins with the simplest and earliest case of marketing by an entrepreneur who was female and French, and who at the beginning of the nineteenth century began to develop marketing methods which are identifiably modern. Pilbeam's account of the history of Madame Taussaud's waxwork exhibitions reveals their origins to have been her own craft as a sculptor in wax and the inheritance in 1794 of a wax exhibition in Paris (for which the models were the live or dead bodies of their subjects) which she had helped to manage with the former owner. Her entry, first as a minor partner with a magic lantern showman in England in 1802, and almost immediately thereafter as an independent touring entrepreneur with her waxwork models, had an enduring impact on the British entertainment industry and established her business's international reputation and customer base. That was constructed on sustained motivation (from need) to make money, craft skills, and an extraordinary flair for publicity. A successful cultivation of a reputation through connections with high society, effective advertising, and a shrewd reading of the taste and life style of middle class consumers was the key to her success. This flair informed decisions concerning both the premises chosen for display and the selection of models most likely to appeal: a combination of royalty, witches, and horror, as well as an eye for the topical. Tussaud was the classic entrepreneur, combining the roles of producer, packer, financier, promoter, and travelling saleswoman. In the 1830s, however, when the transport revolution justified a fixed location in London, her exhibition became a national business institution resident in London; distribution ceased to present a problem.

The larger size, multi-product, and multiple product lines manufactured by leading British and American companies investigated by Church and Clark and by Sally Clarke highlight two (among other) important themes. One focuses on the problem of deciding which products or product lines to manufacture; the other on relationships with distributors. Two of the enterprises examined in Church and Clark's study of J. & J. Colman, Reckitt & Sons, and Lever Bros. also began as single owner-managed businesses formed in the early nineteenth century. The focus, however, is upon their later development as family-dominated limited liability companies, together with Lever Bros., which during the inter-war period was transformed from an owner-entrepreneurial business to

Britain's largest corporate and increasingly bureaucratic multinational manufacturing company. The greater complexity involved in fulfilling the entrepreneurial function in these three firms is demonstrated in the analysis of the processes by which product diversification occurred. The comparison between the three firms reveals the similarities, regardless of size, structure, and organisation, of the centrality of decisions regarding the products the companies should produce; this was during a period of economic depression and stagnation in the markets for some of the companies' products. In each case, this took the form of increasingly systematic, formalised strategies leading to the organisation of new product committees and market research. All three consulted professional advertising agencies which supplied market surveys relating to products or categories of products. The importance of distributors is revealed at the point when Reckitt & Sons diversified into pharmaceuticals, thus risking the company's long-established good relations with grocers by establishing connections with chemists and druggists.

In Sally Clarke's analysis of General Motors' marketing policies between the wars, distribution is the central problem created by the tensions between buyers and sellers: manufacturers, dealers, and consumers. This arose because typically, when consumers purchased a vehicle, the transaction included not only exercising choice on the attributes, real and supposed, of the product, but also trading in a second-hand vehicle and credit finance. These involved costs arising from mismatches between production and dealers' orders and from used car trade-ins intended to increase sales. Financing yielded interest payments. Her analysis of the tensions arising from these market transactions between the three parties involved reveals the efforts each made to ensure that the burdens or benefits were distributed to their respective advantage. However, the exercise of corporate power by General Motors ensured that advantage was taken of franchised dealers who, in turn, manipulated negotiations with consumers to their advantage regarding trade-ins and finance in relation to price. In extending its controlling approach to the British market, the multinational manufacturing company, General Motors, was more typical of foreign entrants into retailing in Britain. This is one of the findings of Godley's comprehensive examination of innovations throughout British retailing between the mid-nineteenth and mid-twentieth centuries. His study shows that of the many foreign entrants into British retailing over the period since 1850, the majority were not retailers, but foreign manufacturers of branded consumer goods who entered the British retail trade in order to overcome the limitations of incumbent independent British retailers. Moreover, and despite several well-known cases, the overall impact of these foreign multinationals on British retailing remained muted. This stands out in clear contrast both to the innovative activity present in British retailing generally at the time, as well as when compared with the diffusion of new technological innovations into British manufacturing introduced by foreign multinationals. Godley concludes that retailers depend especially on less tangible advantages that have been and remain difficult to translate into different cultures.

Cultural differences shaping markets is a theme present in Bakker's demonstration of the emergence of market research in the motion picture industry, a subject also pursued by Church and Clark in relation to manufactured products. However, Bakker compares the marketing of film, which intuitively might appear to be completely different from the problem of marketing manufactured products, with the marketing of fashion goods. He characterises the industry as one which depended upon the constant launching of new products, rather than (as in the case of manufactured consumer goods) of frequent, or moderately frequent, introductions of new products or extension of product lines. The use of market research, in British industries at least, has been an under-researched area which Bakker's enlighteningly detailed account of market segmentation and the systematisation of market research leads to the conclusion that the film industry was a pioneer in appreciating the subtleties and implementation of this strategy. His article also confirms the importance, early in the history of film, of advertising based on the findings of market research.

In Germany, techniques and application of market research and advertising lagged far behind developments in the USA and Britain during the inter-war years. Although the Nazi state, in which campaign-style advertising was a major feature, intervened for purely political purposes, Berghoff's study of the relationships between the advertising industry, professional self-interest, and state control in the Third Reich reveals how professional advertisers welcomed other aspects of intervention. These were the introduction of order through structural and organisational reform, of standards through registration policed by an Advertising Council, of price control, and of professionalisation through education and training. The trade-offs consisted of consumer control and a set of cultural-political guidelines to promote 'Germanic advertising' which, in Berghoff's judgement, produced a net regression in the industry.

The essays which follow encompass an international range and diversity revealing some important aspects of the processes through which modern marketing emerged. Themes present in at least two of these explore aspects of product diversification, product development, selling, branding, advertising goods and entertainment, as well as connections between producers and consumers with market research, regulation, and distribution. In addition to the common themes and diversity of experiences offered in these substantive accounts of the history of marketing, they prompt a broader reflection. They offer a warning to those accustomed to reading, and seeking wholly rational narratives of business history. We believe that theory is a necessary basis for explaining business processes at the most general level and that it justifies the use of neo-classical and evolutionary models and of concepts such as transaction costs, strategy structure, scale, and scope. Theory, however, is not always sufficient for historical understanding. The influence of inherited resources and the role of agency are necessary to understand changes through real time and to proceed beyond generalisation. Whether based on contemporary accounts or on theory-based backward projections, without detailed historical and archival research of the kind presented here, a presumption of rationality and/or structural determinism runs the risk of mistaking plausible explanations for the construction of a more complicated – and richer – historical actuality.

NOTES

1. See J. Sutton, *Sunk Cost and Market Structure: Price Competition, Advertising, and the Evolution of Concentration* (Cambridge, MA and London, 1991), especially Part III and IV. See also a review of the literature from a historian's perspective in R. Church, 'New Perspectives on the History of Products, Firms, Marketing, and Consumers in Britain and the United States since the Mid-Nineteenth Century', *Economic History Review*, Vol.52 No.3 (1999).
2. M.C. Casson, 'Transaction Costs and the Theory of the Multinational Enterprise', in A.M. Rugman (ed.), *New Theories of Multinational Enterprise* (London, 1982).
3. S. Kim, 'The Growth of Modern Business Enterprises in the Twentieth Century', *Research in Economic History*, Vol.19 (1999); and idem, 'The Rise of Multiunit Firms in U.S. Manufacturing', *Explorations in Economic History*, Vol.36 No.9 (1999).

Madame Tussaud and the Business of Wax:
Marketing to the Middle Classes

PAMELA PILBEAM

Royal Holloway, University of London

Wax has been used to represent the human body for more purposes than any other medium, from the crafting of saints and demons to necro-erotic fantasies. It has been crafted into funeral effigies since at least 3000 BC. Body parts have traditionally been made of wax for medical and surgical training. Wax shows probably have the longest history of entrepreneurial entertainment, and certainly the longest history of women both making models and running wax businesses. Wax has never known class barriers; it has always been part of high and low culture. During the eighteenth century there were a number of wax touring shows and exhibitions in London, often run by women like Mrs Salmon, Clark and Bullock, who ran businesses with their husbands and continued as widows. They catered for the sort of popular audience that would also be amused by the assortment of grotesque and glamorous wax figures displayed at fairs. The use of wax bodies and body parts for training doctors became the norm from the sixteenth century. Michelangelo and others both studied anatomy and made anatomical waxes. In the seventeenth century the Italian G.C. Zumbo began to paint his models. During the eighteenth century, the surgeons Pinson and Desnoués made anatomical waxes that were so seductively elegant and erotic that they became collectors' items. The duc d'Orléans amassed a large collection that was inherited by the School of Medicine in Paris after he was executed in 1793. The skilled surgeon-sculptor, Desnoués, sold his figures in exhibitions, such as that of Rackstrow in Fleet Street.

From the seventeenth century, European wax sculptors were producing not merely the wax kings made since the fourteenth century for funeral processions and wax holy figures for churches, but models for the rich to buy for their homes. The Frenchman, Benoîst, made figures both at the court of Louis XIV and at that of Charles II and the later Stuarts. In eighteenth-century England, a number of women sculpted in wax for an elite audience, including the American Patience Wright and Catherine Andras. Mrs Andras' work was shown at the Royal Academy and one of her models is still on display in Westminster Abbey.[1] From 1770, Philippe Curtius made wax the height of Paris fashion in his 'wax salons' in the two most popular centres of the entertainment industry at the time, the Palais Royal and the Boulevard du Temple. Curtius' wax salon has been applauded as 'the greatest show in pre-revolutionary Paris, the centre of a renaissance of marketplace culture'.[2] Wax models fitted the cultural experimentation and variety of that period.

Madame Tussaud began her career as a sculptor in wax in Paris in the 1780s as Marie Grosholz, niece, possibly daughter, of Philippe Curtius. Her mother was his house-keeper. During the 1789 Revolution Curtius and Grosholz prospered, modelling death masks from actual guillotined heads. As the violence and terror escalated, the entertainment industry lost custom. Foreign visitors, who had loved the wax salon, stayed away and French families moved to their country estates. Curtius' artisan customers at his 'Caverne of the Great Thieves' in the Boulevard du Temple were hard hit by the severe war-time economic crisis: the rich no longer bought expensive furniture, clothes, jewellery, and so on. In addition, Curtius failed to keep abreast of the Terror and was reviled for displaying models whose originals had been condemned by the revolutionary leaders.[3] Curtius, and later Marie, sent their more glamorous royal and aristocratic models, which were politically unacceptable in the Revolution, on tour to India, Britain, and Germany. On his death in 1794 Curtius left all his property, including his wax exhibition, to Marie. In 1795, at 34, she married François Tussaud, eight years her junior, an engineer with aspirations to be a theatre entrepreneur. By 1800 Marie had given birth to three children, the eldest of whom, a daughter, died. In 1802, Marie seized the chance of the Peace of Amiens to lead a tour to Britain. The British economy was prosperous and its leisure industry, free from the direct economic impact of war, was still buoyant. Marie was, in her own words, in need of 'a full purse'[4] before she could return to Paris, but her letters home reveal that poor relations with her husband influenced her decision to take the unusual step of leaving her younger son to embark on her first foreign tour.

Madame Tussaud's entry into the British entertainment industry was modest. She came to Britain as a minor partner of Philipstal and his Phantasmagoria, a magic lantern show. Philipstal had performed at the Lyceum theatre, on the corner of the Strand, the previous year and took a lease for a second season. He offered Marie the lower floor for her models. The terms were poor, their agreement guaranteed that 50 per cent of Marie's profits would go to Philipstal and that he would cover advertising and transport costs. Marie calculated that he had more experience of the English market than she had, and took the gamble that, even on disadvantageous terms, she was likely to do better business in England than in Paris.

In Paris, Marie and Curtius had run two wax exhibitions, one focusing on the rich and famous, many of them royals, which appealed to middle-class taste before 1789, and the other a 'Cave of the Great Thieves', full of murderers and other villains. Marie arrived in London with all her best models and the original moulds. In addition to Louis XVI, Marie Antoinette and their two young sons, Marie packed Josephine and Napoleon, whom she had recently modelled in Paris. She took all the death-heads she and Curtius had made, although those of the king and queen were not shown, out of respect for the large number of émigrés in London. Indeed, they did not go on display until after the death of Joseph, Marie's eldest son. Marat, murdered in his bath, had pride of place.

Exhibitions illustrating the iniquities of the Revolution were popular in Britain. What made Marie's unique was that she and Curtius had made the figures from the living, or dead, bodies of their subjects. For the first time, English audiences could really see the features of the guillotined king and queen, whose deaths they had mourned. Less congenial to the British, but fascinating, was their first sight of the actual features, modelled from death, of the leading revolutionaries. People were eager to gaze on their great enemy Napoleon. The tenor of the Tussaud show was distinctly monarchist, as were all waxworks. It was emphatically anti-revolutionary,[5] which appealed to English audiences. That Madame Tussaud, a Frenchwoman, condemned the Revolution, added a delightful piquancy for the British. It was almost as charming as if she were actually anti-French.

Marie was a highly skilled sculptor in wax. In France she had been Curtius' faithful pupil and lived on his reputation. In England she continued to present her show as 'Curtius's Cabinet of Curiosities' until 1808, while she developed her own reputation as a sculptor and a businesswoman. The presence of a large number of aristocratic French émigrés in Britain in these years meant there was a French community in cities like London and Edinburgh. Marie's letters record her attempts to attach herself to the fringes of their society, but she would not have been considered a social equal by the, mainly aristocratic, exiles. They visited her exhibition out of nostalgia, but they did not have the spare cash to buy models. Madame Tussaud consciously reinvented herself in an environment where she was totally unknown. She presented herself to the British as an artist who had moved in high society and politics in France. The final seal to her new persona culminated in 1838 in a volume of published memoirs, appropriately ghosted by a former émigré, Hervé.[6] In these memoirs and in all her publicity, catalogues, posters, and press announcements, she insisted that before the 1789 Revolution she had spent eight years at Versailles as the art tutor to the king's sister, Princess Elizabeth. There is not a shred of evidence for this in the relevant financial records of the royal household,[7] merely a claim in the memoirs, that journalists and others constantly repeated. Marie probably did visit Versailles to give lessons, but not to stay.

Her alleged royal links gave Tussaud stature and a reputation in Britain. They enabled her to present her show as an upmarket entertainment for the prosperous, rather than as a 'tacky' fairground item, which many waxworks were. They also made it easier for her to approach the wealthy and titled to solicit commissions. It was not enough to make models and show them. Private orders made serious money and gave the modeller a chance to claim 'patronage'. Marie courted high society, as Curtius had trained her.

Plugging her own French royal models and connections, Marie worked hard to secure royal backing and was delighted when the duchess of York, wife of George III's second son, agreed to place an order. The duchess had been abandoned by her husband for another woman and had no children, only a house full of dogs. She asked for a model of a little boy. The duchess also agreed that her name could appear on Marie's posters and press advertisements when her model was shown.

When the Lyceum season finished in April 1803, Marie moved to Edinburgh. She did not have another exhibition in London until 1816. She may have been glad to quit London in the spring of 1803, it was uncomfortably close to Paris and she had received a letter from her husband complaining that the Paris waxworks were not making money and that his debts were rising. Before leaving London Marie agreed to instruct her solicitor to make her two French properties entirely over to her husband, so that he could raise yet another mortgage. In these early touring years, a unique insight into both the personal and business side of Marie Tussaud is provided by a series of letters she wrote home. No replies have survived, although Marie makes references to her husband's comments in his letters. Her younger son, her mother and an aunt, to whom she wrote occasionally, were still with her husband in Paris, and Marie always wrote affectionately to them all. However her decision to renounce all control over her French property may have owed less to concern for their welfare than to French marriage law, which at that time was being rationalised and set out in the new Civil Code. A wife gave up all control over the property she brought into marriage. Anything she earned automatically belonged to her husband. A working wife's wages were simply paid to her spouse. Marie steadfastly refused to send any of her earnings in England to her husband. At this stage, indeed, she and Joseph must have been barely surviving. Marie had to fight to persuade Philipstal to release funds to transport her models, herself and Joseph. Marie complained to her husband, 'M. Philipstal treats me as you do. He has left me all alone. He is angry ...'.[8] She had exchanged one poor relationship for another.

Once established in, as always, very 'respectable' lodgings in Edinburgh, Marie was soon boasting of her friendship with the governor of Edinburgh Castle and his French wife, but as the governor was a bachelor, Marie must have made the acquaintance of a lesser official. Edinburgh was a mecca for émigrés, some of whom had moved from England since the outbreak of war between England and France. The Pretender's brother, the comte d'Artois, was living with his retinue in Holyrood Palace.

Marie's Edinburgh exhibition opened on 18 May, timed to coincide with the start of the Edinburgh Horse Show, when the maximum number of visitors were crowded into the city. Marie's show was open from 11am to 4pm and 6pm to 8pm. Marie was pleased with her takings, full details of which she sent to her husband; £3/14/- on the first day, £13/6/- by the eighth. By the eighteenth day she had taken £190 in all and was delighted.[9] As the entry fee was a colossal 2/- per person, she must have had 37 customers on the first day and 133 on the eighth. In less than a fortnight she announced that the exhibition was always full. When the Horse Show finished, Marie reduced the entry fee to 1/-, which was to be Tussaud's standard charge throughout the century and the norm for all similar entertainment. By 23 July 1803 she boasted that the total takings were £420/10/-. The cost of shipping the models from London, rent and posters and newspaper adverts, which amounted to £118/18/-, left Marie with a profit of £301/12/- She also published a catalogue which she sold at the door for 6d. This also became standard practice, but there are no indications of how well they sold until much later, when *Punch* cartoons always showed customers clutching their catalogues. Marie always kept scrupulous daily accounts, listing on one side of the notebook what she took and on the other what she paid out in rent, for candles and materials. Marie reminded her husband that she had been forced to hand over half her profits to Philipstal, 'I have been forced to accept his accounts as he placed them before me … He treats me like a slave'.[10]

Although Marie was to become one of the leading women entrepreneurs in nineteenth-century Britain, in 1803 she was a beginner. Until his death Curtius had run the business and done the lion's share of hustling for customers. Marie's letters to François indicate that she had hoped he would inherit Curtius' mantle, but she was increasingly aware that she had judged ill in choosing him for a husband. Her decision to accept an unequal partnership with Philipstal was no wiser. In Edinburgh it came home to Marie that her agreement to share her own profits with Philipstal, with no return from him except his name, would be binding until she was able to buy her way out. On 26 May she wrote to her husband of Philipstal. 'I know him as my enemy wishing me harm. But I hope in six months to have done with him. His business is in a bad way & he has only my *Cabinet* on which to rely.'[11] In October 1803 the next stop for the touring wax exhibition was Glasgow, less sophisticated and elegant than Edinburgh, but full of monied potential customers with time on their hands and a desire to appear cultured and informed. Marie then followed Philipstal to Dublin. She toured Ireland, following the route of touring theatre companies, until 1808, when she returned to Scotland.

Marie's long absence from England may have been in response to the war-time Aliens' Act. Any foreigner who arrived in Britain after October 1801 had to remain within 13 miles of an agreed residence and not live within ten miles of the coast. There was a three-month limit on their visit. Marie stayed away from England from 1803 to 1808, years when the threat to England from Napoleon seemed at its greatest and anti-French feeling was at its height. When she returned to the mainland in 1808, the chance of invasion had faded and Wellington was beginning to put pressure on French troops in Spain. In the years of greatest war-time tension, Marie may have feared, but apparently never encountered, a hostile reception in England. The only time the Exhibition encountered unrest was in 1831. By pure mischance she had a show in Bristol at the time of the Reform Bill riots and the square in which the Tussauds were staying and showing was torched, but all the models were saved.

In her early touring years in Britain Marie wrote regularly and affectionately to her family in Paris, frequently referring to her eventual return home. She was always full of her success and how well she was received among the elite. She was keen to ensure that Nini (Joseph) was not forgotten by his family in France. She assured them constantly that everyone adored him wherever they travelled.

In Scotland they took his French accent for English, which must indicate that the young boy was already far more fluent in English than his mother was ever to be. She wrote in a firm, large script, not typical of the time. She wrote poor French whose spelling indicates her German origins. Her husband complained that he could not read her letters, so sometimes she dictated the letter to the man who translated the labels she devised to describe her models. Although she sent her husband detailed accounts of her takings, money never crossed the Channel. In late May or early June 1803 François must have written demanding that she return home. Marie firmly replied that she had promised him she would not return until she had made plenty of money. Additionally, the war between Britain and France meant that the ports were closed and journeys between the two countries were difficult. Marie tried to pin her husband down; was he helping with the cooking, was he working hard, was he taking care of François, her mother and aunt, and had he made any changes to the Salon? A lady of firm purpose and sharp tongue and pen, she pointed out that her husband could change the Salon around while she was away.[12] It is easy to infer that François Tussaud was disinclined to shift for himself. Clearly he married a woman much older than himself in the hope of a life of leisure. Marie kept in contact with her husband until she had bought herself out of her agreement with Philipstal. In June 1804 she wrote her last letter to him, although he tried to get money out of her in the 1840s when her business was obviously booming.

Marie was very shocked to be told in September 1808, that her husband had handed over the entire Paris exhibition and the house in Boulevard du Temple to Madame Salomé Reiss to cancel the mortgage Marie took out when Curtius died to keep house and business intact. François was ever eager for the business speculation that would make his fortune. He spent the money he raised on the lease of the Théâtre des Troubadours and the land on which it was built.[13] He moved the family into the smaller house in rue des Fossés du Temple, which Curtius had bought and which had always been let to a tenant. After that her husband had no rental income and there was no suitable property in which Marie could have re-established her exhibition.

In 1808 Marie returned to Scotland, and subsequently toured Scottish and English towns until 1816. She had an acute perception of what would attract customers. In both Scotland and Ireland a small wax Joseph Tussaud welcomed visitors to the show, stressing the family character of the entertainment. The exhibition gradually became more elaborate. It consisted of two rooms, the first devoted to history, Marie always claimed that one of her first duties was pedagogical, to represent the past for adults, but especially for children. For 6d extra the other room contained the revolutionaries, Marat in his bath and death heads of Robespierre, Carrier, and Fouquier-Tinville. Alongside were other items brought from Paris, the models of the Bastille and of a guillotine. In the local paper Marie would offer to make wax models for clients, either from life, or death, assuring readers that the wax effigy of the dead would be very lifelike! Customers liked to see exceptional individuals, if possibly fabulously dressed, whom they would never encounter in life. They enjoyed the sensation that they were learning something new, were fond of a few shocks and thrills, and were fascinated by a topical display. The exhibition was tailored to national taste, as well as capturing people in the news at the time, including outstanding actors – and preachers. The Edinburgh show in 1810 was a typical successful recipe. It highlighted the good-looking Mrs Mary Ann Clarke, the duke of York's mistress. She had spoken up jauntily in her own defence when the duke was charged with selling army commissions illegally at her suggestion. People were talking about her and curious to see what this fine looking woman was actually like. There were, appropriately, new models of old favourites, Mary, Queen of Scots and Bonnie Prince Charlie. The figures of George III and Queen Charlotte were only a few months old. Nelson and Sir John Moore stood with a mixture of English and Irish politicians. Napoleon appeared, bigamously, with both Josephine and a new model of Marie Louise.

As one follows Madame Tussaud's touring career, it is fascinating to see the emergence of qualities that turned it from a short-term visit into a permanent success. In developing her exhibition and adapting it to appeal to a well-heeled British audience, Marie learned from other touring companies, particularly the theatre groups. Crucial to success was where and how the exhibition was displayed. Marie always tried to set up shop in a town's Assembly Rooms, otherwise settling for a Town Hall. In 1824 the theatre pit in Northampton was boarded over level with the stage to make 'one of the largest rooms in Northampton'.[14] Assembly Rooms were ready-made for display, the relatively new playground where the wealthy, respectable middle class lived their indoor public existence, when they were not in church, chapel, shops, or earning the family crust. Most towns were busy erecting Assembly Rooms in the Tussaud touring period. Inside the inevitably imposing exterior, the rooms were long, high-ceilinged, with pillars down each side. This was an impressive backdrop for the 90 or so wax figures and offered opportunities for the prolific displays of candle-lighting which became Marie's trade-mark, as it had been with Curtius. Both particularly relished brilliant lighting because it revealed the impeccable quality of their craftsmanship. Poor wax models might be fudged and concealed by dim lighting.

The Tussaud exhibition invariably announced its arrival in a carefully planned series of advertisements in the local newspaper; tours were mostly confined to fairly large towns with a local press. These advertisements were supplemented by posters and handbills, which were printed to a high standard. In the main this advertising was words. Wood-cut or lithograph illustrations were sometimes used, but the quality was variable and the cost still high. Hence hyperbole and colourful descriptions were the norm. Until cheap good quality lithograph illustrations began to be used in new journals such as *Illustrated London News* and *Punch* in the early 1840s, people relied on wax models to know what the famous (and infamous) people they had heard about actually looked like. This must have been a significant element in the appeal of the exhibition, not just until the illustrated papers hit Europe, but effectively until photography. One can usually follow the Tussaud tours in local newspapers, which presumably charged a fee to reproduce the posters. She personalised her publicity for each town, and each has its own file in the Tussaud archives. Each file contains clippings from relevant newspapers, handbills, and, if available, a picture of the Assembly Rooms which Marie hired.

From 1818, substantial catalogues of each exhibition were published, providing details of each model, and of relevant snippets of highly coloured biography. These were partly financed by advertisements of local firms. At 6d they were very competitively priced. A generation later, the new National Gallery charged 1/- for a catalogue which was a mere list of titles and painters. The 1819 edition of the Tussaud catalogue stressed, as it always would, both the historical authenticity of clothing and other artefacts, and the educational experience to be gained by young visitors.

> Madame Tussaud, in offering this little Work to the Public, has endeavoured to blend utility and amusement. The following pages contain a general outline of the history of each character represented in the Exhibition; which will not only increase the pleasure to be derived from a mere view of the Figures, but will also convey to the minds of young Persons much biographical knowledge – a branch of education universally allowed to be of the highest importance.[15]

Rational recreation, where some education was laced with entertainment, was very much the vogue. The British Museum was criticised for failing to present its huge mass of exhibits in a systematic way or to provide a catalogue. Tussauds never forgot to claim that it was doing its bit, but it took care to keep its 'educational' side light and undemanding, though not unobtrusive.

Catalogues and posters were invariably interlaced with lists of royal 'patrons'. In 1830 the catalogue for the Duffield show identified Madame Tussaud as 'artist to her late Royal Highness Madame Elizabeth, sister to Louis XVIII. Patronised by his most christian majesty, Charles X, Louis XVIII and the late royal family of France; their late royal highnesses the Duke and Duchess of York'.[16] Most of this was pure hyperbole. Madame Tussaud did not meet either Louis XVIII or Charles X when they were kings of France between 1814 and 1830, but it all sounded good.

From 1814 Joseph took an active part in the business, played the piano and led a small orchestra, which played during opening hours. In 1822, François (soon recast as Francis in England), her younger son joined her. He helped her and his elder brother run the exhibition and played harp in the orchestra, now named 'Messrs. Tussaud and the Fishers'. A relative of Madame's memorialist, Hervé, taught Joseph how to make silhouettes. Far cheaper and less space-consuming than a wax figure, the silhouettes were popular and sold well. Family relations were not always harmonious. Francis always complained, with some justice considering that he had been left behind, age two, that Joseph was his mother's favourite.

In her efforts to be recognised and accepted in society, Madame Tussaud was careful to be seen supporting good causes, local and national charities, as long as her contribution was acknowledged. In 1826, when the exhibition was in York, a pre-Christmas ball was held in the same room, separated by canvas screens. When the guests had finished dinner, Joseph Tussaud removed the screens and guests could mingle with the models. The £15/10/- raised was given to 'the distressed Manufacturers of York'.

Because the exhibition paid return visits to towns, Marie was careful to keep her winning formula of coronations and horror up-to-date. The royalism of the exhibition became increasingly accentuated. The Romantic Movement and Sir Walter Scott had a lot to answer for. Coronations were the key. In France, Charles X staged an elaborate pseudo-medieval coronation in Rheims cathedral in 1825, unlike his brother a decade earlier, who had contented himself with a simple swearing-in at Notre-Dame. George IV set the tone in Britain, spending £250,000 on an elaborate, fantastic display of peacockery in 1820. Ludicrous, too, as the popular Queen Caroline bustled around Whitehall, trying abortively to enter the Abbey and claim a crown. The cost and vulgarity of the event itself drew much criticism, but memory was a different matter. People rushed to Westminster Abbey to gaze at the special coronation decorations.[17] In her Manchester show in 1820 Marie staged a tableau of the event, complete with mock-up of both the throne room and the throne itself. The Tussauds played their part in making those unlovable brothers, George IV and William IV, tolerable.

In Liverpool a year later Marie took the opportunity of Napoleon's death to present an even more glamorous tableau of Napoleon's coronation, modelled on David's painting. Characters were increasingly grouped in set-piece dramatic situations as if on stage. In this scene Napoleon is crowning himself, watched by Josephine, the Pope, Napoleon's uncle, Cardinal Fesch – and two mamelukes, Muslim leaders, to remind everyone that Napoleon had fought and defeated them. Journalists were fascinated by the mamelukes. When the opportunity arose later, Marie bought the actual robes that had been worn at the coronations of both George IV and Napoleon, to add an even more authentic touch. She set a fashion for tableaux, placing a group of individuals in dramatic scenes that told a story without movement. Theatres imitated the idea and there were a number of shows dedicated to what were called *tableaux vivants*.

She no longer needed to model directly from the person. Personal observation, combined, where possible, with a famous painting of the subject, was all that was required. Heads, hands, and any other visible parts of a subject were rendered in wax, the rest of the body was a wood or leather frame. The accuracy of Tussaud models was constantly remarked on, and not only in advertisements written and/or paid for by Marie. They did not beautify their subjects, as many wax sculptors did, rendering the model bland, but reproduced them with appropriate wrinkles and imperfections. Models were often spoiled by their unconvincing glass eyes. The Tussauds' eyes were supplied from central Europe until after the Second World War, when a member of the two families who specialised in high quality glass eyes, Mr E. Greiner, moved to Golders' Green.[18] In 1830, on the accession of William IV, Marie's sons, now the chief model makers, constructed a new coronation assemblage. They also revelled in the fact that Marie could repeatedly claim royal patronage – and usually quote the thanks of a popular royal. William IV's sister, Princess Augusta-Sophia wrote to Marie of their 'amusement and gratification' after a visit with her nephew to the exhibition in Brighton in 1833.

Marie had total control of the finances of her business. She always had charge of every penny, sitting in a special cubicle throughout opening hours, taking the money. One of her biggest expenditures was wages. She needed semi-skilled employees, so presumably they travelled with her. Following the fashion of the day, one of her servants was a negro. A violinist in her orchestra was a man who claimed that he was a son of Louis XVI, who had survived imprisonment during the Revolution. Marie eventually established a tight-knit family business, but at the outset she was alone. Another factor was transport. Travelling became somewhat easier during her touring years, with macadamised roads to smooth the journey. As a result, eventually coaches could bat along at ten miles per hour and Marie could be sure of arriving in the next town before the arrival of the 'caravans' transporting the models. Marie transported everything in *Pickfords* caravans. Hiring vehicles was no small expense; she paid £1/4/- for a coach from Leeds to Manchester. Later she bought her own vehicles and transported and advertised at the same time. Her caravans were decorated with gilding and her own name.

Each time she packed up the caravans in the travelling decades it was because her account books told her that in the last weeks fewer people were coming to the exhibition. She would often postpone the move if numbers picked up. Indeed, a press notice that a move had been delayed because the exhibition was attracting large numbers was a standard routine to bring in more customers. It seems clear that she planned her touring route, but left the date when she moved on open. Each destination was calculated on a careful assessment of the potential market. Marie followed the same circuit as the travelling theatrical companies. She always ensured that her visit coincided with a significant date for each town, perhaps a race meeting or the arrival of a theatre group, or simply the high point in the season in that town. Marie only toured towns packed with wealthy middle-class families. She developed a travelling itinerary to take best advantage of the seasonal mobility of the prosperous middle and upper classes in Britain. Bath was a favourite winter haunt for the rich and idle, and she made repeat visits to a number of other cities, including Brighton and Bristol. Bath was such a magnet for those with money to spare that Josiah Wedgwood set up a showroom there.[19] The Tussaud exhibition also paid repeat visits to large cities like Manchester and Liverpool, and medium-sized market towns. The travelling years were successful because in Britain there were enough substantial towns, with suitably impressive public spaces, within fairly easy reach of each other along improving roads.

Marie studied her market assiduously. Her targets were families with leisure, cash, curiosity, and a willingness to accept a smattering of information with their fun. In these years in Britain there were in excess of half a million middle-class families with money to spend on enjoying themselves. The *Liverpool Courier* remarked on the presence at the exhibition of 'some of our first families, who find in this agreeable amusement a most pleasing recreation'. Marie developed her exhibition to be part of the 'public parade' culture of the pre-railway age.

In the early decades of the nineteenth century the British, the French, and probably most Europeans, as we know from the novels of Stendhal, Dickens, and others, liked to spend weekends and evenings, and the season if they could afford it, strolling in carefully designated parts of the heart of their town. They constructed safe, salubrious centres to their cities for this purpose, with churches, public gardens, assembly halls, museums, and, later in the century, department stores, street lighting, and drains. Until the railways were constructed, when they built and moved to suburban villas, middle-class business and professional families lived close to this parade ground and would usually perform the whole circuit on foot, or, if necessary, in their own carriage. They walked, much as a dog will do, both to mark off their territory, after all they would have paid for said gardens and museum, and to emphasise to other families their social and economic equality, or superiority.

Marie ruthlessly exploited and refined this 'promenade' market. She offered more variety than a theatrical performance, which would be almost unchanged through its run. She made new models to catch each topical issue, exploring the snobbish glamour of royalty as well as the thrill of being *au fait* with the latest gruesome murder or assassination. Unlike a museum, a waxworks was a very active cultural experience. Customers could touch the models, study them in detail, discuss them out loud, imagine themselves in relation to the figures, and, if they were rich enough, consider the purchase of a model of themselves. Unlike a theatre, Tussaud clients were not limited to a short interval for nosing around. Customarily the show opened from 11 to 6 and then from 7 to 10. The models were far more brightly illuminated than was a theatre, which created an excellent medium in which customers could study each other without appearing intrusive. The promenade was vastly enhanced by music; a small orchestra of the Tussaud brothers and a few associates played throughout the evening. The music made a backdrop of sound, under which discreet conversations could be conducted with less restraint than in a theatre or concert hall. The Tussauds invented the idea of the promenade concert. Visitors could spend the entire evening 'promenading', strolling around the Assembly Room, without being thought odd. The *Liverpool Observer* noted 'The promenade among the illustrious dead and illustrious living, is truly delightful'.

The exhibition provided a highly interactive experience, offering a vaguely educational reason to wander around, apparently purposefully, being inquisitive about models and fellow guests, socialising and perhaps making preliminary sallies in the direction of business, social engagements, even marriage. It was an informal, yet formal, location for public social contact. You could chat distantly, or more intimately, and the public setting offered the opportunity to walk away without seeming rude, or to establish closer links.

Madame Tussaud was always keen to stress that the exhibition was designed for the middle and upper classes. On the other hand, from time to time she made a great fuss of admitting 'the working classes'. Special sessions were designated at unpopular times, for instance the last hour, up to 10pm, at half price. 'By this arrangement sufficient time will be given for the classes to view the collection without interfering with each other, and they hope that none but those thus situated will take advantage of it.' There are no clues to how many working-class families could afford either the money or were even free to attend. The working day might easily run from 6am to 10pm.

In her pricing strategy, Madame Tussaud followed the norm for the age. Entertainment was class-segregated, mainly by price, although the totally free British Museum sorted out its preferred clientèle by dress and refusing to sell tickets on demand at the door. A 'rational recreation' cost a minimum of 1/-. Only the comfortably off would have paid more per person for a show, but there was plenty to be seen at the cheaper end of the market, although less trace remains of what was available. There were wax and other shows at fairs and in towns costing 1d (old penny).

Before 1835 Madame Tussaud and many other entertainers and theatre companies calculated that they were better off travelling to perform, on the grounds that most customers came for a single visit, although Tussaud found that repeat visits to towns were profitable. In 1835 the exhibition came to rest in London, where it has been ever since. Marie's takings were so good in London that she never moved again.

The Baker Street Bazaar, where the exhibition finally settled, was on the west side of Baker Street between Dorset Street and King Street. It occupied the upper floors of the three-storey building. Downstairs horses and carriages were offered for sale, and later the area was used for the annual Royal Smithfield Club Cattle Show and regular poultry shows. Upstairs was a different world. Unlike the average wax show that was housed in cramped, dark quarters, the Tussaud exhibition did its utmost to resemble a visit to a large, elegant and dazzlingly lit salon. Visitors entered by a small ground floor hall, ornamented with sculpture, both antique-style and modern. A wide staircase led to the saloon, decorated with artificial flowers, scrolled and twirled arabesques and enormous mirrors. Here they were greeted by a lady sitting at a small table, who, until her death, was Madame Tussaud herself.

The next room was the focal point of the Baker Street exhibition, the 'Great Room', which was 100 feet x 50 feet. The walls were covered in plate glass and decorated with draperies and gilt ornaments, in the style of France at the time of Louis XIV. There were statues and groups on all sides, with large tableaux in the centre. There was plenty of space to sash-shay around, and ottomans and sofas for rest and conversation, just as one would expect in an art gallery, or indeed a private drawing room. A balcony over the main entrance housed the orchestra that played during the evening session. At the other end you entered the 'Golden Chamber', the embryo of what was soon known as the 'Hall of Kings', including Henry VIII, Elizabeth, Mary Queen of Scots, Charles I, and Cromwell, plus all the imported Hanoverians. Coronation displays were now a focal point.

Much of the Tussaud wax fare was similar to that in other shows, the royals, assorted witches, and aspects of history, but her models were better made and far more luxuriously dressed and housed than in the average waxworks. Her show was always up-to-date. New models were being added constantly and ones that people walked past without a glance were melted down. You could never say you had 'done' Tussauds. Her premises were spacious and elegant. They offered excellent opportunities for the middle class to 'promenade', and to do so in a protected and very respectable environment. There was never any question of finding whores at Tussauds, aside from a few famous wax examples. There was never a risk that Tussauds would fall foul of the Obscene Publications Act of 1857. They were careful to avoid anatomical models, some of which were sexually explicit, without having any real scientific or medical rationale. They also scored on the question of the demon drink. Their buffet and later their restaurant provided only tea and soft drinks, which must have delighted the censorious temperance movement. This organisation waged war on other popular entertainment, particularly music halls, which sold alcohol and food as well as song, and became very popular with working people. Thus Tussauds fitted in well with the rather puritanical public morality of the Victorian middle class.

In conclusion, it is intriguing to probe why Madame Tussaud's enterprise triumphantly stopped travelling after over 30 years of success. The transport revolution was the obvious explanation, not only for Tussauds, but also for the numerous theatre companies.[20] Tussauds had other reasons to stay put. It gave itself a fashionable museum image. Madame Tussaud, with her acute business sense, was aware that museums and art galleries were becoming increasingly fashionable after the Napoleonic wars, but that the potential customers, particularly the middle classes, were frustrated rather than satisfied by existing establishments. Around 1820 the Tussaud travelling wax exhibition responded by starting to adopt a combination of art gallery and museum characteristics. Gradually the collection acquired so many paintings and other objects that it became less and less mobile and the cost of shipping must have increased considerably. It is noticeable that the last few journeys before they arrived in Baker Street were relatively short and all within the London area. Joseph and Francis devised increasingly elaborate gilded displays, such as the Corinthian Saloon in the Gray's Inn Road. They used enormous gilded mirrors, which showed off the models to perfection, a trick Marie had learned from Curtius. Also following Curtius' example, they haunted auctions and bought precious objects to give authenticity and a museum-like quality with which to surround their models.

Unlike all other wax shows and rival entertainments, Tussauds took the new museums head on. It competed brilliantly with institutions like the British Museum so that within a short time of the opening of the Baker Street exhibition, Tussauds was universally acknowledged to be a 'must' for any tourist, on a par with the Tower of London and Westminster Abbey. Marie assembled the most comprehensive collection of Napoleon relics in the world, at a time when Bonapartism was in the news. Tussauds concentrated on presenting an exhibition free of all the well-known criticisms made of other museums. Madame Tussaud cheerfully admitted anyone holding the required 1/- in their hand, confident that this substantial sum would exclude 'undesirable' elements, because she was more of a snob than most. Paying customers could wander around freely. The catalogue sold at the entrance told them everything Madame wanted them to know about the figures and their history. In contrast to the British Museum, Madame Tussaud concentrated on presenting her collection to its best visual advantage. Unlike many of her rivals, she was aware that museum-gazing made people both hungry and thirsty. She was careful to install a buffet to keep her customers content. Whereas public museums seemed committed to keeping the public out, Tussauds never forgot that their commercial survival depended totally on people lining up at the front door. Above all, Madame Tussaud remembered that her visitors were human. They needed interaction, amusement, and some delighted in being shocked and made slightly afraid – in a safe environment.

The transport revolution made the capital accessible for short visits. London provided far and away the biggest catchment area in Britain, with a population of one million in 1801, rising to a much less densely packed three million by 1861. No other town could rival the size of the capital, and in the early decades of the century there was no really large town north of London. Except for the annual fairs, London entertainment of all kinds was concentrated in the centre, with Leicester Square as the focus. Many of their customers were Londoners, although 'country cousin' and foreign tourist trade was not insignificant. Theatres, exhibitions, and other shows were within walking distance, although the rich might well use a carriage.

The decision to stay in Baker Street, in a highly fashionable central district, close to the most prestigious cluster of retail streets in the world, may have been determined by day-by-day profits, but it was astute and farsighted. The development of transport, in respect not only to speed, but frequency and also cost, made it easy to persuade people to travel to entertainment rather than expect an entertainment to move constantly. Even before the railways, road improvements had made coach journeys shorter. In the 1820s, London to Brighton was cut to six hours, but even an outside seat cost 12/-, so only the rich would ride. Mass movement came with the railways. In 1835, 117,000 made the trip to Brighton by rail. The journey time had shrunk to two hours. Surprisingly, although it was cheaper, the price had only fallen by one-third the coach price of the 1820s.[21] Passengers were drawn mainly from the existing leisured classes, who no longer thought of spending a season in Brighton, when they could go for a day, a week, or a fortnight. Indeed, Victoria was so appalled by the crowds in Brighton that she decamped to the Isle of Wight.

Horse buses brought Londoners to the front door of the new Tussaud venue. Shillibeer's omnibuses provided the first public transport in London in 1829, but only the rich could ride at 6d for a short and 1/- for a longer journey in town. Prices fell as demand increased. A ticket from Charing Cross to Camden Town came down from a prohibitive 1/- to 3d and then 1d. Within a few years the rapid development of the rail network meant customers could travel from all over the country. By 1848 all eight main London rail terminals were built. There was no need to transport the exhibition to people; they came to it. Families who had visited the travelling show made the new venue part of a trip to the capital. The Baker Street site was easily reached from all of the new main stations on the 'New Road', that is, Marylebone Road and its continuation, Euston Road. The permanent exhibition was less than two miles from Kings Cross, St Pancras, Euston and Paddington, while Marylebone station, built towards the end of the century, with its new commuter traffic, was no more than a mile away. The models could now lead a more sedate and restful life. The culture that customers travelled to places of entertainment, to the new municipal art galleries and museums, as well as theatres and waxworks, was quickly accepted. The most rapidly expanding section of the entertainment market was the salaried, rather than the leisured, middle classes. The construction of the rail network, and in London the building of an underground system, tempted them to move out of the centre into the new suburbs. The Tussaud exhibition was in easy reach by a variety of forms of transport.

Tussauds outclassed its numerous rivals in the press coverage it won. It was well-publicised in leading newspapers. At the opening, the *Times* noted that the new exhibition was 'peculiarly imposing and splendid'. The *Court Journal* was equally impressed: 'this is a scene for a pleasant and instructive hour'. Most evocative, perhaps, was *Chambers Journal*: 'we can walk, as it were, along the plank of time'. The Duke of Wellington, an avid museum-goer, was entranced by Tussaud's Napoleon, which was placed facing his own wax self. Dickens gave Tussauds much free publicity, including, in 1840, Mrs Jarley's Waxworks in the *Old Curiosity Shop*. George Cruickshank, the cartoonist, as well as *Punch* and the *Illustrated London News*, regularly documented the attractions of the exhibition.

That the exhibition grew roots in 1835 had nothing to do with human considerations. The fact that at 75 Marie was way past retiring age, or that her sons had 11 young children between them, was irrelevant. It was simply a matter of a total awareness of profitability. Madame Tussaud's artistic skills and sensitivity to public demand would have been as nought without her complete control of money. She still retained close financial control of her business and operated the cash desk herself until shortly before her death. She had well-developed economic antennae. Unlike theatres, she did not give away free tickets, even Queen Victoria had to pay. Like many Victorian entrepreneurs, she employed her family where possible and their wages were very modest. When Marie received a 'request' from Westminster Abbey to help in the restoration of their decrepit wax models, which the Abbey clearly assumed Madame would regard as an irresistible compliment, she replied that she had her own shop to look after, and anyway, she did not work for nothing.

Madame Tussaud was one of the last, not the first, female wax entrepreneurs: wax was a medium a woman could use to make a model, more tractable than stone or wood. Her odyssey was amazing at the time, when almost no married women worked, and when travelling even a short distance was arduous. Marie remained on the road for nearly 33 years in total, visiting 75 main towns and some smaller places. The packing and unpacking alone, without the travelling, and model and costume making, would have been herculean tasks for a young person, but Marie set out when she was already middle-aged, with a tiny child, knowing no-one and speaking not a word of English when she began. She was in her seventies when her touring days ended. This tiny woman possessed self-reliance, courage, and determination to an unusual degree. She was extraordinarily well-organised, paid fanatical attention to detail, particularly in matters financial, and her tiny son must have been a saint. She became as much an attraction at the exhibition as the models themselves, 'one of the national ornaments of the feminine species', according to *Punch*.[22] The *Edinburgh Observer* applauded Marie as an example to other women: 'To the ladies this collection must be highly interesting, from its being the work of one of their own sex: who, in the formation of the numerous groups, has proved what may be done when talent is united with industry.' Her talents were her artistic and financial skills, her imagination and determination to outdo the museums of her day, and her foresight in taking full advantage of the transport revolution.

NOTES

The research discussed here forms part of my book, *Madame Tussaud and the History of Waxworks* (London, 2002). I am grateful to the Arts and Humanities Research Board for a research leave award which enabled me to finish the writing.

1. R. Altick, *The Shows of London* (Cambridge, MA, 1976). Anyone interested in the varied range of different public shows, from art exhibitions to public gardens, should consult this book, an erudite and very readable guide. M. Lemire, *Artistes et mortels* (Paris, 1990), provides an excellent introduction to French wax sculpture.
2. R.M. Isherwood, *Farce and Fantasy: Popular Entertainment in Eighteenth-Century Paris* (Oxford, 1986), p.161.
3. *Almanach général de tous les spectacles de Paris et de la province pour l'année 1792* chez Froullé vol.2 (1792), p.307.
4. Marie wrote to her husband in June 1803 that she would not return to Paris until she had 'a well-filled purse'. Madame Tussaud Archives. London (subsequently MT). I am very grateful to Undine Concannon and Rosy Cantor, the Madame Tussaud archivists who allowed me to use the Tussaud Archive and provided me with much additional good advice.
5. U. Kornmeier, 'Madame Tussaud's First Exhibition in England, 1802–1803', *Object, Postgraduate Research in the History of Art and Visual Culture*, October 1998, pp.45–61.
6. F. Hervé, *Madame Tussaud's Memoirs and Reminiscences of France, forming an abridged History of the French Revolution* (London, 1838).

7. Archives Nationales O1.3787,O1*3789.
8. Quoted in A. Leslie and P. Chapman, *Madame Tussaud: Waxworker Extraordinary* (London, 1978), p.112.
9. Dictated letter to her husband 'my beloved', 9 June 1803, MT.
10. To her husband, 28 July 1803. MT.
11. Copy of the original and a translation, MT.
12. 9 June 1803. MT.
13. P. Chapman, *Madame Tussaud in England* (London, 1992), p.33.
14. L. Warwick, *Theatre Un-Royal or 'They Call them Comedians': A History of the Theatre, Sometimes Royal, Marefair, Northampton* (1806–84 and 1887), p.81.
15. *Madame Tussaud Catalogue* (Cambridge, 1819).
16. *Biographical and Descriptive Sketches of the Distinguished Characters which compose the Unrivalled Exhibition of Madame Tussaud* (Duffield, 1830).
17. Altick, *The Shows of London*, p.177.
18. 'After the War', MT.
19. R. Reilly, *Josiah Wedgwood* (London, 1992), p.210.
20. I am grateful to one of my anonymous readers for this point.
21. J. Walvin, *Leisure & Society 1830–1950* (London, 1978), p.19.
22. Colburn's Kalender of Amusements, quoted in Leslie and Chapman, *Madame Tussaud*, p.163.

Purposive Strategy or Serendipity? Development and Diversification in Three Consumer Product Companies, 1918–39: J. & J. Colman, Reckitt & Sons and Lever Bros./Unilever

ROY CHURCH and CHRISTINE CLARK
University of East Anglia

In a recent review of the literature concerning business leadership and decision-making, Naomi Lamoureaux referred to the temptation for historians to offer rational narratives, to be preoccupied with the optimal, and to disregard historical contingency and alternative historical possibilities. She expressed the view that an antidote to this was a comparative approach.[1] The research reported below predates her address but is entirely consistent with that view.[2] The starting point was a discovery that there is a surprising amount of agreement among economists on the subject of product diversification and its continuing theoretical under-development. Agnosticism provides the common denominator in a literature which reveals that the meanings of diversification are diverse; that how best to define a market or industry conceptually has attracted little attention; that adequate empirical measures of product differentiation have yet to be found; that the present state of theory suggests that with product diversification 'anything can happen',[3] and that, at best, limited progress is being made to indicate only what *may* happen in markets and firms.[4]

Such views signal a shift away from the proliferation of theoretical nuances towards a search for empirical regularities, the approach adopted by Sutton in *Sunk Costs and Market Structure*, in which he fully acknowledged the importance of the historical dimension to the analysis of product diversification.[5] Cynthia Montgomery's survey of the literature on corporate diversification concluded that diversification was likely to elude simple conclusions regarding the relevance of various theoretical explanations advanced when applied to specific firms. She underlined the complexity of the process, arguing for more empirical work to evaluate purposive diversification in the context of resource base and agency.[6] This is consistent with the approach adopted by Edith Penrose nearly 40 years ago when she emphasised the importance of inherited resources and managerial capacities and strategies. She also underlined the absence of empirical research that might add flesh to her bundle of concepts by which she sought to map alternative possibilities from perspectives within individual firms conducting business within specific product markets.[7]

Except as an incidental theme in the biographies of individual enterprises, the lack of progress towards an understanding of the process of diversification is duplicated in the literature of business and economic history.[8] Our approach in addressing this gap is to combine the theoretical framework offered by the model of imperfect competition, which is our starting point, with the resource-oriented concepts and analysis offered by Penrose. Our justification is twofold. As each firm manufactured similar though differentiated consumer goods, the technology for the production of which had reached maturity, the model of imperfectly competitive markets provides a valid *generalised* approximation of the economic context within which the three firms under examination diversified production in the period between the wars. This was also an economic environment in which decisions relating to product diversification and new product development were acknowledged to be imperative for corporate survival and success. At a time when market research was in its infancy, and information therefore imperfect, the increased risk and uncertainty associated with managers' choices of new directions presented challenges to ongoing business routines and customary behaviour. A *specific* analysis of each firm is necessary to secure an understanding of the nature of the adaptive process: the extent to which outcomes were the result of purposive 'rational' action and an evolutionary logic, or were due, at least in part, to serendipity.[9] Resource and agency aspects are of particular relevance to explanations of the directions which diversification and development took and differences in the management of the process in each of the three firms.

There are several justifications for choosing J. & J. Colman Ltd, Reckitt & Sons Ltd, and Lever Bros. Ltd as case studies. Neither Colman nor Reckitt have been the subject of scholarly study; more important, however, is the availability of adequate (though far from complete) archival sources which have facilitated detailed investigation of product changes, a necessary condition for the research. Wilson's *History of Unilever* provides a valuable basis for comparison, though it does not document its relations with the other two companies. For whereas Colman and Reckitt were in direct competition, their managers acknowledged that Lever was a potential competitor. Both formally and informally, each affected the product strategies of one or both of the other two companies.[10] In each case, dominance had been achieved by manufacturing products, the market for which, by 1914, had begun to exhibit characteristics of maturity. After small beginnings in the early nineteenth century, this leadership had seen Colman and Reckitt gradually emerge to become medium-sized firms. In 1909, Colman employed 2,300 compared with the 3,025 employed by Reckitt (2,600 and 5,339 by 1913 after a series of acquisitions).[11] A relative latecomer in 1885, Lever's spectacular growth resulted in the employment of over 6,000 workers in the UK in 1911.[12] These firms belonged to a consumer goods sector of the British manufacturing industry between 1870 and 1939 which has been described as the most successful of all.[13] The formation of Unilever in 1929 marked the emergence of the first and largest M-form corporate structure in Britain, while Colman and Reckitt merged to form Reckitt & Colman in 1938.[14]

In several respects the three firms shared similar experience of changes to their economic environments. Each was a manufacturer of household consumer goods trading in markets which since the late nineteenth century had become increasingly competitive, albeit in the context of rapidly expanding demand. Each had also become a corporate predator to achieve and maintain market dominance. After the post-war boom, increasing international competition intensified the effects of stagnating or declining product markets for which other factors peculiar to the companies' product mixes were responsible. Colman's success in acquiring competitors in the mustard trade before 1914 helped to offset the difficulties presented by a mature product market. The prospects for growth in the starch and blue trades were similarly constrained as changes in textile technology and the introduction of synthetic fabrics, the development of detergents, and changing fashion adversely affected consumer demand for traditional products.[15] The increasing importance of the bagwash system, in which the operators of machine-using laundries were the potential purchasers of starch and blue, coincided with an advertising campaign by Lever which claimed that blue was unnecessary when Persil washing powder was used.[16] Following five years of exceptionally high sales immediately after World War I, from 1923, sales of starch and blue fell.[17] Likewise, after W.H. Lever's death in 1925, his successor D'Arcy Cooper predicted gloomy prospects for the traditional trade in soap as a consequence of intensified international competition.[18]

In a market environment in which no technical breakthrough occurred and where each firm was, even in a limited sense, a first mover, the other principal strategy was the defence of market shares/profits. Advertising and promotion were two responses, though these warrant separate treatment elsewhere, and, in any case, tended to be employed to support rather than initiate diversification. The major strategies were those of collusion; the acquisition of other firms' proprietary technologies or of their products which were close substitutes for those manufactured by the predator; or investment in new product development.[19] Within such a context, and as far as data allow, resource- and agency-oriented concepts are applied to analyse the directions and managerial dynamics of the process of product diversification in the three companies. First, we compare their general marketing strategies and, second, their approaches to product innovation. The concluding section examines the connections between resources and agency in the process and considers how far the pattern of diversification can be interpreted as the outcome of purposive strategies and the reflection of differences and developments in corporate structures and organisation.

II
HISTORICAL PROFILES

Both Colman and Reckitt began as sole proprietorships. Jeremiah Colman set up as a flour miller in Norfolk in 1804, adding mustard, which required a similar production process, in 1814. In terms of sales and profits, this became the firm's major product until after World War II. Using flour as an input, starch was added in the 1830s, soon becoming the second largest selling product, followed, from the 1850s, by washing blue for whiter laundry. Isaac Reckitt commenced starch manufacture in his new business venture in Hull in 1840; starch and washing blue (added in 1852) were the main products until shortly before World War I. By that time, polishes, the first of which was black lead introduced in 1855, had emerged as the third important product line. By 1914, Reckitt's starch and blue sales had overtaken those of Colman; Reckitt now dominated the polish market, though Colman's virtual monopoly of the mustard trade remained. Thanks to Wilson's study, the early history of Lever is well known. By adding the manufacture of soap to the family's retailing business in 1885, W.H. Lever laid the foundations for the growth of an enterprise which, by 1919, produced 60 per cent of all soap made in Britain, at the same time having established a major presence in the US. Important differences between the three companies can be summarised by comparing their structure as presented in Table 1.

Shares other than those owned by the Colman family were in the hands either of trusts or banks. The holdings of voting shares, together with the composition of the directors, reveal complete control of the Board by family members. Throughout the inter-war period the chairman was Sir Jeremiah

TABLE 1
SIZE, OWNERSHIP AND CONTROL OF THREE COMPANIES, 1935/36

	J. & J. Colman Ltd	Reckitt & Sons Ltd	Lever Bros/ Unilever
Capitalisation	£3.5m	£5.1m	£60.8m
Net tangible assets	£5.1m	£7.1m	£80.5m
Voting shares held by 20 largest shareholders	49.2%*	35%	20.4%
Voting shares held by directors	27.5%	13.1%	7.2%
Employment	3,325 (1920)**	8,103	60,000

Notes: * Among whom three members of the Colman family owned 24.2% and Basil Mayhew, son-in-law of senior director Russell James Colman, held 5.7%.
    **Probably a maximum figure for 1935/6. The number employed at Carrow (i.e. excluding those employed at the Farrow business in Peterborough) in 1938 was 1800.

Sources: P. Sargant Florence, *Ownership, Control, and Success of Large Companies, 1936–1951* (London, 1961), pp.203, 209, 212. Financial data refer to 1936, employment figures to 1935. Colman's employment figures are from Mottram, 'A History of J. & J. Colman and J. & J. Colman Ltd. of Carrow and Cannon Street' (unpublished typescript, c 1950), n.p; *Eastern Evening News*, 3 April 1938, p.7.

Colman. He was aged 59 when World War I ended; Russell James Colman, aged 57, was the other active senior director. From 1922, together with W.H. Slack, a director of Reckitt, Colonel F.G.D. Colman was in joint charge of the joint committees through which the two companies organised and co-ordinated their overseas trade and pooled profits. Partner in a London accountancy firm and an auditor of the company's accounts, Sir Basil Mayhew became a director in 1935 following his marriage to the daughter of Russell Colman; he replaced Captain Geoffrey Colman, who died that year aged 42. Family dominance was a tradition. Since 1896, when the partnership had become a private limited company capitalised at £1,350,000, the Rt Hon. James Stuart, the first Professor of Mechanism and Applied Mechanics, had been admitted to the Board in 1898 at the age of 53 after marrying the daughter of Jeremiah James Colman. Jeremiah James was described by his successor as 'a soft-hearted gentleman' who, from the establishment of the business at Carrow in Norwich in the 1850s (which he dominated until his death in 1898), had adopted 'the more polite and gentle methods' of managing a country partnership.[20] F.G.D. Colman, aged 21, joined the Board in 1903, as did Jeremiah 'Jack' Colman in 1909 at the age of 23. Both held responsibilities on the sales and advertising side of the business based at the London offices. The first incomer possessing no family connection was E.B. Southwell. He had joined the office as a clerk in 1875, a moderniser who introduced a statistical department to the company and rose to become general manager on the death of Jeremiah James in 1898. Not until the death of James Stuart in 1913 at the age of 66 was Southwell dissuaded from retirement and made a director. This elevation was accompanied by the appointment of Southwell's son-in-law, James Barclay, to the position of general manager. Formerly an accountant with Price Waterhouse, he had joined Colman in 1901. When Southwell retired from the Board in 1919, Barclay did not succeed him. Geoffrey (Captain) Colman, Russell's eldest son, became a director in 1916, aged 23, after being invalided out of the army. Alan Rees Colman, Russell's younger son, became a director in 1922 at the age of 21. In the list of Colman's directors serving on the new Board of Reckitt & Colman in 1938, five were Colmans, Mayhew was related by marriage, and H.A.G. Salter had no connection with the Colman family. The latter had been a manager at Colman in Carrow until 1926 when he was appointed general manager of R.T. French, an American firm of mustard, spice, and birdseed manufacturers, jointly acquired by Colman and Reckitt. He returned to Carrow in 1935 as general manager and was appointed to the Board of Directors in 1938. The amalgamation agreement stipulated that when either Sir Jeremiah Colman Bart, then aged 79, or Russell J. Colman, aged 77, ceased to be a director, he was not to be replaced.[21]

Several important differences are revealed between the corporate structures of Reckitt and Colman. Reckitt had been a public company since 1888, though only 45 per cent of the total issued capital of £450,000 was sold to the public.[22] Lower percentages of voting shares rested with the 20 largest shareholders, including the directors, who were primarily members of the Reckitt family which continued to dominate the Board of Directors. Between 1888 and 1917, Francis Reckitt (who died in 1917, aged 89) and Sir James Reckitt were chairmen of the company in alternate years. Although from 1919 he had ceased to attend Board meetings, Sir James continued in the office of chairman – and influenced policy – until his death, aged 90, in 1924. In addition to Sir James, five of the directors were Reckitts at that time. Among these were three who joined the Board in 1904: Arnold, the works engineer and son of Francis; Albert, whose father George had been in charge of the London sales office; and Philip, son of James both of whom conducted the commercial activities in Hull.[23] On entering the firm following training at the engineering works or at university, each had been 'able to pull his weight and be immediately useful'.[24] A rapid expansion and diversification of the company's activities followed this infusion of new blood.[25] However, in contrast to the executive management at Colman, non-family directors also played important roles. T.R. Ferens was acknowledged to be the driving force of the company during the early twentieth century, following in his mentor's footsteps. Ferens, who had joined the firm in 1868 as confidential clerk to Sir James, was appointed works manager in 1874 at the age of 27 under a profits-sharing agreement, becoming the first company secretary when the private company was formed in 1879. By the time he became a director in the new public company in 1889, he had assumed much of Sir James' commercial executive role,[26] and in 1903 displayed commitment to, and confidence in, the firm by purchasing £45,000 of Reckitt shares with a bank loan.[27] In 1931, his 200,000 ordinary shares valued at £800,000 were not regarded as an 'outside' shareholding; neither were his votes, which, when added to those controlled by the Reckitt family, gave 'insiders' roughly one-third of the total.[28]

As Liberal MP for Hull East between 1906 and 1918, his executive role was compromised, though he became joint chairman with Arthur Reckitt, Francis' older son, in 1924 and remained until the latter's death aged 65 in 1927. Ferens, then aged 79, succeeded to the chairmanship until 1930.[29] Like Ferens, each of the other non-family directors was elected in recognition of his past and potential contribution as a successful manager.[30] Ferens' progress suggests that this practice had become part of the culture of Reckitt's Board by 1879. Moreover, that this was by choice rather than as a result of a shortage of Reckitt family members is suggested by the concurrent appointment, in 1904, of three Reckitts plus W.H. Slack, the overseas sales manager. In 1901 he decided to diversify into metal polish, an idea which proved fundamental to the company's subsequent diversification. In 1914, two more senior managers joined the Board. In 1935/36, the Board included five from the Reckitt family and six who were not. All except one resulted from the promotion of senior managers of sales, advertising, accounting, manufacturing, and research departments; the remaining director resulted from the acquisition of a firm of polish manufacturers.[31] Throughout the period, Reckitts and their insider non-family directors controlled the business within a hierarchical committee structure.

The complex history of the evolving management structure of Lever/Unilever in our period, analysed in detail by Wilson, has been described as defying summary.[32] Until 1919, Lever was wholly owned and controlled by the founder, W.H. Lever. By 1919, as a result of single-minded, expansionist, commercial policies, his firm accounted for 60 per cent of soap production in Britain. A financial crisis resulted in the intervention of the company's bankers and auditing accountants, the outcome of which was a reform of the organisation, masterminded by the accountant D'Arcy Cooper. William Lever remained in full control of his worldwide organisation. The sheer size and geographical dispersion of the Lever business empire offered greater scope for the emergence of senior managers from outside the Lever family. Nonetheless, it was not until after his death in 1925 that his unremitting personal control of the firm's development was diminished. Formal restructuring, resulting from the merger with the Dutch Margarine Unie in 1929, accelerated the influx of managers from diverse backgrounds, some of whom were graduates, others possessing experience of other businesses, some in the US.[33] During the 1930s, the structure and management of Unilever has been described as a professional, largely non-family-managed hierarchy.[34]

Throughout this period, the sales and profitability of each of these companies was perceived by managers to depend primarily on marketing in general and product diversification in particular. This prompts several questions: when, why, and how did diversification take place? Precisely what form did it take and with what effects? How systematic was the process of product innovation and development? What long-term effects did it have on a firm's product profile and general marketing policy? What was the role of scientific research and development? Differences in the quality and volume of information relating to the product histories in the three firms preclude a wholly thematic analysis of these processes category by category. It is possible, however, to compare approaches to marketing and to product innovation in the three companies before attempting to generalise in the concluding section.

III
APPROACHES TO MARKETING AND PRODUCT DEVELOPMENT

Colman's approach to marketing was the most informal and the least successful. It can be described briefly; a Home Sales Committee consisting of senior salesmen (though excluding the advertising manager) met with directors to discuss marketing strategy with respect to products, packaging, prices, and advertising. Traditionally, a basic principle adhered to by the directors had been that diversification outside the company's traditional products and distribution channels was to be avoided.[35] By World War I, the company's heavy dependence on mustard for 62 per cent of profit,[36] together with a declining market for starch and blue, began to put pressure on the directors to search for new products, departing from traditional concerns though utilising traditional resources. The first initiative followed the acquisition, jointly financed with Reckitt, of R.T. French & Co., a successful American manufacturer of mustard, spices, and birdseed whose problem of owner-management succession had led the brother owners to offer the business to Colman to expand their American mustard sales. Together, Colman and Reckitt acquired French for £750,000 in 1926, the management of which was given to Colman's former production manager, H.A.G. Salter. After a visit to the US, Captain Colman proposed to the Sales Committee at Carrow that Colman should enter the birdseed market (by chance, Norwich was a centre of canary breeding).[37] The American business had obtained the Steenbock patents relating to the production of irradiated ergesterol, a potent source of vitamin D. It was suggested to Captain Colman that this substance could be used to develop a market in Britain as well as in the United States for vitamin-enhanced birdseed to be sold under the R.T. French brand. The Colman salesmen argued that while French's mustard, spice, and custard products were familiar as grocery staples, British grocers would not distribute birdseed in a trade which was already supplied through a different distributive route. This view, however, was over-ruled by Captain Colman and research for development began. Long after initial research at the Carrow Research Department, where new products were tested, revealed the vitamin to have minimal or no effects on the body growth of canaries, Britain's first industrial aviary continued to accommodate a large canary flock. The birdseed initiative failed completely.[38]

Again in 1930, salesmen failed to dissuade Captain Colman from entering the pastry mix trade which had impressed him while in the US. He argued that success in Britain was assured because the product was unique, labour saving, and aimed at a mass market. A £25,000 advertising campaign to launch 'Krusto' in 1930 resulted in sales worth £45,000 in 1931. Difficulties in maintaining quality and competition from the large flour producers saw sales plummet and led to withdrawal of the product.[39] It was not until after the merger with Reckitt in 1938 that Colman introduced a Research and New Products Committee duplicating the Reckitt model.

Reckitt directors showed a similar concern to preserve traditional distribution through an extensive network of grocers' shops which had long sold the company's household cleaning products. Since 1864, these had included Reckitt's 'Diamond Black Lead' made from graphite. In 1904, by which time paste had superseded traditional blacking, the Reckitt's general manager claimed that the company was the world's largest manufacturer of black lead for domestic use.[40] From this position in the trade, Reckitt extended the product by developing a liquid metal polish suitable for cleaning brass and copper. This innovation originated from a visit by the company's senior traveller, W.H. Slack (a director from 1904) to the company's branch in Australia in 1901, where he discovered such a product in use.[41] Samples from Australian and American producers were analysed by Reckitt's chemists and by 1905, under the trademark 'Brasso', liquid polish was being sold initially to railways, hospitals, hotels, and large shops. In 1914, a similar motive led to experiments to produce a silver liquid polish,

'Silvo', the trade-mark name acquired with the goodwill of a small business in liquidation.[42] The progress of Reckitt's diversification away from starch and blue to include polishes of all kinds is indicated by sales figures between 1900 and 1914, when Reckitt's UK aggregate sales rose from £377,959 to £1,137,709. After only eight years in production, polishes other than lead accounted for 27 per cent; the proportion of total sales accounted for by starch dropped from 43 per cent to 21 per cent, and blue from 25 per cent to 15 per cent.[43]

Diversification was to take a different direction after the war, though based on new development within the same class of cleaning products. Imitating proprietary products introduced by other smaller companies lacking the marketing infrastructure, resources, and connections of Reckitt was early established as a route to product development. In 1921, the directors instructed Reckitt's chemists to try to replicate the formula for 'Dry Clene', a proprietary window cleaning preparation which had entered the market. The result was 'Windo',[44] which in 1923 was changed to 'Windolene' after Reckitt's acquired the assets and trade mark from a small and struggling business.[45] Because it was found that Reckitt's Windolene formula was effective for cleaning enamel as well as glass, travellers were asked to canvas grocers' views on the potential for selling Windolene as a bath and stove cleaner as well as for windows. A divided response and concern expressed about its competitiveness against 'Vim' and 'Kleanoff' (produced by Lever), was followed by sampling among consumers in Salisbury and other towns. Windolene for cleaning windows was launched in 1927.[46] The product survived for many years, though it never exceeded five per cent of total sales.[47] 'Steamo', a preparation for cleaning steamed up windows, was introduced in 1926, achieved few sales, and was withdrawn in 1940.[48]

In 1923, in response to a suggestion made by Sir James Reckitt, the nonagenarian chairman, the directors confirmed a long-standing policy not to trade through chemists because the management of transactions through two separate channels would be uneconomic. Because they did not regard bath salts as groceries, the directors resolved not to act on Sir James's suggestion that the company should experiment with methods used to manufacture blue and starch in tablet and crystal powder form in order to add bath salts to the product range.[49] Within these self-imposed constraints, marketing strategy continued to be developed through discussions between the senior salesman and the general manager, T.R. Ferens; he reported the outcomes to the Board of Directors, with whom responsibility for decision-making lay. When the war ended, the directors instructed the laboratory staff to research and report on a moth preparation, a baking powder, and an aluminium paint, though nothing came of these.[50] In the absence of new products, the directors returned to the strategic issue raised by Sir James' proposal regarding bath salts distribution. In 1925, the directors agreed that considerable scope existed for introducing shampoo powders, cough emulsions, 'week-end pills', and similar toiletry products sold through chemists.[51] While initially the product achieved limited sales, in breaking into the chemists' distribution chain this tentative initiative began a trend towards more radical marketing policies for which a reformed organisation concentrating specifically on new product search and development was considered imperative. This was introduced in 1927 in the form of a Research Committee which henceforward assumed responsibility for systematically searching for new opportunities by investigating new lines with a view to their introduction. In addition to assessing the suitability of products for manufacture, the committee was also charged with evaluating (with reference to financial considerations as well as competitive or complementary product mix) companies which might be suitable for acquisition.[52] A Technical Committee was formed in 1928 which comprised the heads of the manufacturing departments in addition to three members of the Research Committee – Arnold Reckitt, W.H. Slack (head of sales), and N.H. Joy. Meetings were held at least twice monthly. This committee's role was to consider the feasibility of manufacturing products proposed by the Research Committee before the recommendations were presented to the Board. Packaging became a major consideration of the Technical Committee, which explains why the head of the canister works (purchased in 1907) was a member.[53] Though not always adhered to, typically the sequence was as follows: first, the screening of new suggestions for new lines (wherever they originated) by the Research Committee; second, recommendations for experimentation were passed to Management Committee and the Board of Directors, from whom successful proposals would be referred to the laboratory for experiment; third, subject to satisfactory outcomes, the Technical Committee carried out feasibility and costing analysis, including that of packaging. The Technical Committee and the Sales and Advertising Committee reported back to the Research Committee, and, finally, firm recommendations from the Research Committee proceeded to the Board of Directors for decision on action. Cutting across this, in 1930, the directors instructed the Technical Committee to experiment with more of the company's products 'with a view to recommending standard lines for uses other than the ones they are normally put'.[54] This resulted in suggestions for alternative uses for starch: as tooth cleaner, for sunburn,[55] and for use in baths to effect slimming.[56] None was pursued. Even so, the Research Committee was of central importance to corporate strategy, playing a major role in successfully widening the product range by increasing sales and profitability during the 1930s. Impressed by the company's past success in distributing various types of cleaning products sold through grocers and the increasingly para-chemical character of production, the Research Committee persuaded the directors to reopen the question of introducing a car polish, a lavatory cleaner, and a household disinfectant to the product range. These products were to transform the company's product base.[57] Largely through the persistence of Langthorp and Stabler of the Advertising Department, the Research Committee revived the bath salts idea in the form of a perfumed effervescing tablet which was introduced into the market in 1927.[58] In 1931, Reckitt's chemists produced a preparation with a view to competing with 'Harpic'. Technically, feasibility of production was confirmed, but further inquiries into Harpic's market position led the Board to conclude that the strength of the brand rendered purchase preferable to competition. This led, in 1932, to the acquisition by Reckitt of the small Harpic Manufacturing Company formed in 1921.[59] Harpic toilet rolls (introduced by the Harpic Company in 1930) were also taken on to compete with the market leaders, 'Sanitas' and 'Bronco'. Again imitating the manufacturers of these brands, Reckitt's toilet line included medicated and perfumed rolls, though they achieved little success.[60] 'Sanpic', a drain cleaner manufactured by Harpic, was discontinued, but in 1935 the trademark was applied to a pine disinfectant for household use.[61]

Until his death in 1925, Lord Leverhulme was entirely responsible for determining the marketing strategy of Lever. Lever, like Reckitt, assessed their own products in the light of those manufactured by competing firms before deciding which to imitate or acquire. His travels, especially in North America, were a source of numerous ideas for new products or the marketing of existing ones. Since the 1880s 'Sunlight Soap' had been the basis of Lever's success, and from 1894 'Lifebouy', a disinfectant soap, took second place.[62] The success of 'Sunlight Flakes', developed in Lever's laboratory in 1899 and renamed 'Lux Flakes' in 1900, owed its huge commercial success less to the nature of the product (flaked soap was known from the mid-nineteenth century) than to the market research, presentation, and promotion carried out by the J. Walter Thompson advertising agency. The responsibility for introducing advanced American marketing methods to the company was that of Francis A. Countway, who from 1912 was the general manager of Lever's American subsidiary whose business was then largely confined to New England. Supported by Lever's personal financial resources as well as from the British business and by borrowing, the extensive national campaign that began in 1915 saw the sales of Lux rise from a few thousand boxes to more than a million within four years; sales of Lifebouy also doubled. Initially, the boxed Lux was advertised to middle-class women as a luxury soap for washing woollens. During the 1920s, when silk became more fashionable, the high-class brand was reinforced by advertisements linking Lux to washing silk.[63] In 1925, Countway introduced Lux toilet soap using similar methods and achieving a similar success, turning annual losses of £20,000 into a profit of £300,000 a year. In 1928, when the London office of J. Walter Thompson won the Lux account, this strategy of market research and positioning in the middle-class luxury market, supported by very large advertising expenditure, was successfully applied to the British market.[64]

A policy of multiple acquisition of other competing companies, culminating in the merger between Lever and the European Margarine Union in 1929 to form Unilever, resulted in an organisation comprising 49 associated manufacturing companies. Decisions concerning products, production, and marketing were under the control of each of the companies which in some markets were often in competition with each other. D'Arcy Cooper, Lord Leverhulme's successor, tackled the problems arising therefrom, first through a programme of reorganisation and rationalisation. A Technical Committee was set up to plan a programme of research 'directed to commercially profitable results' and to ensure co-operation between the technical experts of the associated companies.[65] Beginning in 1930, product areas were divided into three under the powerful central Special Committee of the Board. Divided into home and overseas, each product area was controlled by an executive body: for soap, margarine, and oil and fats. Control over product development and marketing remained with each of the manufacturers, whose numbers were drastically reduced by rationalising the product mix of the associated companies, concentrating on the strongest brands manufactured in a small number of profit centres.[66] In 1930, the transformation of the Advertising Department into a Market Research and Information Department marked a shift towards a more systematic, centralised marketing organisation, though associated companies were free to engage external agencies.[67] Details of the Market Research Department have not survived. It seems likely, however, that because of the emphasis on reducing brands within the organisation, the department's primary role was that of providing market intelligence and advertising to strengthen surviving product lines.[68]

IV

PRODUCT INNOVATION, R&D

Colman's first laboratory was opened in 1924 and heralded a shift of emphasis in product development.[69] Whereas hitherto a small number of researchers had been employed in an advisory role relating to traditional milled products focused on quality control, henceforward they were to become responsible for the implementation of higher levels of scientific control and experiment. The origin of this trend was twofold. In the context of difficulties in the trade in starch and mustard, the decision to utilise rice gluten, a by-product from the starch factory, was perceived as a route to diversification into the growing market for baby food. Development in this direction also offered Colman the opportunity to exploit the well-established reputation in that field of one of its subsidiary companies, that of Keen Robinson & Co. The acquisition of this business in 1903 had been for the purpose of removing competition in the mustard trade. However, that company also possessed a long history of a large trade in Robinson's patent barley and patent groats for infants.[70] Production of these was transferred to Norwich in 1925 to consolidate research on infant and invalid food products.[71] After a false start by one of Colman's chemists, a former employee of the Ministry of Food, the Colmans sought the advice of the Cambridge Professor Frederick Gowland Hopkins, a pioneer in the formulation of the vitamin concept and an influential figure in the history of nutrition.[72] On his advice, in addition to exercising strict scientific control over the manufacture of their food products, the company's researchers began to investigate the nutritional value of Colman's products. The appointment of Leslie Harris from Gowland's Department of Biochemistry in 1925, followed by the appointment of three other researchers to form a team, marked a significant step in the company's approach to new product development.[73] Scientific control was important in developing a method of retaining Vitamin C in soft drinks and in discovering the fungicide properties of mustard with a view to use it for medicinal purposes, though the latter did not prove commercially successful. However, the primary research objective set for Harris and his team was to develop a substitute possessing the nutritional composition of mothers' milk, thereby competing with Glaxo's fortified dried milk. An extensive study undertaken by Colman's chemists of infant feeding and nutrition which involved live animal experiments to test growth-promoting effects resulted in a product marketed through Keen & Robinson under the brand name 'Almata'.[74] A powder soluble in water, and in that respect novel, it was initially advertised as an infant food, though subsequent research aimed at stretching the product to justify recommending use by invalids and even puppies. Employing the language of nutritional science to describe the new product and the growth-promoting qualities claimed for it, Colman's heavy advertising of 'Almata, the complete infant food' was targeted especially at nursing mothers and general practitioners.

In fact, neither the quality of scientific research nor the substantial investment of resources into researching and advertising Almata prevented the commercial failure of an otherwise outstanding technical success (as it was perceived by the firm's scientists and managers).[75] Harris left in 1927 to lead the Dunn Nutrition Research Laboratory in Cambridge, though the remaining researchers stayed at Carrow, continuing to conduct research as well as advising on advertising copy. Subsequent nutritional research projects were both less ambitious and smaller in scale and potential. Attention was given to the addition of vitamin D to barley and groats and to the vitamin C content in a variety of fruit products, while the possibilities for making vitamin sweets and concentrates was another direction taken by the search for new products.[76]

More productive and more commercially successful was the branch laboratory and pilot established in Peterborough in 1928 in connection with the development of the trade of Joseph Farrow & Co. Ltd. An erstwhile competitor in the mustard trade, which had been based on heavy advertising at home and overseas, Colman had taken over the company in 1912, partly anticipating that the CWS (which had already begun to manufacture self-raising flour, thereby competing with Colman) was about to enter the mustard trade.[77] Again, as in the case of Keen & Robinson, which brought Colman into the infant and invalid food and drinks market, the acquisition of Farrow influenced the subsequent direction of Colman's search for new products at a time when product innovation became imperative for corporate survival. Farrow was a long-established firm specialising in the production of ketchups and processed vegetables and fruit, to which Colman later added the production and processing of peas and other vegetables for sale in cans. In 1932, an agreement with Smedley's Wisbech Produce Canners Ltd and British Canners Ltd resulted in the formation of a joint company, British Canners & Colman, capitalised at £0.25m.[78]

Although managers regarded research as central to the search for products which were either new or improved, a retrospective report on the company's R&D carried out in 1944 concluded that, although the quality control contribution was vital and the technical quality of research had been high, the commercial outcome from scientific research in the form of new products had been insignificant. The laboratory was regarded as having fallen well short of the standard expected of a leading food manufacture, and the report advised that the Chemical Research Department and the Control Section should be combined with a newly established Market Research Department, separate from the Sales Department. Implying past failure, the recommendation was that the newly created Research and Development Department would work to a director responsible for policy implementation. An outline strategy for the future emphasised the need to redirect efforts towards the development of new lines and the improvement of existing products.[79] This suggests that the belated introduction of Colman's New Products Committee in 1938, charged with 'finding, enquiring into, and reporting upon new products, new uses for existing products etc.', together with a Housewives' Panel, had yet to bear fruit.[80]

Reckitt's first qualified chemist was appointed in 1894[81] for the purpose of testing raw materials and controlling quality of starch and blue products. Another was appointed in 1898 'purely for research work and saving of by-products'.[82] Following the provision of laboratory facilities in 1900, including those in the polish manufacturing factories in Chiswick, the company employed possibly 16 chemists by 1914.[83] While quality control of raw materials and products continued to be their main role, a significant amount of internal research was applied to the search for new formulae to improve existing products. Borax and bi-carbonate were introduced to starch manufacture and carbon black into grate polishes. Experiments with potential new lines included those with boot polish, a notable if modest success.

The development from carbon blacking to other cleaners, together with the acquisition of polish-producing companies and the commercial success of Reckitt's metal polishes, notably Brasso, shifted the company's technical and research interests towards the chemistry of cleaning fluids. Thus, in 1927, Albert Reckitt proposed the development of a household disinfectant to be marketed through grocers. Though not anticipated at the time, this was to prove a turning point in the company's manufacturing and marketing history. While originating in research conducted in Reckitt's laboratory, the breakthrough was the work of an elderly bacteriologist, Dr Reynolds, formerly employed as a chemist by Jeyes, the long-established manufacturer of household disinfectant. Evidently seeking to develop a disinfectant at a higher level of bacteriological sophistication, his rebuff by the Jeyes directors in 1929 prompted Reynolds to offer his services to Reckitt.[84] Within the period of an initial three-month contract, a household disinfectant had been prepared possessing a coefficiency of three and qualities which rendered it excellent for household use. On a five-year contract Reynolds continued the experiments, developing a final product ready for testing outside the laboratory. A germicide based on para-chlor-meta-xynol was compounded with essential oils to produce a pleasant smell not normally associated with bacterides.[85] In 1930, the London Press Bureau and the London Press Exchange were consulted on the market for disinfectants,[86] a field which Reckitt's Research Committee felt was 'entirely new' to the company. A 1931 report confirmed Albert Reckitt's initial suggestion that disinfectants for general household uses offered a growing market opportunity.[87] Initial experiments conducted by Reckitt's chemists were aimed at developing a mild disinfectant suitable for household use which would possess a pleasanter odour than the disinfectants sold by Jeyes and Lysol, the market leaders.[88] The acquisition in 1928 of the Suffolk Chemical Company, the firm's supplier of methylated spirits used in making metal polish, was envisaged as the location for production. Distribution was intended to be through grocers, building on established connections.

Reynolds' research had a long-term impact on the work carried out in the Reckitt laboratories. Shortly before Reynolds joined the company in 1928, H.A. Scruton, chief chemist at Reckitt's Kingston Works, had observed that whereas there was no distinction between industrial and scientific research in the laboratories, a difference should be made between fundamental and empirical research: 'Although we ourselves do not do much fundamental work, we are interested in the results of such work in different fields and attempt to utilise these results wherever possible.'[89] Based on the rationale that scientifically qualified staff could contribute both to the process of routine control and therefore quality as well as to creative activity, until the development of pharmaceuticals in the 1930s no distinction was drawn between research and development and chemistry applied to control. Separation began to take place as the complexity of the company's products increased and the specialisms required of scientists grew.[90] The laboratories were clearly important in enabling the company to innovate. Like members of the Technical Committee, the chemists were responsible for implementing the Board's decisions in support of the recommendations of the Research Committee. Once a new product entered the experimental phase, the Board received monthly reports from the laboratories and referred those aspects they considered required action to the relevant committee: Research, Sales and Advertising, or back to the Technical Committee.[91]

In the absence of statistical data, it is impossible to compare the size of R&D expenditure at Colman and at Reckitt with that at Unilever, one of the largest spenders in Britain during the 1930s.[92] Before 1914, the search for new materials, rather than the development of new products, had been characteristic of the research conducted by Lever's chemists.[93] The company's capacity to do this was expanded considerably in 1919 with the acquisition of Joseph Crosfield & Co. and the accompanying research laboratory located in Warrington, which possessed a strong record of research.[94] Amalgamation of the two laboratories in the early 1920s resulted in an 'extensive research laboratory with an annual cost of more than £20,000'.[95] Unless a dramatic change in attitude occurred during

World War I, it appears that the expanded research facilities failed to impress Lord Leverhulme. In 1915 he had expressed the view that research was 'absorbing rather than making money', even excluding research staff from the company's profit-sharing scheme because of this.[96] Even so, the possibility of concentrating soap-related research at Warrington and the decision to manufacture edible fats in 1915 marked a change in the character of research at Lever's Port Sunlight laboratory, from the empirical and technical to the scientific.[97]

Until 1914, product developments and acquisitions at Lever were directly soap-, oil-, and fats-related in order to control raw material supplies for manufacture. Thereafter, a classic instance of vertical integration effected in that year resulted in the diversification into edible fats through the production of margarine. The origins of this development lay in the outbreak of World War I and the government's attempt to anticipate the adverse effects on supplies. Specifically in order to minimise the expected effects of disrupted margarine supplies, the government approached Lord Leverhulme to explore a possible solution. The result was the formation of Planter's Margarine Co., a joint venture with Watson, one of Lever's major competitors. Lever acquired complete control of the company in 1915.[98] Except during the artificially created wartime boom, Lever's margarine trade remained limited until after the merger with European Margarine Union producers to form Unilever in 1929, in part because of the taste of vegetable oil. Nonetheless, D'Arcy Cooper's conviction that the static state of the soap trade since 1924 would continue is crucial in explaining why he decided to concentrate research into the 'unknown possibilities' of the edible fats trade.[99] Under his management, the pioneering research begun at the Port Sunlight laboratory in 1915 in an attempt to make the vitamin content of margarine comparable with that of butter[100] eventually bore fruit. Under the brand name 'Viking', the new margarine containing vitamins A and D was launched in 1927 and marketed as 'an expensive article with special claims', a pricing strategy intended to imply close comparability to butter.[101] This research by Unilever's chemists led to two vitamin concentrates, 'Essogen' and 'Advita'. Essogen was, in effect, trialled in 1933, when the vitamin supplement was distributed to all Unilever staff during the influenza outbreak of that year. In 1935, all employees were issued with both. By that time, the company magazine claimed, the supplements were in regular widespread use (though it was not clear whether this referred only to company employees or to the public).[102] By 1935, the quality of the concentrate was sufficiently consistent to extend it to all branded lines of margarine, which in 1936 accounted for 25 per cent of margarine sales. Of even higher quality was 'Stork Margarine', produced in 1938. Tasting competitions at which consumers were invited to try to distinguish 'Stork' from butter and the setting up of a cookery school to promote the culinary qualities of the product contributed to the rapid growth in sales.[103] Thereafter, the development of edible fats was due primarily to internal research, though Van Den Bergh's 'Blue Band' came into the Unilever product range through the 1927 merger. In 1937, a repositioning of margarine was attempted through a Lintas advertising campaign to sell Lever's Stork margarine as a spreading fat, rather than as a butter substitute. Advertising copy stressed the 'energy-giving freshness' to be gained from the 'sunshine vitamins' contained in Stork.[104] Although annual research expenditure rose to £85,000 in 1938,[105] in a memorandum prepared by Unilever's technical director in 1942, the commercial achievements of the company's research were considered to have been modest. He argued that because the company enjoyed such a dominant position in the markets for its products, any inventor with a relevant discovery invariably offered it to the company; one result was to slow research and development,[106] though not expenditure.[107] In 1939, evidence of concern to pay greater attention to product development is the formation of a sales and service section, the purpose of which was 'to criticise our products with a view to improvements, the need for which is not ordinarily obvious'.[108]

V

PRODUCT DIVERSIFICATION AND DEVELOPMENT: THE ROLE OF INHERITED RESOURCES AND AGENCY

The history of product development in the three firms reveals important similarities and differences in their responses to similar economic environments. Table 2 highlights the similarities in the characteristics of product innovation and development under conditions of imperfect competition.

This is an attempt to distinguish between (1) products introduced possessing truly innovative attributes from (2) those which while new to a firm's product range did not, and (3) those which were no more than variants of existing lines.

TABLE 2
THE CHARACTERISTICS OF PRODUCT DIVERSIFICATION AND DEVELOPMENT

Firm	1 A completely new product	2 A product or product line new to the company incorporating novel features or in different form	3 A new item in the company's existing product line or a modification of an existing product in the form of novel features, dispensing, or packaging	Developed through acquisition of another business or purchase of patent rights
Colman's	1	3	10	4
Reckitt's	1	8	12	9
Lever/Unilever	0	12	16	8*

Notes: * One is not known. The complete list of products for each company is presented chronologically in Appendix 1.

The table shows that only two products fall into the first category. It also shows that most diversification took the form either of adding product lines (sometimes in the form of variants), or by extending existing lines through product development and marketing, for example, by varying flavour, colour, dispensing, or packaging was the most frequent form of diversification. The table also indicates the relative importance of acquisition of other businesses or purchase of patent rights in the process compared with internal development. The data presented for Colman is misleading in the sense that although internal development accounts for all except four of the products listed, this is because the products deriving from Farrow's and Keen & Robinson's product range were only developed and marketed by Carrow long after the businesses had been acquired.

The structure and organisation of firms and the strategies pursued by their respective managers and directors were critical factors explaining differences in direction and extent of diversification. The driving force behind Colman's strategy was the defence of its almost monopolistic position in the mustard trade (in the mid-1920s this accounted for 85 per cent of the company's profits) though at the same time they hoped for new products to emerge from the laboratories.[109] This partly reflected the company's failure to hold on to its dwindling market share in the starch and blue trades, not least because of competition from Reckitt.[110] With the agreement of Colman's directors in the course of discussions of merger, in 1930, the Reckitt directors examined Colman's internal records to assess the company's performance. They were critical of Colman's 'lavish' experimentation with proprietary lines supported by heavy expenditure on advertising which the figures showed to have been unprofitable.[111] This policy was compared with Reckitt's own approach to product development. During discussions leading up to merger, one director reported: 'again and again we ... referred to our fixed policy that we would have nothing to do with proprietary lines unless they yielded a substantial profit'.[112] This referred to the policy, formalised by the Research Committee in 1927 but originating in 1919, that profitability should take precedence over sales volume in product planning. As a method of achieving this, lines shown to be either uncompetitive or in overall decline should be replaced by products for markets which were profitable and expanding.[113] It was not until 1938 that Colman set up a New Products Committee along Reckitt lines as well as a Housewives' Panel to advise on marketing problems.[114] Colman's continuing heavy, albeit diminishing, dependence on its staple product was confirmed in a review of the home trade carried out during 1947 and 1948. This showed 50 per cent of the company's profit to have been derived from the sale of dry and prepared mustards, peppers, and spices; starch and blue accounted for 11.5 per cent. The markets for these lines showed a declining trend. Of the 'new' lines believed to be possible sources of expansion, invalid and infant foods accounted for 15 per cent of profit and cereal products (oats, flakes, pastry, and semolina) eight per cent. Only soft drinks, which contributed 16 per cent, were expected to increase sales and profitability substantially.[115]

Table 3 in Appendix 1 presents a chronological list of products introduced by Colman. The two products which were completely new to the company, the innovative Almata powdered food for infants in 1922 and Krusto pastry mix in 1930, were both commercial failures. Relatively successful was the development of variants of products already made by the company but developed through the introduction of new items in the existing line and by branding and advertising. However, the origin of this development was the acquisition in 1903 of the substantial long-established London business of Keen Robinson & Co. While the motive for acquisition had been to end damaging competition from Keen's mustard, the new acquisition brought with it 'Robinson's Patent Barley Water' and 'Robinson's Patent Groats' for infants. These continued in production at the London plant until 1925, when relocation in Norwich was followed by intensive advertising campaigns and product development.[116] Under the Robinson brand, 'Old Heathers' Barley Water' was launched in 1928, Lemon Barley Water in 1935 and Lemon Barley Crystals in 1936. Lime and orange flavours were added in 1937 and 1939. The acquisition of another competitor in the mustard trade, the Peterborough firm of Joseph Farrow & Co Ltd, was also to be the source of product diversification into processed foods, though again only in the longer term.[117] In 1932, the formation of British Canners & Colman, a joint company in association with Smedley's of Wisbech, established a foothold for Colman in the processed foods trade.[118] Thus, as in the case of Keen & Robinson, the diversification of Colman's product range resulting from the takeover of Farrow was actually the outcome of an historically defensive policy of acquisition focused on staple products and was, in effect, an unintended development. The failure of intended diversification must be attributed in large measure to the failure of management. In 1919, following Stuart's death, Sir Jeremiah Colman, from the London side of the family and already 60 years old, had been chairman since 1900 and considered himself to be the only director who was either interested or knowledgeable regarding company matters. Sir Jeremiah referred to the only other senior director, Russell James Colman, two years older and from the Norwich side of the family, as having withdrawn early from his responsibilities: 'to him a day spent in the office, at Board meetings, signing papers and looking at sheets of figures was a day wasted.' Russell James preferred field sports and local politics.[119] Longstanding intra-family tensions between the London and Norwich branches of the Colman family as well as generational and successional problems were also tackled by Sir Jeremiah.[120] But despite his introduction of meetings where junior as well as senior directors were invited (a novel development just before World War I) in order to acclimatise the juniors to business matters, the younger generation expressed no desire to become involved in the day-to-day management of the business.[121] Sir Jeremiah had considered conversion of the business into a public company as a method of introducing 'new ... as well as eminent young blood into management' as early as 1913.[122] The war intervened. When the younger Colmans returned after the war they expressed complete opposition to the idea of 'sinking their individuality' which they perceived merger or conversion would involve. In Sir Jeremiah's words, 'the new directors were quite content to jog along and maintain their position'.[123] After Sir Jeremiah wrote his private memoir in 1925, the younger generation did become involved in decision-making, Captain Geoffrey being personally associated with the ill-fated Krusto and birdseed initiatives. His demise aged 42 in 1935 led to a renewed attempt to prepare for merger, preferably with Reckitt, to which end control as a condition was waived by the remaining directors. Conversion from private to public company, another facilitating step, also occurred in 1935.

Acquisition followed by internal product development is also characteristic of Reckitt's more systematic marketing strategies which were sensitive to the importance of concentrating on profitable growth markets. This explains why the corporate acquisitions which occurred within the inter-war period were developed immediately after takeover. Table 4 in Appendix 1 lists the product developments at Reckitt. The technology of starch and blue did not provide a good basis for product stretching or development. Reckitt's leading Robin brand starch had been re-packaged under the name Robin toilet powder immediately before 1911 and offered as a foot powder for soldiers in 1914.[124] The failure of both was attributed by salesmen to distribution through grocers rather than chemists. Bath salts survived throughout the period but with only small sales, though by making the breakthrough into distribution through chemists the experiment had long-lasting significance for the company's product history. Polishes provided a much better basis for development. The demand for paste polish for stoves was slow to decline. However, the new liquid polishes answered the growing demand from the owners of brass furniture, brass and copper fireplaces, and brass and plated ornaments, which from the end of the nineteenth century became fashionable among and affordable to a wide range of consumers.

Metal polishes were profitable and they were also important in shifting the company's competence in increasingly complex industrial chemistry, which led to the appointment of specialist chemists to control and improve quality.[125] The route, however, from polish to disinfectant was circuitous. In 1921, Reckitt began to market 'Zebo', a liquid grate polish which exploited the association with the firm's Zebra paste.[126] In 1926, the sales staff in the Australian branch reported the replacement of black lead on stoves by aluminium paint.[127] The option of following the trend by substituting paint for black lead was rejected, however, after a financial assessment estimated profits would fall below 33.3 per cent on selling price,[128] an important criterion affecting decisions relating to product innovation. Instead, attention turned to variations in packaging and dispensing as ways of maintaining profits from a declining black lead trade, specifically the development of a new lead paste dispensed from tube containers. Trials to compare packet, liquid, and tube lead were conducted by a newly formed Housewives' Jury.[129] Meanwhile, increasing sales of lacquered and oxidised articles which did not require polishing dealt a further blow to Reckitt's lead polish sales. By contrast, metal polish sales grew and in the 1930s accounted for roughly one-half of Reckitt's polish sales and more than one-third of the company's UK sales. Reckitt held about 80 per cent of the UK market.[130] The acquisition of competitors and the resulting extension in the kinds of polish sold, partly accounts for this. So, too, does internal product development.

Impressed by the potential for growth in the market for a polish suited to the cellulose finish of cars, floors, and furniture, in 1925, the directors allocated finance for experimental work in the laboratory of the Chiswick Polish Company. This was a joint enterprise formed in 1913 that comprised three other wax polish firms – Master Boot Polish Ltd, William Berry Ltd, and the valuable Cherry Blossom brand (hitherto solely owned by the Mason family). Initially, Brasso had been advertised as suitable for use as car polish, but that ceased in 1926 when the inventor of 'Carlustre' offered Reckitt's the manufacturing rights. After chemical analysis of the product and development in preparation for volume production, it was introduced to the market as 'Karpol' and was distributed mainly through garages.[131] In the early 1930s, Karpol held roughly 50 per cent of the car polish market.[132] However, sales declined rapidly thereafter, a consequence of improvements in coachwork finishes, the increasing provision of washing and cleaning facilities at garages, and (probably most important) the failure of Reckitt's chemists to solve the continuing problem of producing a polish in volume which did not remove colour from paintwork. Attempts in the laboratory to modify the new polish formulae for use in households on paint, varnish, and fabric also failed.[133]

Polishes and cleaners were the main products which sustained the company from the early years of the twentieth century until the 1930s. It was then that the company diversified in a completely different direction from household goods and toiletries, though the search had begun in pursuit of a cleaning disinfectant for household use. 'Dettol' originated from considerations similar to those which led the Research Committee to revive the Harpic initiative, and by a circuitous, initially unintended, route were to take the company into the pharmaceutical trade.[134] Building on the chemistry of cleaning fluids, a strong marketing organisation through grocers, and the possession of several market-leading brands, in 1927, Albert Reckitt proposed that the company should produce a household disinfectant. A market research report confirmed the potential for such a product where a growing market existed[135] and the research for development began.[136]

However, a dramatic re-positioning came under consideration on the advice of Charles Hobson, a self-employed advertising agent, who from 1927 had handled accounts for Reckitt's bath cubes and Karpol car polish. He persuaded the directors to seek scientific evaluation by expert bacteriologists and to agree that, subject to convincing them, the product should be marketed as an antiseptic for human use. He suggested midwifery as a starting point.[137] Tests conducted at the Bernhard Baron Research Laboratories at Queen Charlotte's Maternity Hospital in London proved to be so favourable that Hobson's strategy was adopted. It was agreed that medical use should form the basis of the initial marketing campaign for 'Dettol', the name chosen by the directors because it sounded 'vaguely scientific, was brief, memorable, had no particular meaning, and was acceptable in most languages'.[138]

In 1931, consultation between the Research Committee, the Advertising Department, and the laboratory resulted in a list of the main uses for which the product was considered suitable and which would determine marketing strategy in phase one. In rank order, medical uses included: 1. cuts and bruises, feminine hygiene, general surgical purposes, bath and toilet purposes (cleaning false teeth), and children's epidemics. In phase two, which was planned to begin once medical uses had been firmly established in the public's mind, advertising was to draw attention to general purposes: for use in sinks, drains, dustbins, and lavatories (as a disinfectant cleaner), also for washing floors, laundry uses, and for washing dogs.[139] Hobson satisfied the directors' request for the design of a 'unique container' with the curved-shouldered Dettol bottle with black Bakelite screw cap. His distinctive label consisted of a black background, white sword (denoting protection), lettering on a green strip and the reassuring legend: 'Germicidal, antiseptic, non-poisonous, non-irritant.' The new product also marked a turning point in the firm's history since it was agreed that, because it was designed for medicinal use, it was necessary to forsake the grocers and to penetrate the network of chemists and druggists with whom some grocers were trying to compete. Chemists and druggists regarded themselves as a profession which, through its organisations, had hitherto successfully protected members against price-cutting and encroachments by grocers, and to a lesser extent the growth of multiples. One result was that the mark-ups on products sold by chemists and druggists were typically higher than on goods sold by grocers. This was another advantage to offset risking grocers' traditional goodwill towards Reckitt.[140]

'Confidential information' regarding Lysol's intention to market a similar product hastened the launch that took place at exhibitions attended by chemists, druggists, and medical practitioners in London in January 1933.[141] The £80,000 advertising campaign to launch Dettol received an unsolicited boost by the medical profession which reflected an effective pre-marketing testing and education programme (not least in preparing a new sales force) before the actual launch. Maternal mortality had been the subject of a recent government inquiry and was the context in which a paper on this subject in relation to antiseptics researched by Drs Colebrook and Maxted appeared in *the Journal of Obstetrics and Gynaecology of the British Empire* in 1933. In a subsequent booklet entitled *Antisepsis in Midwifery*, Dettol was specifically recommended. In 1936, a foreword to a more extended study of antisepsis included Sir Comyns Berkeley's reaffirmation of the superior efficacy of Dettol for use in obstetrics. A report which appeared in the *British Medical Journal* in 1937 by Drs Garrod and Keynes likewise praised Dettol cream for its effectiveness and convenience in use for midwifery. Dr Nixon's article 'The Prevention and Control of Puerperal

Sepsis', published in *The Practitioner* in 1938, was described in Reckitt's magazine aimed at overseas branches and agents as 'valuable propaganda' and offered 1,000 copies for 14 shillings.[142] Such public authoritative statements from independent medical experts provided perfect copy for use in testimonials distributed to hospitals and to medical professionals generally by the specialist medical sales representatives recruited at the beginning of the initial campaign.[143] The company was quick to extend the Dettol product line by introducing obstetric cream, surgical and instrumental antiseptics in 1934, and 'Dettolin' mouthwash in 1935.

The commercial success of Dettol did not end the Research Committee's search for new products sold either through grocers or chemists. In 1934, one employee was placed in a grocer's shop and another in a chemist's to monitor customers' behaviour and preferences.[144] Staff in Reckitt's overseas branches and sales representatives overseas were invited to suggest new lines which might be profitable in their respective markets. A poor response led the Committee to suggest an indigestion powder (similar to 'McClean's'), or skin creams and oils (like 'Nivea').[145] Home representatives' conferences produced suggestions which included laxatives, firelighters, flycatchers, wallpaper glue, and steel wool. An even wider range of suggestions was elicited through a general staff questionnaire from which only a new gas cooker cleaner, a non-abrasive bath cleaner, and a 'U-need-this' pine-scented soluble tablet for use in the cistern proceeded to experimental stage in the laboratory.[146]

The final successful product to be developed before World War II was 'Steradent'. The origin grew out of the Research Committee's conviction of the advantage to be gained from extending the Dettol line, following Dettol obstetric cream, surgical and instrumental antiseptics added in 1934, and Dettolin mouthwash in 1935. With this intention, Reckitt's chemists set out to develop a toothpaste. This focus on dental hygiene evidently alerted staff, for in 1935 Board Minutes recorded that 'several individuals in the office' gave good reports of Steradent Denture Cleaner, a product launched by a small company of the same name in the previous year. The directors ordered testing in the laboratory, on the basis of which the chemists returned an unfavourable verdict on quality grounds. A year later, the Steradent company was producing to an improved formula, resulting in rising sales. Reckitt's directors reacted quickly. Trials of the improved Steradent were carried out, though this time the directors ignored the chemists and tested among 50 of Reckitt's office and factory employees. Positive evaluation led to the purchase of Steradent Ltd in 1937 for £1,000, an acquisition which marked the introduction of a long history of this new Reckitt product, though retaining its brand name.[147] When in 1937, D. & W. Gibbs (a Unilever subsidiary company) introduced 'Dentabs', Reckitt's plans to produce Steradent in tablet form were brought forward.[148] A panel of 45 employees undertook to test the tablets and to use them strictly in accordance with directions, submitting to regular examinations of their dentures to test the efficacy of the tablets. The outcome was deemed sufficiently successful to proceed, but World War II brought further development to a halt.[149] The Steradent experience had repercussions. While the in-house 'consumer survey' had proved useful, in 1938, the Research Committee agreed to abandon this method of testing reactions to new products, replacing it with a Housewives' Jury consisting of 1,000 women, none of whom should be Reckitt employees.[150] Initial screening of ideas for new projects, whether from laboratory staff, staff from elsewhere, members of the Research Committee, other directors, inventors, sole proprietors, or from members of the public remained the responsibility of the Research Committee. Some indication of the scale of this task is its rejection of 50 such proposals in 1938, some after experimentation in the laboratory and testing, though summarily in other cases. Most were aimed at the pharmaceutical and toiletry markets.[151]

Before 1939, Dettol was aimed almost entirely at the home market and accounted for eight per cent of total UK sales (but at minimal profit).[152] This compared with sales of starch (11 per cent), of black lead (21 per cent), and metal polishes (20 per cent). The latter two were the biggest profit earners (both profit on sales of over 30 per cent, and total). Harpic sales (eight per cent) and Steradent (seven per cent) were to grow after the war, as did Windolene. During the war, sales of Dettol products grew, exceeding 25 per cent (at a rate of profit between 20 and 30 per cent), though sales and profitability fell to around 20 per cent during the 1950s. Metal polishes and a revival of starch were the other major post-war growth points.[153] As a matter of policy, product development came to be focused primarily on pharmaceuticals.

While very much larger than the other two companies – even when the companies amalgamated to become Reckitt & Colman in 1938 – the pattern of diversification and the process by which it occurred are similar for Lever (see Table 5, Appendix 1). A mixture of corporate acquisitions to defend or expand market share in established markets was a feature of the early period. Later, some of the products of companies taken over were developed by the acquiring companies, either in the company's laboratories or through modification and 'improvements' in the presentation of existing products. Unilever's historian referred to this process as 'diversification under distress'.[154] The outcome was a product mix which, in 1937, was directed towards the markets for soaps and other detergents, toilet preparations, and perfumes (22 per cent); for margarine, edible fats, and salad oils (22 per cent); and for foods for human consumption, other vegetable and animal oils, and fats (22 per cent.).[155] Perfumery and toothpaste were new lines inherited by Unilever through acquisition which began to be developed as a matter of policy during the 1930s, though especially after World War II.

Foods for human consumption were developed through enterprises purchased privately by Lord Leverhulme between 1918 and 1921 after he had become the owner of the Scottish islands of Lewis and Harris. To handle the products of the islands' fisheries, he purchased the Macfisheries retailing chain. As fishmongers also sold sausages, he also bought the Wall's company which, in addition to making sausages, manufactured ice cream.[156] Initially, these businesses, whose acquisition has been described by Unilever's historian as 'economic madness',[157] were completely separate from the company and unrelated to the firm's corporate strategy. In 1922, however, financial pressures led Lord Leverhulme to divest himself of these 'personal extravagances' and they passed into the hands of Lever as part of the company's diverse underdeveloped assets. Under the rationalisation strategy introduced in the reorganised structure during the 1930s, Lord Leverhulme's former private enterprises began to emerge as a basis for a single group of food products in which manufacturers shared common problems in preserving, technology, and marketing.[158] This trend intensified immediately after the end of World War II when Unilever acquired Batchelors Peas Ltd (one of the largest vegetable canning plants in Britain) and a controlling interest in two other firms manufacturing frosted foods.[159] This acquisition shifted the balance of diversification towards the manufacture of processed food other than edible fats and oils. It also underlined the increasing threat to Colman in the market for prepared and processed foods. Lever had long set the limits to the diversification possibilities open to Colman and Reckitt in the laundry trades and affected decisions concerning acquisition (in overseas markets, too) as well as internal development of washing blue. When, in 1925, the Research Committee considered the idea of producing a cleaner for artificial silk, the question one director raised was whether this would trouble Lever. The response was that as the product would be spirit-based it could be regarded as a different line from a soap cleaner, though further investigation (which came to nothing) should proceed with care.[160] In 1928, Reckitt's directors resolved to avoid tri-sodium-phosphate-related new lines for cleaning fluids because they would be interpreted as conflicting with Lever's interests. Also in 1929, Reckitt's directors rejected a complaint from Lever that advertising Karpol as suitable for cleaning paint as well as cleaning cars was 'entering Lever's territory'.[161] In 1931, an agreement was reached for a period of 15 years whereby Lever undertook not to handle starch, blue, or polishes and sold to Reckitt its blue and stove polish interest in a subsidiary company in Australia. In return, Reckitt undertook not to enter the soap, soap powder, scourer, or margarine trades,[162] though the sheer difference in the size of the two companies made the last possibility extremely remote.

Competition and collusion of this kind, therefore, including, as Penrose suggested,[163] expected actions of competitors, were part of the external environment influencing constraints on product diversification. So, too, was the perception of the costs of changing distribution channels, from grocers to chemists. Reckitt's directors found the logic compelling, following the development first of bath cubes and later of Dettol, the latter leading to direct sales to hospitals and through medical practitioners. Colman remained firmly committed to grocers, even after the diversification into food and drink products intended for infants and convalescents. Both also found it necessary, despite hostility from grocers, to sell through the new multiples, even the Co-op. Lever's larger scale commitment to the toiletry trade made distribution through chemists inevitable. From the 1920s, the mass marketing approach of Liggett and Boots began to transform the sale of pharmaceuticals and toiletries, offering an appropriate channel for Unilever's increasing range and volume of toiletry products in the 1930s. Unilever's problem was not the *lack* of product diversification, but the task of rationalisation and more focused marketing of the wide range of products which the company had accumulated primarily through acquisitions culminating in the 1929 merger.

VI
DIVERSIFICATION, DECISION-MAKING AND CONTINGENCY

The model of imperfectly competitive markets in which production technology had reached maturity approximated the economic context within which the three firms under examination operated between the wars. The characteristics of each of the companies' economic environments were similar, as were the incentives to diversify (or, in Lever's case, alter the balance between existing products). Penrose maintained that the two factors within a firm most affecting perceptions of solutions and the directions which, as a consequence, diversification takes, are (1) inherited resources, both physical and knowledge-based, and in the form of established business and commercial connections, and (2) the capacities and skills of existing managerial personnel, the management 'team'.[164] She also maintained that the direction diversification takes is heavily influenced by the areas of specialisation developed by an organisation which has little to do either with scale or size of firm, but more to do with 'the nature of the basic position that it is able to establish for itself' and that it can defend in depth.[165] In this process, industrial research is seen as a rational development in the search for new products, though she emphasised that the essentially speculative character of such research, was an 'act of faith'.[166] Penrose was also critical of the view that regards acquisition and merger as significant primarily as a means of reducing competition or establishing monopolistic dominance, an emphasis which she regarded as simply wrong.[167] How far do these generalisations illuminate the history of our three firms?

In the sense that at least one of the principal products manufactured by the companies originated either from the beginning of the nineteenth century (Reckitt's and Lever's cleaning products) or from the early nineteenth century (Colman's food and cleaning products), the companies continued to trade within the same product classes for a very long time. Within these classes the new product lines introduced required limited changes in resources in the form of materials, capital, technology, skills, and distribution networks employed. In each case, specialisation was not primarily dependent on technical economies of scale or the size of firms except inasmuch as each developed a basic defence of positions in markets through acquisition of competitors and advertising, strategies which, by the twentieth century, the smaller companies they acquired could not emulate. This process occurred partly through the exploitation of the goodwill accompanying trademarks either acquired from enterprises taken over or purchased for the name only. Albeit at different speeds and on a different scale, Lever and Reckitt, followed by Colman, extended their market position beyond a limited range of corporate brands within one or more product classes to construct multi-brand product portfolios. However, multi-branding using non-descriptive terms was also introduced to market products developed internally, beginning with Lever's Sunlight Soap from 1887, and Reckitt's Zebra grate polish from 1890. In the case of Colman and Reckitt, the perception of constraints on the extent of diversification beyond an inherited familiarity and accumulated connections throughout the grocery trade proved to be most enduring at Colman and a hindrance to Reckitt's diversification into pharmaceuticals and toiletries. Lever was large enough to acquire its own distributive connections outside the grocery trade.

Perceptions regarding the limits to diversification and the directions it should take, however, were powerfully influenced by the capacities and skills of owners and managers. Colman emerges as an extreme example of the stereotypical dysfunctional family firm. It maintained a closed structure (directors and the family holding more than 50 per cent of the ordinary voting shares in 1938) and was a hierarchical organisation which, until the early years of the century, did not even hold meetings that included 'junior directors', let alone managers. The management of production was completely separate from marketing functions, the separation being geographical with a history of divided family interests and loyalties. A succession problem was in part due to war, but much more important was the haemorrhage of second- and third-generation Colmans from management because they favoured a sporting life and politics over days spent in the office. Geographical and functional division was also a feature of the Reckitt organisation; however, the intra-family tension that produced this arrangement during the first generation of entrepreneurs had disappeared by the late nineteenth century. As for the younger Colmans' reluctant entrepreneurialism, no parallel existed at any time in the Reckitt's history. Although the Reckitts, and T.R. Ferens, were also involved in politics and country life, they showed a hard-headed approach to the need to recruit directors as well as managers from outside the family and made the most senior positions open to them. While the Reckitts' level of control was much less than the Colmans', the family continued to dominate the Board and the organisation remained hierarchical. Even so, during negotiations, Ferens and Arnold Reckitt used the company's status as a public company in their argument for insisting on a more disciplined approach to business by Colman before merger could take place. Reckitt's directors, the Colmans were told, needed to protect share prices to retain the confidence of shareholders and therefore ensure profitable trading.[168]

In theory, the Reckitts were open to external influence on business policy, in fact, they and their insider non-family directors controlled the business. They did, however, also display an appreciation of the importance for succession of promotion, based on ability and performance, rather than on family membership alone. Again, unlike the management at Colman, the organisation of management within a hierarchical committee structure involved those best able to contribute to policy formation and implementation. Such a management team enabled the company to promote and successfully manage growth through acquisition and diversification.

Lever's transition from autocratic hierarchy to professional, largely non-family-managed hierarchy was sudden, more spectacular but nonetheless, as far as decisions regarding product diversification and development were concerned, was accompanied by problems and approaches to solutions not dissimilar from those encountered by Reckitt. The same could be said of all three companies with respect to the application of science (though on completely different scales) to industrial research. The outcomes, however, reveal that science contributed more to control and modification than to the development of entirely new products. As in the period between 1870 to 1914, the overwhelming proportion of product developments were those introducing a new product into an existing product line sold in an existing market (a change in flavour or brand) or with added features, or involving modification affecting, shape, colour, size, packaging, or dispensing. Not one of Lever's products introduced between 1919 and 1939 was new to the world, though roughly one-third of them was new to the company. Colman's Almata was a product entirely new to the company, developed through science-based research and marketed by using the goodwill of Keen & Robinson. However, 'Keen's complete infant food' ran into competition from Glaxo, whose image of modernity and aggressive management soon offset Colman's first-mover advantage. Much the same happened to Krusto, the instant pastry mix, another product new to the company though quickly taken up by the large flour millers. Reckitt was exceptional in introducing and establishing enduring leadership in the development, production, and marketing of a new product – Dettol – resulting from scientific research. Dettol was exceptional inasmuch as it was the only product (rather than a variant) newly introduced to any of the companies which achieved major commercial success within the period.

The employment of the British Press Exchange to report on the likely response of consumers to Dettol marked Reckitt's transition from directors' reliance on salesmen's advice to that of professional market researchers. In this respect, Reckitt followed both Lever and Colman, each having engaged the services of J. Walter Thompson earlier in the 1920s.[169] Fitzgerald's study of Rowntree, a British company pioneering the use of market research, includes a description of product-oriented and marketing-oriented firms. In the former, production functions, costs, and availability of machinery and labour determined which products were made while production functioned with little reference to the sales marketing-oriented firm, product planning occurred according to consumers' wants identified through market research.[170] Even if we accept this sequence from production to marketing orientation stereotypes,[171] the characteristics of marketing and product development revealed in the history of the three firms place them between the two extremes. Defining 'new' products as those described in categories 1 to 3, the overwhelming preponderance of development in the lower categories of novelty were symptomatic of a process of competition through imitation and differentiation, and therefore involved minimal risk of misinterpreting completely consumer demand. Sometimes successful and sometimes not, salesmen's advice through contact with retailers was highly regarded as an important input in decision-making. Intelligence regarding consumers' responses to new products introduced by companies in the US and Australia was another fruitful ingredient in the process of finding significantly novel products. Consumer testing among employees was a primitive form of research (though there is evidence of a similar approach in the preparation of JWT's reports) yet it did reveal an appreciation of the need to satisfy consumers. So, too, did the sampling of new products among populations in locations chosen according to income, observed regional preferences, or other relevant characteristics (hard and soft water, for example).

Systematic searching for new products did not begin with professionalised market research through market surveys which took consumers as their starting point. This was preceded by an intermediate stage when the search process, albeit constrained to a degree by inherited resources and competencies, was consciously directed towards satisfying consumers' perceived wants in addition to diversifying a productive base under competitive pressure. However, neither in the phase of organised research and development nor in the early stages of systematisation of market research were the essential characteristics of product development patterns transformed. Inherited resources and reputation, rather than reported consumer preferences, continued to explain the *initiation* of new products and new product lines within each company's committee structures. When market research was employed it was to test internally generated ideas.

Inherited resources and reputation are also fundamental to an explanation of the persistence of product classes. However, they neither explain entry into new product classes nor account for the introduction of every new product line. In the case of Lever, the transition from being a soap-manufacturing company to a producer of food and toiletries owed more to Lord Leverhulme's personal ventures in 1919, undertaken for reasons unrelated to corporate strategy, than to planned new product development. The introduction of margarine in 1914 was in response to a government initiative. Colman's addition of infant food, health-related soft drinks, sauces, and canned vegetables to the product range was the outcome of its acquisition of Keen Robinson and Farrow, competitors in the mustard trade, the objective in each case being monopolisation rather than diversification. Reckitt's entry into the pharmaceutical trade (and therefore a new product class) was the result of internal research and development to produce a superior household disinfectant, an extension of traditional cleaning fluid products. Advice from an advertising agent at a late stage in this process led to an alteration in the direction of development work and market research. The outcome was a transformation of both the company's product mix and the construction of a marketing capacity through the pharmaceutical trade. In each of the three cases uncertainty regarding competition led to acquisition. Perceptions of maturing markets prompted the search, varying in the extent to which search was systematic, to find new products and explore possibilities of existing product development, again to different degrees; each firm looked to market research to reduce the level of risk involved in launching new products. The outcome of this activity, however, was also affected by the unintended acquisition of extended product ranges which, as the pressures to diversify intensified, were internally developed. Rational purposive strategy *and* serendipity are necessary to explain the contingent directions that diversification took.

APPENDIX 1

Tables 3, 4 and 5 show the changing product range in chronological order in the three companies and their classification in accordance with the categories used in Table 2. A detailed account of the methodology underpinning the construction of these tables is given in the authors' study of the three companies' histories of product development between 1870 and 1914.[172] For the purposes of exposition, the three categories used to define new product development above were derived from five employed in the earlier article.

TABLE 3
J.& J. COLMAN, PRODUCT DEVELOPMENTS, 1914–39

Product	Date of Launch	Rating	How Developed
Almata	1922	1	D
Salad Cream	c.1925	3	D
Old Heathers Barley Water	1928	3	A+D
Krusto	1930	2	D
Canned Fruit and Vegetables	1932	2	A+D
Veterinary Mustard	1932	3	D
Picnic Mustard	1934	3	D
Lemon Barley Water	1935	3	D
Lemon Barley Crystals	1936	3	D
French Mustard	1936	3	D
Lime Barley Water	1937	3	D
Three Bears Oats	1938	3	P + D
Orange Barley Water	1939	3	D
Farmers Glory Wheat Flakes	1939	2	P + D

Notes: A = by acquisition of company; P = purchase of patent rights; D = developed internally.

Sources: Unilever Historical Archives; *Carrow Magazine*; *The Advertising of J & J Colman: Yellow, White and Blue* (Colmans, 1977).

TABLE 4
RECKITT & SONS, PRODUCT DEVELOPMENTS, 1914–39

Product	Date of Launch	Rating	How Developed
Globe Metal Polish	1917	3	A
Zebo Liquid Grate Polish	1921	3	D
Windo	1923	2	D
Windolene	1924	3	P + D
Screeno Windscreen Cleaner	1925	3	D
Zebo (French quality)	1926	3	D
Steamo (window de-steamer)	1927	3	D
Karpol Car Polish	1927	2	P + D
Bath Powder	1928	3	D
Bath Cubes	1929	2	D
Harpic Toilet Rolls	1932	2	A
Harpic	1932	2	A
Dettol	1933	1	P + D
Dettol Obstetric Cream	1934	2	D
Dettol Surgical Antiseptic	1934	3	D
Dettol Instrument Antiseptic	1934	3	D
Peggy Blue	1934	3	A or P
Flypic Spray	1934	2	A
Sanpic	1935	3	D
Dettolin Mouthwash	1935	3	D
Steradent	1937	2	P + D

Notes: A = by acquisition of company; P = purchase or patent rights; D = developed internally.

Source: Reckitt Archives, Hull.

TABLE 5
LEVER BROTHERS, PRODUCT DEVELOPMENTS, 1914–39

Product	Date of Launch	Rating	How Developed
Plate Margarine	1914	2	D
Skipper Brand fish products	1919	2	A
Sailor Brand fish products	1919	2	A
Tea Time Brand	1919	2	A
Sausages	1919	2	A
Ice Cream	1919	2	A
Chocolate	1919	2	D
Persil	1919	3	A
Omo	1920	3	D
Rama Margarine	1924	3	NK
Olva	1924	3	D
Lux Toilet Soap	1925	3	D
Suma Soap Powder	1926	3	D
Viking Margarine	1927	3	D
Radion	c.1930	3	D
Lux Flakes (finer flakes)	1932	3	D
Lifebuoy Toilet Soap	1933	3	D
Essogen (vitamin supplement)	1934	2	D
Advita (vitamin supplement)	c.1934	2	D
Gibbs SR Toothpaste	c.1934	2	D
Cold Water Lux	1935	3	D
Blue Band	c.1935	3	A + D
Cookeen	1935	2	D
Spry	1936	3	D
Stork	c.1938	3	A
Sunlight Flakes	1938	3	D
Olavina Edible Oil	1939	2	D
Improved Persil	1939	3	D

Notes: A = by acquisition of company; D = developed internally; NK = not known.

Sources: Unilever Historical Archives; C. Wilson, *The History of Unilever*, Vols.1–2 (London, 1954);
            History of Advertising Trust.

NOTES

We are pleased to express our gratitude to the Leverhulme Trustees who funded the research project on which this article is based (F/204/R, 1997–2000), to the anonymous referees for their careful and constructive advice, and to the archivists of each of the companies studied for their valuable assistance.

1. For interesting general reflections on these issues see the Business History Conference presidential address by N. Lamoureaux, 'Reframing the Past: Thoughts about Business Leadership and Decision Making under Uncertainty', *Enterprise & Society*, Vol.2 No.4 (Dec. 2001), pp.632–59.
2. See acknowledgements above.
3. M. Waterson, 'Models of Product Differentiation', in S. Davies *et al.* (eds.), *Economics of Industrial Organisation* (London, 1998), p.133.
4. J. Cable, 'Recent Developments in Industrial Economics', in J. Cable (ed.), *Current Issues in Industrial Economics* (Basingstoke, 1994), pp.1–10; Davies *et al.*, *Industrial Organisation*, pp.50–63; B.C. Eaton and R.G. Lipsey, 'Product Differentiation', in R. Schmalensee and R. Willig (eds.), *Handbook in Industrial Organisation* (Amsterdam, 1991), pp.720–27; Waterson, 'Models of Product Differentiation', pp.105–33.
5. R. Sutton, 'Sunk Costs and Market Structure' (unpublished MA dissertation, University of Cambridge, 1991).
6. C. Montgomery, 'Corporate Diversification', *Journal of Economic Perspectives*, Vol.8 (1994), pp.163–78.
7. E.T. Penrose, *The Theory of the Growth of the Firm* (London, 1966), especially chapters V to IX.
8. Channon's *Strategy and Structure of British Enterprise* (London, 1973) focused on the period post-1945. The limitations imposed by the data and the associated methodological problems referred to above (and not least the insufficient disaggregation of analysis based on SIC codes) warn against using his findings as a frame of reference for comparison with developments in the preceding period which is the subject of this paper.
9. Lamoureaux, 'Reframing the Past'.
10. Ibid. In 1995, Unilever's subsidiary food company, Van Den Berg, acquired the Colman food and soft drinks business from Reckitt & Colman which became Reckitt Benckiser.
11. Staff census, 1909–61. Reckitt & Colman Archives (hereafter R&CA), R 48; R.H. Mottram, 'A History of J. & J. Colman Ltd of Carrow and Cannon Street' (unpublished typescript, c.1950, unpaginated).
12. R. Church and C. Clark, 'Product Development of Branded, Packaged Household Goods in Britain, 1870–1914: Colman's, Reckitt's and Lever's', *Enterprise and Society*, Vol.2 No.3 (Sept. 2001), p.506; C. Wilson, 'Management and Policy in Large-Scale Enterprise: Lever Brothers and Unilever, 1918–1938', in B. Supple (ed.), *Essays in British Business History* (Oxford, 1977), p.125.
13. A.D. Chandler Jr, *Scale and Scope The Dynamics of Industrial Capitalism* (Cambridge, MA, 1990), pp.262–74.
14. On the formation of the organisation the current assets of Colman's averaged over the period between 1934 and 1936, were valued at £1,194,780 compared with the figure for Reckitt's of £1,090,926. However, Reckitt's profits averaged 65.6% of the combined companies' profit. Agreement between Reckitt & Sons Ltd and J. & J. Colman Ltd, 4 May 1938. R&CA, R 368.
15. A survey of usage carried out in ten towns in 1927 revealed a growing popularity of artificial silk and improved linens which did not yellow and therefore did not require blueing. This was one reason why less blue was being used by the population in these towns. R&CA, R 225, Minute Book (Board) 12, 5 May 1927.
16. R&CA, R 223, Minute Book (Board) 10, 3 Feb. 1927.
17. R&CA, R 301, J.& J. Colman Ltd correspondence overseas trading, No.2, 26 Oct. 1920; R 221, Minute Book (Board) 8, 7, June 1923; R 25, Record of UK sales, 1861–1954.
18. C. Wilson, *History of Unilever* II (London, 1954), p.341.
19. Church and Clark, 'Product Development', pp.503–42.
20. Jeremiah Colman of Gatton Park, 'J. &. J. Colman, 1883–1925' (unpublished typescript, Jan. 1925).
21. C. Colman, *Jeremiah James Colman: A Memoir* (London, 1905), genealogical table, p.465; H.

Edgar, 'The History of J & J Colman' (unpublished typescript, c.1974); Mottram, 'A History of J. & J. Colman Ltd'; 'Sir Basil E. Mayhew', *Carrow Magazine*, Vol.12 (1967), p.23; 'Colonel F.G.D. Colman, O.B.E., T.D., *Carrow Magazine*, Vol.17 (1969), p.34; 'The late Sir Jeremiah Colman, Bart', *Carrow Magazine* (1961), pp.2–4. Amalgamation Agreement Reckitt & Colman & Sons Ltd. R&CA. R 368.

22.   B.N. Reckitt, *The History of Reckitt and Sons Limited* (London, 1951), chapters VI and VII and appendix II, pp.94–105.
23.   Ibid., appendix I.
24.   Ibid., p.49.
25.   Ibid., p.90.
26.   Ibid., pp.34, 37.
27.   Ferens to Townsend, 9 May 1905. R&CA, R 293.
28.   J. & J. Colman correspondence. R&CA, R 302.
29.   Reckitt, *History*, appendix I.
30.   Ibid., p.54.
31.   Ibid., appendix I, pp.54, 80–81.
32.   L. Hannah (ed.), *Management Strategy and Business Development* (London, 1976), p.186.
33.   Wilson, 'Management and Policy', pp.124–40.
34.   Hannah, *Management Structure*, p.286.
35.   E.B. Southwell letterbook, 19 Sept. 1912, Unilever Historical Archives, Port Sunlight (hereafter UHAPS). J. & J. Colman Collection.
36.   J. & J. Colman Ltd correspondence, R&CA. R 300.
37.   Colman's contributed £250,000 and Reckitt's £500,000 to the purchase price. R.H. Mottram, 'History of J. & J. Colman', n.p.
38.   Directors and Managers Meetings (hereafter DMM), 30 July, 1929. UHAPS, Colman Archive.
39.   Ibid., 28 May 1930.
40.   R&CA, R 293, Letterbook, 6 Jan. 1904.
41.   Reckitt, *History*, p.55.
42.   R&CA, R 271, 9.5.12; 6. 12, 12; 30. 1. 13; R271 4.12.14; 9.4. 15; Reckitt, *History*, p.55.
43.   R&CA, R 25, T.A. Upton, Record of UK sales by product 1861–1954.
44.   R&CA, R 220, Minute Book (Board) 7, 20 March 1921.
45.   Reckitt's directors issued a threat to launch 'Windo' in competition unless their purchase offer was not accepted. R&CA, R 221, Minute Book (Board) 8, 30 April 1922; 5 Oct. 1922.
46.   R&CA, R 224, Minute Book (Board) 11, 24 March 1926; 6 July 1926; 3 March 1927.
47.   R&CA, R 222 3 Nov. 1924; R 25, T.A. Upton, Reckitt's 'Record of UK Sales by Product 1861–1954'.
48.   R&CA, R 222, Minute Book (Board) 9, 5 March 1925; 11 Feb. 1926.
49.   Minute Book (Board) 9, 1 May 1924; 5 June 1925. 0, 12 Feb. R&CA, R 223; Minute Book (Board) 12, 5 Feb. 1925. R&CA R 225.
50.   Minute Book (Board) 10, 3 Oct. 1926. R&CA, R223; Reckitt, *History*, p.73.
51.   Ibid., 5 June 1925.
52.   R&CA, R 224, Minute Book (Board) 11, 3 March 1927.
53.   R&CA, R 236, Technical Committee Minutes, 19 June 1930, 5 Dec. 1930.
54.   R&CA, R 226, Minute Book (Board) 13, 4 Dec. 1930.
55.   Members of staff were asked to try 'Robin' during their holidays and report back.
56.   R&CA, R 226, Minute Book (Board) 13, 16 March 1932, 8 July 1932, 19 Oct. 1932; R 227, Minute Book (Board) 14, 21 May 1935.
57.   See below.
58.   Reckitt, *History*, p.73.
59.   The directors had considered such an acquisition in 1924 though the asking price of £250,000 was then deemed excessive. R&CA, R 224, Minute Book (Board) 11, 1 Aug. 1924, 6 Nov. 1924.
60.   Ibid., 6 Oct. 1932; 3 Aug. 1933; 20 June 1933; R 227, 18 Feb. 1937; R 228, 24 March 1938.
61.   The purpose was to distinguish the product from 'Dettol'. See below.
62.   Wilson, *Unilever*, pp.50–56.
63.   Ibid., pp.205–6, 224–5.
64.   A 760, 1928, A 720, 25 Oct. 1929. J Walter Thompson archive, History of Advertising Trust (hereafter HAT); 'Round the Square', 3 (1929), A 693. J. Walter Thompson archive, HAT; A 687, 9 Feb. 1937.

65. Ibid., I, pp.299–303.
66. Ibid., II, p.346.
67. *One Hundred Years*, pp.11–13.
68. UHAL, Supplementary Documents 3768, 3 May 1939.
69. *Carrow Magazine*, July 1927, p.87,
70. Church and Clark, 'Product Development', p.519.
71. Mottram, 'History of J & J Colman Ltd', n.p.
72. H. Kamminga and A. Cunningham (eds.), *The Science and Culture of Nutrition, 1840–1940* (Amsterdam, Atlanta, 1995), pp.10–11.
73. *Carrow Magazine*, July 1927, p.87.
74. S. Horrocks, 'The Business of Vitamins: Nutrition, Science and the Food Industry in Interwar Britain', in Kamminga and Cunningham (eds.), *Science and Culture*, p.247.
75. E. Jones, *The Business of Medicine*, pp.32–3. Colman's initiative in deciding to pursue vitamin research was contemporaneous with that of Glaxo, and that, like 'Almata', Glaxo's innovative product, 'Ostelin' vitamin D, was likewise 'not an outstanding success'.
76. Ibid., p.249.
77. *Advertising World*, Vol.6 No.2 (1909), pp.145–50; Colman, 'J & J Colman, 1883–1925', p.12; UHAPS, Business correspondence, Southwell's letterbooks, 24 July 1912.
78. Farrow's mustard production was switched to Carrow. UHAPS, Colman archive, DMM, 9 Sept. 1931, 27 April 1932.
79. LBM 16 Aug., 13 Oct. 1944.
80. Unilever Historical Archives, London (hereafter UHAL), Special Committee Minutes, 7 Sept. 1938.
81. Edward Elliott possessed relevant experience in Germany.
82. E. Chicken, 'Ultramarine: A Case Study' (unpublished Ph.D. thesis, Open University, 1993), p.179.
83. R&CA, R 48, Staff Census, 17 Dec. 1909.
84. Interview with Basil Reckitt, 11 Oct. 1997.
85. R&CA, R 226, Minute Book (Board) 13, 2 Nov. 1933.
86. R&CA, R 236, Technical Committee Minutes, 19 June 1930.
87. In 1938, the London Press Exchange reported on the market for stomach powders and laxatives. Reckitt's began to experiment with laxatives, which were later to become an important line. R&CA, R 251, 29 March 1938.
88. R&CA, R 225, Minute Book 12, 6 Nov. 1929.
89. *Ours*, Vol.6 (1928), p.10.
90. E.V. Wright, 'History of Reckitt & Colman' (typescript c.1990), pp.4, 15.
91. Ibid.
92. D.E.H. Edgerton and S.M. Horrocks, 'British Industrial Research and Development before 1945', *Economic History Review*, 2nd Series Vol.47 (May 1994), p.227.
93. Though in 1908 at Port Sunlight a chemist had developed a means of preparing soda in small crystals which provided the basis for a perfumed bath preparation. Taylor, *Unilever Research*, pp.3–6; UHAPS Lever Correspondence, 12 June 1908.
94. A.E. Musson, *Enterprise in Soap and Chemicals: Joseph Crosfield & Sons Ltd., 1815–1965* (Manchester, 1965); Wilson, *Unilever*, Vol.I.
95. UHAPS, Lever Correspondence, 8663, 17 June 1921; 16 Feb. 1923; Musson, *Enterprise*, p.293.
96. UHAPS, Lever Correspondence, 7322, 22 July 1915.
97. Taylor, *Unilever Research*, p.6.
98. Wilson, *Unilever*, Vol.I, pp.227–9.
99. Ibid., p.305.
100. Ibid., pp.306–7.
101. Ibid.
102. *Progress*, Vol.35 (1935), pp.43–4.
103. Wilson, *Unilever*, Vol.II, pp.331–2, 9.
104. *One Hundred Years: The Lintas Story* (privately printed, 1990), pp.35, 51. See below.
105. 213 research staff, of whom 79 were postgraduates, were employed. UHAL memo re 'Research and Industry: Report of the FBI Industrial Research Committee', 2 June 1943.
106. Ibid., Supporting Documents to Special Committee of Unilever, 4868, 1 April 1942.
107. Ibid., memo to FBI re 'Research and Industry', 2 June 1943.

108. Ibid., Supplemenary Documents 3768, 3 May 1939.
109. R&CA, R 302, J. & J. Colman Ltd, correspondence overseas, W.H. Slack to Albert Reckitt, 9 Oct. 1930.
110. Ibid., Report of interview, J. and R. Colman, A. Reckitt, T. Ferens, and W. Slack, 9 Jan. 1930.
111. Report to the directors on a meeting with Colman's directors regarding pooling agreement and amalgamation, 9 Oct. 1930. R&C, R 302.
112. Ibid. Between 1926 and 1930, losses on Almata alone amounted to £100,000.
113. Minute Book (Board), 20 March, 2 May, 6 June 199. R&C, R 219.
114. UHAL Special Committee Minutes, 7 Sept. 1938.
115. UHAPS Board Reports, 12 Oct. 1948.
116. Church and Clark, 'Product Development', p.519.
117. See above.
118. 'Joseph Farrow & Co Ltd', *Advertising World*, Vol.5 (1909), pp.145–50; Colman, 'J & J Colman, 1883–1925', p.12; business corrspondence of E.B. Southwell, 24 July 1912. UHAPS.
119. Colman, 'J.& J. Colman, 1883–1925'; Mottram, 'History of J. & J. Colman', pp.53–4.
120. Colman, 'J. &. J. Colman, 1883–1925'.
121. Ibid., Report of Interview with Sir Jeremiah Colman, Ferrens to Sir James Reckitt, 31 Dec. 1912. R 300 R&CA.
123. Ibid., Ferrens to Sir James Reckitt, 21 Feb. 1913.
124. Sir Jeremiah Colman to Ferrens, 9 Jan. 1930, 28 Nov. 1929. R&CA, R 302.
125. Minute Book (Board) 5, 4 Sept. 1914. R&CA, R 218.
126. R&CA, R 214, Minute Book (Directors') 1A, 19 March 1903, 21 June 1904; R 213, Minute Book (Directors') 2, 9 Dec. 1904; 9 Aug., 4 June 1907; R 216, Minute Book (Directors') 3, 6 Feb. 1910. A similar sequence of development resulted in the launch of a boot polish. A Board discussion of market opportunities in the wake of the sales managers' reports from the US and Canada, analysis of competitors' products by Reckitt's chemists was followed by the development of a formula suitable for production. The purchase of the small, but well-established Master Boot Polish Company of West Bromwich, enabled Reckitt's to exploit its reputation. R&CA, R 217, Minute Book (Board), 5 Sept. 1912; 1, 11 Nov. 1912. The purchase price of Silvo was £54,357.
127. Reckitt, *History*, p.72.
128. R&CA, R 223, Minute Book (Board) 10, 5 Nov. 1925; 4 Nov. 1926; 2 Dec. 1926.
129. Ibid., 2 Dec. 1926.
130. R&CA, R 225, Minute Book (Board) 12, 2 Jan. 1930; 5 June 1930; R 226, Minute Book (Board) 13, 29 June 1932; R 250, Minutes of Research Committee, 1 Dec. 1938.
131. Some of these were 'own name' brands sold by Army and Navy Stores and Woolworth's. R&CA, R 226, Minute Book (Board) 13, 2 June 1932; 9 March 1933.
132. R&CA, R 223, Minute Book (Board) 10, 5 Nov. 1925; 2 Sept. 1926.
133. Minute Book (Board) 10, 1 Sept. 1927 R&C, R 223; Minute Book (Board) 14, 4 April 1935. R&C, R 227.
134. R&CA, R 225, Minute Book (Board) 12, 6 June 1928; R 226, Minute Book (Board) 13, 5 June 1930, 2 Oct. 1930.
135. Reckitt, *History*, p.86.
136. R&CA, R 236, Technical Committee Minutes, 19 June 1930.
137. R&CA, R 251, 29 March 1938.
138. R&CA, R 225, Minute Book (Board) 12, 6 Feb. 1930, 5 June 1930.
139. Ibid., 5 Dec. 1930.
140. Ibid., 12 Feb. 1931.
141. H. Brindle, 'Developing the Pharmaceutical Side of the Business of a Chemist and Druggist', *Chemist & Druggist*, 4 March 1933, p.227; 'Whither Pharmacy?', *Chemist & Druggist*, 29 Aug. 1936, p.249.
142. Ibid., 2 March 1932, 29 July 1932, 1 June 1932.
143. *Overseas Advertising News*, Vol.5 (Jan. 1939), Vol.8 (April 1939).
144. R&CA, R 227 Minute Book (Board) 14, 5 May 1934; S.E.S, 'History and Development of Dettol', *RCH Magazine*, Vol.3 (1961), pp.27–33.
145. R&CA, R 227, 2 Nov. 1934.
146. R&CA, R 250, 26 June 1934.
147. R&CA, R 250, Minutes of Research Committee, 24 July 1934, 26 Nov. 1935, 23 Jan. 1936, 1 Jan. 1937. None proceeded further but several were revived after World War II.

148. R&CA, R 222, Minute Book (Board) 14, 28 March, 4 April 1935; 30 Oct., 27 Nov., 3 Dec. 1936.
149. Ibid., 2 Sept., 29 July 1937.
150. Ibid.
151. This followed the practice introduced by Colman's with which Reckitt's merged in the same year. R&CA, R 250, Minutes of Research Committee 1 Dec. 1938.
152. Report of Research Committee, Minute Book (Directors), 1 July 1938. R&CA. R 227.
153. T.A. Upton, Record of UK Sales, 1861–1954. R&CA, R 25; 'History and Development of Dettol', *RCH Magazine*, Vol.3 (1961), pp.27–33.
154. Upton, Record of UK Sales, 1861–1954. R&CA, R 25; HRW, 17 Dec. 1962, Profits, 1938/39–1962/63.
155. Wilson, 'Management and Policy', p.134.
156. Wilson, *History of Unilever*, Vol.II, p.378.
157. Wilson, *History of Unilever*, Vol.I, pp.261, 274–5.
158. Ibid., p.261.
159. Wilson, *History of Unilever*, Vol.II, p.341.
160. Ibid., p.377.
161. Minute Book (Board Meetings), 30 July 1925. R&CA. R 222.
162. Minute Book (Board Meetings), 6 Dec 1928, 7 Feb. 1929. R&CA. R 225.
163. Directors' Minutes, General Export Committee, 9 July 1931. R&CA. R 263
164. Penrose, *Growth of the Firm*, chapter VII, 'The Economics of Diversification', pp.104–52.
165. Penrose, *Theory*, pp.77–82.
166. Ibid., pp.137–141
167. Ibid., p.116.
168. Ibid., p.155.
169. Minute Book (Board) 17 March 1930. R&CA, R 302.
170. 'J. & J. Colman' Microfilm 16, J. Walter Thompson archives, William J. Hartmann Collection, Duke University, NC.
171. Ibid., pp.31–2.
172. For critical comments see Church, 'New Perspectives', pp.405–13.
173. Church and Clark, 'Product Development'.

Closing the Deal: GM's Marketing Dilemma and Its Franchised Dealers, 1921–41

SALLY CLARKE

University of Texas at Austin

Since the early years of the automobile industry, dealers have mediated between manufacturers and motorists. With a smile and a handshake, they stood ready to sell you a car. They promoted new features and styles; negotiated the price of a trade-in; and worked out the details of instalment financing. Local retailers thus brought to fruition a firm's marketing efforts: they closed the deal.[1]

Among auto makers, General Motors distinguished itself for its marketing techniques. GM managers led the field during the 1920s with their new focus on advertising, instalment financing, and the art of styling low-priced automobiles.[2] The company also capitalised on the systematic use of industrial research and flexible methods of mass production so as to increase consumers' choices and change styles each year.[3] These factors became easily recognised ingredients in explaining GM's dominance: compared to a 12 per cent slice of the US market in 1921, by 1927 GM held 43 per cent of sales and claimed about 40 per cent of the market through the depressed 1930s.[4] Still, it was left to the local car dealer to translate these marketing efforts into car sales. Alfred P. Sloan, Jr., the chief executive officer of General Motors in the years before World War II, understood the critical role dealers played. Calling dealer relations so important as to be almost a 'specialisation' for his job, Sloan outlined the origins of dealer policies in his 1964 autobiography.[5] Accounting procedures were put in place in the 1920s to track dealers' sales, inventories, and profits. Using market data, GM began allocating dealers relative to the size of their markets. And the General Motors Acceptance Corporation (GMAC), established in 1919, assisted dealers in purchasing automobiles. Sloan thus labelled dealer relations friendly and efficient, and he left no hint of conflict, no sense that dealer relations were so bad by the 1930s as to prompt the Federal Trade Commission (FTC) to launch a major investigation and then the Justice Department to surprise GM with an antitrust suit.[6]

The FTC's investigation indicated that GM was typical. Interviews with Ford and Chrysler dealers yielded similar accounts, and the Justice Department filed suit against the Big Three auto manufacturers. Ford and Chrysler signed consent decrees, but GM stood trial and was convicted of antitrust violations.[7] While the three firms shared similar policies, GM remains the focus of my study because I can turn to records from both the FTC and the Justice Department. I also focus on GM because Sloan's autobiography became a classic in business management: Sloan presented a narrative for the efficient organisation and performance of GM as a model for the modern corporation.[8] The federal investigations invited a different narrative, however. Their records indicated that Sloan's account was accurate, but also incomplete: it overlooked the tensions between dealers and managers born out of the particular details in marketing automobiles – details that added up to what I call consumers' marketing dilemma.[9]

Perhaps more than other modern consumer goods, automobiles drew attention to familiar tools in marketing. Consumers, of course, selected from among a number of models, colours, and accessories. Being so expensive, most cars were bought on instalment plans and most owners traded in an old vehicle in the hope of bargaining down the new machine's price. What is important to recognise is that each of these activities posed potential conflicts between dealers and managers. As consumers' design choices proliferated, for instance, GM faced a more complex job in producing vehicles. Inaccuracies in co-ordinating the production of cars with dealers' orders or consumers' demands resulted in unwanted cars (and costs) that either dealers or GM shouldered. A higher allowance for a used car meant lower profits for dealers and, should dealers reduce their demand for new cars, lower profits for manufacturers. And, while car buyers financed their purchases, GM and its dealers squared off as to who wrote the loans and pocketed the profit from financing sales. Given the details in marketing automobiles, it was not just that management addressed the question of profitability in terms of efficiency, but they also focused on profits in terms of market transactions – how dealers worked with the factory in ordering cars, and how they negotiated with consumers in selling cars. The three parties – consumers, dealers, and management – faced tension to the extent that one party's profit came at the expense of another party.

Had GM relied on salaried employees to sell cars, these conflicts would have remained inside the firm, but the manufacturer defined its method of distribution through a network of franchised retailers. Whereas Sloan had outlined accounting and credit policies meant to create an efficient system of distribution, my intent is to ask how GM managers used franchised retailers to cope with the tensions resulting from marketing cars. Managers and dealers tried different tactics, but they never settled the question of how profits or costs would be distributed among parties to the market transactions. Regulatory intervention modified but still did not resolve tensions.[10] Implicit in the process of marketing autos, then, was the question of trust between buyers and sellers. As market mediators, traders of all stripes have been suspect in the eyes of consumers, even high-brow middlemen like the auction houses of Christies and Sotheby's.[11] Yet, unlike nineteenth-century traders, car dealers were aligned with a manufacturer through a franchise contract.[12] This method of mass distribution pointed to a modern basis of distrust inasmuch as tensions between dealers and consumers were traced back to the conflicts dealers and management faced in coping with consumers' marketing dilemma.

II
FRANCHISED DEALERS AND THE MARKET FOR AUTOS

GM defined its relations with dealers in terms of a franchise contract: dealers bought cars from GM at a discount to the retail price and then resold the cars to consumers; they were assigned a specific sales territory; they agreed to maintain proper service facilities and perform operations to the satisfaction of the manufacturer. Franchises became a distinctive feature of the modern US economy: by 1986 franchised dealers claimed roughly a third of all retail sales, leading a congressional report to call franchising 'the most dynamic business arrangement since the emergence of the corporation a century ago'.[13] Where the retailer was not a salaried employee but an independent business, parent companies faced common problems in measuring their retailers' performance. For instance, manufacturers needed to determine whether their franchised agents fully exploited their market in selling their goods and whether they provided the kind of service that sustained the manufacturer's 'good reputation' with its customers. These examples fit under the general category of cases in which dealers failed to satisfy management's standards for effective operation.[14] There was also a second potential source of conflict: cases in which dealers' strategies for turning a good profit were at odds with the parent company's profit strategy. Alfred Sloan addressed dealer relations in terms of the first possible source of conflict, but the FTC and Justice Department found that the second possible source of conflict also applied to GM's dealers – thanks to dealers' problems in marketing cars.

Soon after Sloan joined General Motors in 1918, the management introduced several policies intended to establish an effective dealer network for an emerging mass market.[15] One key provision was the exclusive sales arrangement. If dealers only marketed GM vehicles, such as Chevrolet or Buick, they would devote all their energies to GM products.[16] Officials also worried that too much competition among dealers could hurt their profits and, by extension, cause them to neglect service and to damage GM's reputation among car owners.[17] To avoid this situation, management decided to limit the number of dealers in any given territory. GM contracts also carried a threat: the firm claimed the right to cancel a dealer's contract with little if any notice.[18] Still, cancellation was a blunt instrument, and rather than only elect this course of action, GM officials chose to increase their bureaucratic oversight.

As an initial step, management allocated dealers to regions based on the size of a given market. This meant that officials developed indices to measure the size of demand in a given territory (say a city or county) so as to determine the number of dealers to place in that market area. As a second step, managers developed various accounting procedures, and by 1927 all of some 15,000 dealers were required to follow GM's standardised accounting system.[19] Officials assembled data for each dealer's sales of new vehicles, used vehicles, and accessories, revenues and costs tied to service, a dealer's debts, the percentage of net working capital in receivables, the used car inventory, and fixed and variable expenses. Managers used the data to assess on a monthly basis each dealer's profits and losses. For instance, in 1930 minutes of GM's General Sales Committee cautioned that used cars which lingered on a car lot for more than 90 days signalled a dealer headed for trouble. The old vehicle tied up working capital and, as it continued to depreciate, foretold greater losses. The balance between sales and profits for new as compared to used cars could indicate dealers who were too cautious, or, conversely, too 'greedy for business'. Officials as a matter of routine organised data by cities and zones to keep track of the overall percentage of profitable dealers, undercapitalised dealers, and other measures used to compare retailers and identify troubled firms.[20]

Aside from using accounting data to assess dealers, managers found the information valuable in co-ordinating production and distribution. Sloan, for instance, noted that managers tabulated on a ten-day basis the level of dealers' inventories so as to keep production in line with retail demand. M.E. Coyle, the general manager of the Chevrolet Division, offered one example when he testified that in November of 1937 dealers' ten-day reports indicated a sudden increase in inventories and slowdown in sales. Based on this data, GM cut its production of new cars.[21] Another tool in co-ordinating production and distribution was GM's credit agency, the General Motors Acceptance Corporation (GMAC). It assisted dealers in purchasing automobiles. But, as Martha Olney has detailed, in helping dealers, GMAC allowed factory managers to cope with the tendency for car sales to be concentrated in the spring and early summer of each year. While manufacturers wanted to keep assembly-line production relatively stable, and lacked storage space to stockpile cars for each sales season, they began the practice of selling cars to dealers who had storage space. Insofar as dealers may have lacked the cash to finance these purchases, GMAC provided wholesale credit.[22] In this regard, GMAC was more than a credit agency: it helped the factory in 'regularizing production'.[23]

Behind its ten-day and monthly dealer reports stood an array of managers, known to dealers as factory representatives. By 1938 Chevrolet supervised about 9,000 dealers with roughly 5,000 factory managers.[24] They checked to make sure dealers filled out their many forms according to GM standards. They watched expenses to see that dealers put enough – but not too much – money into reconditioning used cars. They reviewed customer complaints to single out dealers who failed to provide helpful service. They tracked the rate of turnover of used cars, seeing that working capital was not 'frozen' with used cars sitting on car lots. On these and many other topics, factory representatives kept a watchful eye.[25] Presumably, as Sloan wrote, this system ensured 'a group of sound, prosperous dealers as business associates'.[26] Still, Sloan's account did not preclude the possibility that the interests of managers and dealers differed, or, worse still, that one party's gain came at the other's loss. Beginning in the mid-1920s, records reveal that managers used accounting data and GMAC financing not only to assess dealers by presumed objective standards, but also actively to shape dealers' businesses.

One source of tension concerned new car sales, and dealers' monthly reports proved valuable in the management's active process of encouraging dealers to sell as many cars as possible. At first glance, this task seems obvious. But the question of new sales was complicated for dealers, given the role of used cars. Depending on the old car's allowance, the losses on the used car's resale could more than absorb the gross profit earned on the new car. Once the deal was 'washed out' (meaning the trade-in resold), the retailer could have increased revenues but decreased profits.[27] For dealers, then, not every sale was a good one. For management, a profitable dealer was not a sure sign of one who had done the most to sell GM products. As one response, GM closely watched new car registrations. Managers obtained data from R.L. Polk & Company, which distributed figures for the sale of cars at their local site of registration.[28] These data permitted GM officials, like their counterparts at other auto manufacturers, to track dealers' sales on a ten-day basis to determine whether they were selling a given 'percentage of cars in their price class'. Those who fell behind were 'ripe' for receiving 'special pressure'.[29]

Pressure took different forms. In 1938 William Holler, the general sales manager for Chevrolet, used the Joe Louis–Max Schmeling championship boxing match to set up paired contests among his dealers. Winners of each bout (determined by who sold the most cars) received a banquet dinner on the night of the official fight.[30] Sales pressure of this sort was not peculiar to automobiles, nor did dealers find it pernicious.[31] But dealers complained about pressures to take more cars than their territory justified. One dealer recounted: 'if you [the factory] engage a dealer long enough', then he will 'capitulate' for the extra stock. Where 'factories have been guilty of loading the dealer beyond his capacity and the potentialities of his territory', he concluded that dealers 'sell new cars for less than a fair return in order to satisfy the manufacturers' demands for percentage of price class'. The FTC found that some 30 per cent of Chevy dealers reported that prior to 1938 GM had 'oversupplied' them with cars.[32]

Just as dealers and managers differed when it came to the topic of selling new cars, they diverged when it came to the problem of matching production and distribution. The goal of efficiency in co-ordinating mass production and mass distribution remained elusive inasmuch as efficiency implicitly depended on knowing car buyers' 'tastes and preferences' when car buyers could select many features in buying a vehicle. Robert E. Griffin, the distribution manager of the Olds Motors Works, stated as one example that the 1938 Oldsmobile included two engine series – a six cylinder and an eight; ten colours plus three types of trim; two rear axle gear ratios; and several accessories.[33] Based on a consumer's selections, a dealer wrote a purchase order and placed it with a factory. Presumably the factory filled the order as specified. Problems at the factory, however, made any smooth co-ordination of orders and output unlikely. Joseph M. Hendrie, the distribution manager for Chevrolet, stated that in dealing, for example, with an order for ten cars, production might proceed as expected for five cars, but parts might be delayed for the other five. So, Hendrie offered, the factory substituted cars to fill the order.[34] The start of a new model year also posed problems. M.E. Coyle, the vice president and general auditor of Chevrolet Motor Company, recalled that production was estimated against the sales department's projections so the initial distribution of cars did not necessarily match local market demands. Finally, given the scale of production, cars could only be parked on the 'drive away yard' for one or two days before being shipped out.[35] Each of these details in the production process meant that factories shipped cars that dealers did not necessarily order or want.

Factory representatives in turn leaned on dealers to take unpopular cars. A Buick dealer reported that the factory (GM) often would 'insist' on sending cars with radios or other accessories to push up their sales. The FTC cited an Oldsmobile dealer who took 'unwanted cars' so as to get 'cars on order for customers'. As a result of labour strikes in 1937, a Chevy dealer at first did not receive cars and then 'received a few too many, resulting in forced sales at losses'. Another dealer lamented that the year-end close out resulted in factories pushing cars on dealers, and dealers in turn offering large discounts in order to 'clean up' for the next model year. The FTC reprinted a memo from 1925 in which Alfred Sloan noted that 'just before the close of the season' dealers were forced to take cars 'that they couldn't possibly sell except at a loss'. He continued: 'This loss had been sufficient in some cases to absorb their profits for the entire year.'[36]

The potential for conflict in all of these matters was further aggravated by the topic of credit. By the late 1930s 50 per cent of GM dealers financed all vehicle purchases and another 26 per cent financed at least half their cars with GMAC.[37] Former GM officials testified that credit and sales managers swapped information so that they could identify dealers who did not use GMAC financing.[38] Beginning in the mid-1920s, dealers complained of being 'coerced' to rely on GMAC or risk some form of retribution. In his opinion regarding the Justice Department's suit against GM, Judge Lindley recounted specific examples. A Pontiac dealer had 'desired to finance his wholesale purchases and retail sales through a discount company owned by a personal friend, but he was required to agree to use GMAC 100 per cent as a condition precedent to securing his franchise contract'. In 1936 GMAC stopped providing a Buick dealer with wholesale credit 'because of his failure to give GMAC a sufficient amount of retail paper'. When the Buick dealer began using a local finance company, he 'experienced a great deal of trouble receiving the models he ordered'. Other dealers in his area had no trouble, however. When a Chevy dealer began using a local finance company, 'he was shipped cars of different model and design from those ordered'. Another Chevy dealer used GMAC, but not for at least half his loans. In his case, cars with 'unordered accessories in great quantities were forced on him'.[39] Robert Smith had held one of the largest franchises in San Francisco in the 1920s and ran his own financing company which cleared $15,000 a month in profits. He testified in the antitrust case that GM officials forced him to shut down his finance business.[40]

Whether dealers used their finance company or GMAC represented a conflict of interest. Part of the conflict concerned dealers' ability to sell cars. For example, farmers might want to 'pay a third down, and wait six months and pay the other two-thirds balance in one payment'. But dealers reported that GMAC would 'insist' on monthly payments.[41] Judge Lindley recalled the example of a dealer who had many customers who 'were employees of a local discount company, and hence it was easier to sell to them by using the facilities of their employer'.[42] From GM's perspective, however, dealers who used GMAC financing served GM in two regards: they channelled earnings directly into the corporation's coffers, and they reduced the cost of GMAC having to solicit new business. GMAC also served as a tool to check on dealers. The Justice Department's lawyer in his closing statement recalled the experience of a Pontiac dealer who gave GMAC 80 per cent of his business. The factory had 'him in their grip' and shipped him cars he had not ordered. He did not object since his capital was 'tied up in the business and he does not want to have his franchise canceled'.[43] Without independent financing, would dealers put up less fuss about accepting unpopular models? Would they be more agreeable to taking cars at the year-end clearance?[44]

At the root of the conflicts between dealers and management was the market relationship between dealers and consumers. Managers and dealers squared off over the question of fully exploiting markets given the practice of used car trade-ins. And, the difficulties dealers and managers faced in co-ordinating a factory's production with dealers' sales proved more complex as consumers could choose from a wide range of colours, accessories, and other items. In one sense, Sloan described the accounting policies and credit financing as key tools for creating a healthy dealer network. But as the firm saddled dealers with extra vehicles, the accounting reports did not simply serve as an objective measure of a dealer's ability to run the business, but represented an artifact of the particular costs managers shifted to dealers given the difficulties GM faced in co-ordinating production with consumers' demands. The impact of federal regulators was mixed. The Justice Department convinced the courts that GM had pressured dealers to rely on GMAC financing, but other problems persisted.

III
TRYING TO SHAPE THE MARKET'S DEMAND SIDE

As GM developed its credit and accounting systems to shape dealer relations, managers and dealers also tried to condition market relations between dealers and car buyers. During the 1920s, the very growth of the mass market contributed to a burgeoning supply of used cars, and by the late 1930s GM reports found that 90 per cent of new Chevrolet purchases entailed trades.[45] Trade-ins were at the heart of dealers' profitability since large allowances on used vehicles could mean reselling the old car at a loss – potentially absorbing the gross profits earned from the new car's sale. One 1927 GM study concluded that trade-ins induced 'a highly destructive' competition among dealers for which their profits could be 'diminished if not wiped out altogether'.[46] The problem mattered to GM since dealer losses on used cars cut back 'the ability of dealers to purchase new cars'.[47] Together then, GM and its dealers experimented with policies intended to restrict consumers' ability to negotiate the elements of a car's purchase: trading the used car, setting the new car's price, and working out the details of the finance plan.

As unlikely as it may sound, in the mid-1920s Chevrolet introduced a plan to permanently destroy 'junkers'. They wanted to reduce the supply of the oldest cars, thus curbing buyers' chances of using them to bargain down prices on new vehicles. Under the 'Chevrolet Used Car Disposal Plan', Chevrolet increased each new car's price by $5 'and allowed the dealer a rebate of $25 to apply on a junk car when five new cars had been purchased'.[48] At least by 1926, a junking programme was standard in Chevrolet's dealer contracts.[49] The junkyards were employed throughout the country. By 1929 the plan was broadened and sponsored by the National Automobile Chamber of Commerce, Inc., the forerunner to the Automobile Manufacturers Association.[50] And dealers gladly told FTC investigators the party line that old cars were 'unsafe' on highways and should be eliminated. This was a new twist on safety, since in both cases the intent was to demolish each 'junker', as GM's sales executive Richard Grant instructed, so that 'it cannot be repaired and resold. To accomplish this purpose, smash starting motor, generator and coil, carburetor and manifolds, cylinder head, cylinder block, and transmission. ... Break the radiator, head lamp, and instrument board and drive the grease plug into the rear axle. The dealer may then sell the car for junk'.[51]

The junkyards did not stop trade-ins, and company-run plans disappeared at the end of 1933 when the National Recovery Administration (NRA) went into operation. Dealers anticipated that the NRA's minimum price codes for used cars would alleviate the trade-in menace.[52] But the NRA expired in 1935, and dealers tried other tactics. One dating back to the late 1920s was the co-operative work of so-called 'appraisal' bureaus. Dealers set up local bureaus in order to share information about the prices of used vehicles. A Los Angeles dealer told a FTC investigator that they had established their bureau in 1935 and all local Chevrolet dealers were members. When a customer asked about a trade-in price, the dealer could call a central phone number to learn what bids other dealers had made. Dealers acknowledged the system's obvious limitations to the extent any member could bow out and undercut the effort to fix prices. Still, the bureaus offered some help, otherwise dealers would have had no incentive to support them. The LA dealer who discussed his bureau with the FTC interviewer noted that the local dealer association had GM approve the plan and that factory officials (a point the FTC sustained) and other dealer organisations asked for information so as to set up bureaux in other markets. The secretary of the Illinois dealer association reported that many bureaux were in use and had helped eliminate what he called 'the over-allowance evil'. This dealer asserted that the practice did not entail price fixing. The FTC countered that the practices may not have been violations of interstate commerce but were still unfair under state laws. What the FTC did find was that dealers ran bureaux in several states, including Michigan, Wisconsin, Minnesota, Pennsylvania, Illinois, Missouri, and Virginia.[53]

Dealers also tried to alter prices through 'padding' car sales. They offered a large allowance on a customer's trade-in but made up this loss by padding the new vehicle's price. In an internal letter, Sloan observed that this action was premised on the idea that 'psychologically speaking, a big allowance for a used car is more effective in selling a new car than a lower price on the new car'.[54] The padding worked to the extent that GM advertised cars as the factory price plus freight and taxes, for which the sum for freight and taxes was not specified. The FTC noted the 'frequent practice of either motor-vehicle manufacturers or dealers of adding to the factory price a transportation charge ... greater than that actually incurred by the manufacturer'. It called for 'regulation' to provide 'each retail purchaser with an itemized invoice showing in detail the components of the cash sale price' including transportation and advertising fees, federal, state and local taxes, the cost of accessories, and all other charges.[55] It took nearly 20 years, but in 1958, as Sloan reported, Congress passed a new law requiring manufacturers 'to affix a label on the window glass of each new car shipped to a dealer' with 'detailed information' about 'the manufacturer's suggested retail price'.[56]

At the same time, the FTC found that since 1929 roughly 60 per cent of all new and used cars were sold with instalment financing, and it charged dealers with 'packing' interest fees on car loans.[57] Here they worked with finance companies to raise payments, counting that a car buyer could not calculate monthly payments and so would not identify the extra fees.[58] The executive vice president of GMAC, Ira McCreery, testified in 1940 that GMAC refused such loans because they would result in consumers losing confidence in GM.[59] Still, to the extent that dealers used other financing agencies, they could and did pack prices. Sloan concluded that 'dealers in a community will get together and all agree to pack certain amounts. We, of course, keep after those things ... but it does happen, no matter how aggressive we may be'.[60]

In the autumn of 1935, GM introduced a new finance campaign, under the title 'the 6% plan'. The plan tried to put an end to dealers' packs while boosting GM's finance business. It offered consumers a lower rate of interest than competitors' plans, a point Sloan declared and the FTC verified. But the plan ran into trouble in its wording. The reference to '6%' was not a reference to a six per cent rate of interest, since the rate varied depending on the length of the loan. A multiplier of half of one per cent applied. A 12-month loan carried a six per cent rate, but an 18-month loan had finance charges of nine per cent and a 24-month loan came with a rate of 12 per cent. The FTC put an end to this advertising in 1938.[61] In the meantime, the plan brought other complaints. GM tried to stop dealers' packs, which initially gave dealers an incentive to work with independent finance companies. GM tried to make this choice futile by educating consumers about finance plans. If consumers could spot packs, then dealers would have no reason to use them and no reason to turn to independent finance companies. Still, dealers protested that GMAC had 'coerced' them to rely on the factory-controlled finance division. Further, they contended that GMAC could set lower rates to the extent that its cost of soliciting business was lower because dealers were forced to rely on GMAC. Independent finance companies charged they had been cut out of business and their complaints helped bring indictments against the Big Three auto makers. Thus, while GMAC worked to lower interest rates for consumers' benefit, the gain came through coercive relations with dealers and anticompetitive practices with independent finance companies.[62]

In the end, dealers persisted in padding prices and packing loans. In response to the FTC's investigations, GM managers oddly enough found themselves defending their dealers. Neil Borden, a Harvard Business School professor, wrote that by 1939 GM 'started a magazine campaign which stated very plainly the policy of the corporation and its dealers on delivered prices'. The firm also initiated a 'plainview price tag' – dealers hung in their showrooms signs listing clearly a car's price, its taxes, and transportation and accessory fees. A new advertising campaign pictured a friendly dealer chatting with Mr and Mrs Car Buyer, in which a smaller insert carried the theme: 'You can see the Value ... And you can see the price.' GM kept up its campaign in 1940 and 1941, calling the GM dealer 'a fine businessman and a leader in his local community'.[63]

Buying a car meant haggling over specific details: the old car's trade-in value, the new car's price, and the terms of instalment loans. The FTC discovered that for each activity dealers tried to tilt the negotiations to their favour. When it came to used cars, they had tried to destroy jalopies at company-run junk yards, had relied on the NRA's price codes, and had established their own appraisal bureaus. For new car prices, the ambiguity in transportation and other fees allowed retailers to raise prices. Finally, financing terms were more complicated, but dealers could and did pack loans. If car buyers remained suspicious of dealers, the FTC also linked complaints to GM since the manufacturer had worked with dealers so that their interests were aligned. In the case of used cars, for instance, dealers' losses limited their demand for new cars. And, while GM took exception to dealers' attempts to pack loans, it tried to boost GMAC's revenues – a strategy that ultimately backfired. The problems consumers faced were of a scale that exceeded any one buyer's ability to redress. They needed the state to intervene in the market. The FTC had halted the misleading advertising of GM's 6% plan, and federal legislation in 1958 made new car prices transparent. The problems of valuing trade-ins and finance charges were more difficult to legislate on, and remained sources of contention long after the Depression.[64]

IV
RETHINKING THE RELATIONSHIP BETWEEN DEALERS AND CONSUMERS

If dealers felt squeezed by GM's pressures to sell more cars and consumers' determination to lower the price of a new vehicle, they also linked these two concerns to a third problem: competition in their own ranks. GM allocated a given number of dealers to a geographic territory based on the estimated demand in that region. But dealers complained to FTC investigators that 'fringe' dealers outside their assigned regions 'stole' their business. Some retailers attributed this practice of crossing into another dealer's territory to a dealer's attempt to meet unreasonably high sales quotas. Others faulted undercapitalised dealers who 'trade[d] wild' in used cars.[65] Whatever the cause, the competition demoralised dealers, and, in this context, William Holler, the general sales manager of the Chevrolet Division, tried an alternative approach in his focus on dealers' commitment to a specific market.

Since the 1920s GM had allocated a given number of dealers to a local market territory. Determining the optimal number of dealers in a region meant estimating the demand or 'potential' for cars in that territory. Further, measuring dealers' performance in sales and profitability also required an objective measure of demand since a dealer's low profits could follow from mismanagement or from a region's limited potential (meaning too many dealers relative to consumers' ability to purchase cars).[66] In the early 1920s, GM officials created an index of consumer demand for each county in the nation. Still, the index left unanswered how to cope with variations in consumers' cost of living or variations in the distribution of income.[67] With the onset of the Depression, as demand collapsed, William Holler decided to reassess the official market size used to allocate Chevrolet dealers.

Testifying in 1940 for GM's antitrust case, Holler recalled that whereas in the 1920s Chevrolet had simply expanded the number of dealers as its sales rose, in the early 1930s, once markets collapsed, its dealers suffered terribly. In 1933 he decided to create a new basis for allocating his sales force, such that dealers not only prospered in flush times but also survived depressed markets. In order to assign a given number of car dealers to a particular geographic territory, Holler returned to the task of estimating the level of demand in each local territory. He recounted having 'two field crews of statisticians' – one for the eastern half and one for the western half of the United States – travel to cities and counties where they gathered 'all the statistics with reference to crops and business and economic conditions'. Once the figures were converted to estimates of demand for each market, Holler set new targets for the optimal number of dealers. 'If we have eight dealers in the field, in that territory', Holler noted as an illustration, but estimate that only six can survive in good times and bad, 'we so notify the region and zone people that they can have ample time to consolidate or to liquidate the account'.[68] In other words, rather than err on the side of too small a potential, Holler chose the reverse, and effectively gave dealers greater opportunity to turn a profit.

Holler also expected dealers to take greater responsibility for their territory. In early 1937, one memo declared that Chevrolet wanted each dealer 'to capitalize on local goodwill and become a figure in the community. This takes an investment of time and money on the dealer's part'. Chevrolet offered its help. On the demand side, shoppers could hurt dealers if they went in search of the best bid on their used cars. Whereas more dealerships translated into more places where a buyer could play dealers against each other, Chevy managers had reduced the number of dealers. On the supply side, officials noted that the shape of retailing was changing. Dealers located in the heart of cities were finding it difficult to sell used cars. Evidently, used car buyers tended to 'avoid "marble fronts"'. Although the dealers wanted to set up used car lots outside their cities, sales managers worried that this option would spark new 'brother-dealer' competition.[69] Management put some teeth into its protective efforts in the late 1930s. Dealers could now sign agreements with GM whereby any retailer who encroached on another dealer's market would be fined $25 per car. The same LA dealer who told the FTC interviewer that all the area's Chevy dealers supported a used car appraisal bureau also reported that the city's dealers supported the 'protected territory' programme.[70]

In 1941 Holler reported that Chevy had trimmed its dealers by nine per cent from 1929 to 1936 and another 12 per cent by 1940. Yet sales per dealer increased by 31 per cent in these same years. With the exception of 1937, Chevy kept its sales well ahead of Ford and Plymouth. From 29 per cent of its price class in 1929 (an off year), its market share rebounded to 41 per cent in 1936. Further, despite their protests to the FTC, Chevy dealers had earned a profit each year since 1933, averaging $5,760 per dealer in 1936 and $6,626 per dealer in 1940. After 'years of constant work', Holler credited the Chevrolet Dealer Organization as 'the strongest and best organization in the field today'.[71]

As a management problem, Holler's strategy never addressed the pressures dealers faced. It did not stop car buyers from negotiating their trade-ins. It did not alleviate the costs dealers faced in terms of problems in co-ordinating production and distribution, or the pressures to sell more cars. All of those problems remained. But Holler had given dealers more breathing room to cope with the sources of tension. He had essentially left more money on the table for dealers and he had reduced the number of dealers requiring supervision, thereby reducing managerial costs.

V

CONCLUSION

Thirty-eight years after Sloan published his autobiography, John McDonald, who had worked for *Fortune* and had edited Sloan's book, published his own memoir. McDonald surprised readers by telling them that despite Sloan's standing as having directed the firm's rise to prominence, lawyers inside GM nearly blocked publication of the retired CEO's manuscript. Curiously, Sloan's autobiography would never have seen the light of day had McDonald not sued GM. In his memoir, McDonald recounted his work for Sloan, whom he admired, and his strategies for freeing the manuscript from GM's lawyers. Throughout, he puzzled over the question why the lawyers wanted to block publication. Obviously they objected to something in the book, but he could not spot the problem. One hint came when a retired GM lawyer, Daniel Boone (related to *the* Daniel Boone), told McDonald that if the book had been his publication, GM would not have objected, but being Sloan's publication and recognising that Sloan was an officer of the corporation, the firm worried that 'anything in the book could be put directly into evidence in a government suit against General Motors'.[72]

Sloan in all likelihood did not need this warning. McDonald reported that problems in the text were inadvertent – the sort of thing that an overly anxious lawyer might construe as an example of monopoly power.[73] In other words, the retired CEO recalled his years not as a story of corporate power but as someone intent on putting management on a 'scientific basis'.[74] Still, Sloan's narrative, while accurate in many specific details or topics, was still incomplete. Naomi Lamoreaux cautioned business historians to 'avoid the trap of the rational narrative', by which she meant the narratives managers have given in hindsight as logical explanations for their decisions and their firms' subsequent performance.[75] McDonald's experience offered one reason to heed this advice: GM's lawyers had good reason to exclude accounts that could be used in a suit against the firm, which implied fudging questions about corporate power. In his discussion of dealers, Sloan reported little about the state's investigations during the 1930s, and when he did address the FTC and Justice Department, he predictably emphasised GM's strong points without fully outlining the basis of conflicts, and thus offered no reason to doubt management's authority.[76]

Instead, Sloan focused on GM's internal operations and explained the development of its network of franchised dealerships as a set of decisions to carefully co-ordinate production and distribution, and to maintain a network of healthy retailers. To this end, he declared: 'Uncertainty and efficiency are as far apart as the North Pole is from the South.' He singled out 'proper accounting' as the key to seeing that each dealer knew 'the facts about his business'.[77] Reports for dealers' sales, costs, earnings, balance sheets, and inventories brought clarity to their operations. Managers trusted the numbers to systematically identify retailers' 'soft spots' and correct their operations.[78] The data also helped GM match production with shifts in the level of demand. Sloan outlined a similar role for GMAC. The corporation's financing division both assisted dealers in purchasing cars wholesale and smoothed the flow of automobiles from the company's factories to dealers' showrooms. Sloan thus outlined a set of tools for assessing dealers 'objectively' and achieving efficiency in the co-ordination of production and distribution.[79]

The FTC and the Justice Department's records invited an alternative explanation for how GM relied on franchised retailers. The federal agencies first altered the problem to be explained: rather than account for a healthy network of dealers and an efficient method of distribution, they pointed to what I have called consumers' marketing dilemma. Behind the tools meant to entice buyers were problems for managers and dealers: who shouldered the costs that followed from inaccuracies in matching production with dealers' orders? Who absorbed the costs of used car trade-ins relative to achieving greater new car sales? And who earned the interest from financing cars? Different implications followed from recognising consumers' marketing dilemma and the question of how profits or costs would be distributed in market transactions.

One implication concerned the key accounting and credit policies. Faced with the task of sharing profits or costs, GM managers not surprisingly exerted power in trying to allocate costs to dealers: they pushed cars on their retailers, encouraged retailers to take cars at the end of a model year, shipped cars not ordered, and shipped cars loaded with accessories. From this perspective, accounting and credit policies acquired a different image. Accounting policies offered not an objective measure of dealers' performance, but reflected the effects of management's effort to shift unwanted cars from themselves to dealers. The numbers represented artifacts of the power management exerted in reallocating costs to dealers. Credit also carried a different meaning. Aside from offering dealers a means to finance wholesale purchases, GMAC reallocated profits from dealers' financing agencies or local communities' finance companies to GM directly. Further to the extent dealers relied on GMAC financing, access to credit offered management a tool in pressurising dealers to take orphaned cars. From Sloan's perspective, accounting and credit represented tools for objective management; acknowledging the marketing dilemma GM faced, accounting and credit reflected the power managers exerted in their relations with dealers.

A second implication concerned dealers' relations with consumers. FTC investigators uncovered various dealer practices that had justified consumers' suspicions. From the late 1920s through the 1930s, dealers had tried to curb consumers' ability to negotiate a car's price by destroying used cars at company-run junk yards; they had used appraisal bureaux to share information about consumers' trade-ins; and they had padded new car prices and packed car loans. Taking the franchise contract at face value, dealers purchased cars at a discount to the retail price and had no need to squeeze consumers over the new car's price. But given the marketing dilemma as seen in used cars and given management's pressures in pushing unpopular or year-end models on dealers, as well as management's pressure to set high sales quotas, dealers tried to recover their profits by squeezing dollars out of car buyers' wallets and purses. In other words, car buyers' distrust of dealers reflected a modern method of distribution and a modern system of marketing. Further, while consumers attributed their grievances to dealers, GM managers had shared in the goal of restricting buyers' negotiations because dealers' prosperity benefited the company's fortunes.

A third implication addressed the role of the state. Sloan had paid little attention to the state in his autobiography, implicitly suggesting regulation had little relevance for understanding the modern firm or this consumer market. The conflicts in marketing automobiles, however, prompted dealers and consumers to call on the state to alter market relationships. Dealers were the most vocal, and, as pressures intensified in the worst years of the Depression, their complaints first prompted the FTC's investigation and then the Justice Department's antitrust suit. Still, the conflicts did not end with the Depression, and, as Stuart Macaulay recounted, dealers continued to turn to the state to curb manufacturers' power in shaping their relationships.[80] Much like dealers, consumers also found relief in federal legislation. The 1958 law requiring window stickers was intended to make information about prices transparent for car buyers, and to limit dealers' padding of prices. In each of these many details of the market's operation, the state served as a crucial, if imperfect, restraint on management's pressure on dealers or dealers' pressure on consumers.

GM responded in different ways to the political investigations. When the FTC publicised dealers' pricing tactics, managers initiated a marketing campaign to assert dealers' trustworthiness in their local communities. What effect such claims had is hard to ascertain. A second response came from William Holler. His approach worked to avoid the consequences of political investigations and sought to ease the pressure between dealers and management. His answer was simple: he reduced the number of dealers and enlarged their markets. He thus mitigated the tension between dealers and GM without ever resolving consumers' marketing dilemma.

NOTES

I am grateful to the editors Roy Church and Andrew Godley, and the many colleagues in seminars at Johns Hopkins University, the Economic History Group, Research Triangle, NC, UCLA, and the Wharton School, University of Pennsylvania. Research for this article has been sustained through the generous financial assistance from the Alfred P. Sloan Foundation, the Radcliffe Institute for Advanced Study at Harvard University, the University of Texas at Austin, and the National Endowment for the Humanities.

1. As Alfred Sloan observed, the dealer 'makes and closes the deal that sells the car'. A.P. Sloan, Jr., *My Years with General Motors* (New York, 1964), p.280.
2. GM is singled out in specific studies of advertising, styling and public relations. Consider R. Marchand, *Advertising the American Dream* (Berkeley, CA, 1985); C.E. Armi, *The Art of American Car Design* (University Park, PA, 1988); D. Gartmann, *Auto Opium* (London, 1994); R. Marchand, *Creating the Corporate Soul* (Berkeley, CA, 1998); L. Calder, *Financing the American Dream* (Princeton, 1999); S. Clarke, 'Managing Design: The Art and Colour Section at General Motors, 1927–1941', *Journal of Design History*, Vol.12 (1999), pp.65–79. Overviews of GM's competitive use of marketing are found in S. Tedlow, *New and Improved: The Story of Mass Marketing in America* (New York, 1990), pp.112–81; and Sloan, *My Years with General Motors*, pp.149–68, 219–37.
3. For GM's history, consult A.D. Chandler, Jr., *Strategy and Structure: Chapters in the History of the American Industrial Enterprise* (Cambridge, MA, 1962), pp.114–62; A.D. Chandler, Jr. and S. Salsbury, *Pierre S. du Pont and the Making of the Modern Corporation* (New York, 1971), pp.433–604; and A.D. Chandler, Jr., *Giant Enterprise: Ford, General Motors, and the Automobile Industry: Sources and Readings* (New York, 1964). On GM's system of mass production, see D. Hounshell, *From the American System to Mass Production* (Baltimore, MD, 1984); and D. Raff, 'Making Cars and Making Money in the Interwar Period', *Business History Review*, Vol.65 (1991), pp.721–53. For GM's early promotion of industrial research, see S.W. Leslie, *Boss Kettering* (New

York, 1983). And, for GM's competitive prowess, consult A.J. Kuhn, *GM Passes Ford, 1918–1938* (University Park, PA, 1986); R.F. Freeland, *The Struggle to Control the Modern Corporation: Organizational Change at General Motors, 1924–1970* (New York, 2001).

4. US Federal Trade Commission, 'Report of the Motor Vehicle Industry', 76th Congress, 1st Session, House Document No.468 (Washington, DC, 1939), pp.22, 27.

5. Sloan, *My Years with General Motors*, pp.136–9, 279–312, quotation on p.279.

6. One reference comes in regard to GMAC. Ibid., p.309. On dealers' complaints as motivation for the investigation, see US Federal Trade Commission, 'Report of the Motor Vehicle Industry', 76th Congress, 1st Session, House Document No.468 (Washington, DC, 1939), p.147.

7. E. Hawley, *The New Deal and the Problem of Monopoly* (1966), p.433. US Federal Trade Commission, 'Report of the Motor Vehicle Industry', pp.4–5.

8. McDonald quoted an article from *Fortune* (16 Jan. 1995) in which Bill Gates rated Sloan's autobiography as 'probably the best book to read if you want to read only one book about business'. J. McDonald, *A Ghost's Memoir: The Making of Alfred P. Sloan's My Years with General Motors* (Cambridge, MA, 2002), pp.ix–x, 188–9, quotation on p.189.

9. Various scholars have studied how firms have come to grips with questions about consumers. See R. Blaszcyzk, *Imagining Consumers: Design and Innovation from Wedgwood to Corning* (Baltimore, MD, 2000); A. Forty, *Objects of Desire* (London, 1986); J.L. Meikle, *American Plastic: A Cultural History* (New Brunswick, NJ, 1995); R. Weems, Jr., 'The Revolution Will be Marketed: American Corporations and Black Consumers During the 1960s', *Radical History Review*, Vol.59 (1994), pp.94–107; C.M. Goldstein, 'Mediating Consumption: Home Economics and American Consumers, 1900–1940' (unpublished Ph.D. dissertation, University of Delaware, 1994); S. Clarke, 'Consumer Negotiations', *Business and Economic History*, Vol.26 (Fall 1997), pp.101–22.

10. The FTC investigation was submitted as US Federal Trade Commission, 'Report of the Motor Vehicle Industry'. For a summary of the antitrust charges, see C.M. Hewitt, Jr., *Automobile Franchise Agreements* (Homewood, IL, 1956), pp.103–6. The court's opinion is found in *United States v. General Motors Corporation, et al.*, 121 F.2d 376 (7th Cir. 1941). On dealer-manufacturer relations after World War II, see S. Macaulay, *Law and the Balance of Power: The Automobile Manufacturers and Their Dealers* (New York, 1966); G.K. Hadfield, 'Problematic Relations: Franchising and the Law of Incomplete Contracts', *Stanford Law Review*, Vol.42 (1990), pp.927–92.

11. The two auction houses faced antitrust charges for conspiring to fix 'commission fees charged to more than 130,000 customers over six years'. C. Vogel, 'Indictment Names Two Ex-Chairmen of Auction Houses', *New York Times* (3 May 2001), p.A1; C. Vogel, 'Sotheby's Guilty Plea Brings Collusion Case Closer to End', *New York Times* (4 Feb. 2001), p.C5.

12. Traders are suspect in part because they typically (but not always) claim more information needed to appraise goods and the market than the other party. Still, traders have been subject to suspicions for being outsiders, for instance, being Yankee peddlers in southern markets. Traders further have been made the subject of negative stereotyping, such as anti-Semitic images of Jewish merchants. My point is that in the case of automobile dealers, their conflicts with consumers were traced not to dealers' actions as individuals, but to the marketing dilemma associated with automobiles, and in turn, the modern method of distribution. J.T. Rainer, 'The "Sharper" Image: Yankee Peddlers, Southern Consumers, and the Market Revolution', *Business and Economic History*, Vol.26 (Fall 1997), pp.27–44.

13. Franchises serve as an alternative to firms that maintain their own sales force or retail outlets. By 1986 franchising had also moved abroad, accounting for 11% of retail sales in Great Britain and 10% of retail sales in France. 'Franchising in the U.S. Economy: Prospects and Problems', Committee on Small Business, House of Representatives, 101st Cong., 2nd sess. (Washington, DC, 1990), pp.14, 16–20. J. Katz provides a recent overview of issues in 'Franchise Nation', *Regional Review*, Federal Reserve Bank of Boston (1996), pp.6–10. T. Dicke reviews case histories of various franchises in *Franchising in America* (Chapel Hill, NC, 1992). For a treatment of the early history of auto franchising, see Hewitt, *Automobile Franchise Agreements*. Current legal problems are surveyed in Hadfield, 'Problematic Relations'; Sloan, *My Years with General Motors*, pp.280–82.

14. Economists have studied agency or control problems that shape relations between the franchisor and its franchisees. Examples include P. Rubin, 'The Theory of the Firm and the Structure of the Franchise Contract', *Journal of Law and Economics*, Vol.21 (1978), pp.223–33; A.W. Dnes, 'The Economic Analysis of Franchise Contracts', *Journal of Institutional and Theoretical Economics*,

Vol.152 (1996), pp.297–324; F. Lafontaine and M.E. Slade, 'Retail Contracting and Costly Monitoring: Theory and Evidence', *European Economic Review*, Vol.40 (1996), pp.923–32; P.J. Kaufman and F. Lafontaine, 'Costs of Control: The Source of Economic Rents for McDonald's Franchises', *Journal of Law and Economics*, Vol.37 (1994), pp.417–53; G.F. Mathewson and R.A. Winter, 'The Economics of Franchise Contracts', *Journal of Law and Economics*, Vol.28 (1985), pp.503–26.

15. Sloan, *My Years with General Motors*, pp.129–39, 279–312.
16. Hewitt, *Automobile Franchise Agreements*, p.88. Other manufacturers began to monitor their dealers more closely, beginning in the early 1920s. US Federal Trade Commission, 'Report of the Motor Vehicle Industry', p.288.
17. Manufacturers could also pack more dealers into a market, but this option ran the risk of having weak retailers undercut their healthy counterparts. See Dicke's discussion in *Franchising in America*, pp.67–79.
18. Sloan, *My Years with General Motors*, p.293; Dicke, *Franchising in America*, p.72; Hewitt, *Automobile Franchise Agreements*; and for the industry in general, the US Federal Trade Commission, 'Report of the Motor Vehicle Industry', pp.110–21, 123–5, 140–45, 254–8, 289–94.
19. Sloan, *My Years with General Motors*, pp.136, 287. For General Motors and the industry in general, see the US Federal Trade Commission, 'Report of the Motor Vehicle Industry', pp.110–14, 118–21, 123–5, 140–45, 254–8, 289–94. For inventories, see Chandler, *Strategy and Structure*, pp.145–53; and A.J. Kuhn, *GM Passes Ford*, pp.203–9.
20. US Federal Trade Commission, 'Report on Motor Vehicle Industry', pp.222, 242 and in general, pp.173–6, 215–22, 240–45, 288–91. In 1938, for example, Pontiac reported that used car losses must be kept to a minimum by maintaining a 30-day turnover. R.A. Dickinson, Business Management Department, 'Monthly Report on Dealer Operating Results – May 31, 1938', Box 3156; E.J. Hogan to Regional, Assistant Regional and Zone Managers, 28 April 1938, Box 3156; H.B. Hatch to H.L. Horton, 8 Oct. 1937, Box 3156, Record Group 122, Entry 7, 'Economic Investigations File, Motor Vehicles 1915 – 1938', National Archives, Washington, DC (hereafter RG 122, NA).
21. 'M.E. Coyle Testimony', *U.S. v. General Motors Corporation*, Case No. 7146, Transcript of Record for the US Circuit Court of Appeals for the Seventh Circuit, Box 1003, pp.1779, Transcript of Record, 26 April 1940, Record Group 276 (hereafter RG 276), April 1940, National Archives, Great Lakes Region, Chicago (hereafter NA, Chicago). Sloan, *My Years with General Motors*, pp.129–39.
22. M. Olney, *Buy Now, Pay Later* (Chapel Hill, NC, 1991), pp.119–28.
23. 'Donaldson Brown Testimony', Transcript of Record for US Circuit Court of Appeals for the Seventh Circuit No.7146, Box 1003, Record Group 276, pp.997–8, April 1940, NA, Chicago.
24. 'Government's Summation by Mr. Baldridge', Case No.7146, Transcript of Record for US Circuit Court of Appeals for the Seventh Circuit. Box 1003, RG 276, p.1862, April 1940, NA, Chicago. US Federal Trade Commission, 'Report on Motor Vehicle Industry', p.112.
25. The FTC collected various examples. W.E. Cabeen, Zone Manager, to Claude Simmons, Dallas Motors, Inc., 25 Aug. 1937, Box 3156; M.I. Noll, Office Manager, to Wm. Carson, Indianapolis, Indiana, 25 May 1938, Box 3156; Service and Mechanical Manager to J.H. Bates, Weburn, Massachusetts, 10 June 1937; H.J. Walsh, Zone Manager, to E.B. Hatch, Detroit, 23 Nov. 1936, Box 3156; Assistant Zone Manager to E.B. Mohr, Mohr Chevrolet Company, Dallas, Texas, 10 May 1937, Box 3156; H.B. Hatch to H.L. Horton, 8 Oct. 1937, Box 3156, all in RG 122, NA. I discuss factory representatives in 'Consumer Negotiations', *Business and Economic History*, Vol.26 (Fall 1997), pp.106–8.
26. Sloan, *My Years with General Motors*, p.280.
27. J.J. Baney, 'Field Report for C.M. Woodward', 26 and 28 June 1938, p.5, Box 3108, RG 122, NA.
28. US Federal Trade Commission, 'Report on Motor Vehicle Industry', pp.179–80, 222, 241–4; Sloan, *My Years with General Motors*, p.136.
29. US Federal Trade Commission, 'Report on Motor Vehicle Industry', p.180. GM records given to the FTC indicate that dealers' sales were assessed based on a percentage of a given price class. See, e.g., H.L. Horton to R.G. Schulte, 17 Nov. 1938, Box 3156, RG 122, NA.
30. H.L. Horton to W.E. Holler, 14 May 1938, Box 3156, RG 122, NA.
31. J.J. Baney, 'Field Report for C.M. Woodward', 26 and 28 June 1938, pp.6–7, Box 3108, RG 122, NA.
32. J.J. Baney, 'Field Report for J.E. Harris', 19 Sept. 1938, pp.4–5, Box 310; 'Field Report of Joseph

A. Schlecht', p.3, 2 Aug. 1938, Box 31087, RG 122, NA. US Federal Trade Commission, 'Report on Motor Vehicle Industry', pp.204, 206, 208, and 275. More cases are reported in the FTC's report and provided in the US government's antitrust suit against General Motors. Macaulay called attention to these problems in *Law and the Balance of Power*, pp.17–18.

33. 'Robert E. Griffin Testimony', Transcript of Record for US Circuit Court of Appeals for the Seventh Circuit No.7146, Box 1003, RG 276, pp.1175–6, March 1940, NA, Chicago.

34. 'Joseph M. Hendrie Testimony', Transcript of Record for US Circuit Court of Appeals for the Seventh Circuit No.7146, Box 1003, RG 276, pp.1018–38, Feb. 1940, NA, Chicago.

35. 'M.E. Coyle Testimony', Transcript of Record for US Circuit Court of Appeals for the Seventh Circuit No.7146, Box 1003, Record Group 276, pp.1760–81, April 1940, NA, Chicago.

36. Sloan stated that GM began offering dealers allowance for year-end models in 1930 up to 3% of the dealer's estimated supply of cars for the following year. But the policy was apparently inadequate as dealers complained of having cars forced on them at the end of each selling season. Sloan, *My Years with General Motors*, pp.285–6. US Federal Trade Commission, 'Report on Motor Vehicle Industry', pp.174–7, 204–9, 271–7, quote pp.174, 205, 209, 275; J.J. Baney, 'Field Report for J.E. Harris', 19 Sept. 1938, p.8, Box 3107, RG 122, NA.

37. US Federal Trade Commission, 'Report on Motor Vehicle Industry', p.286, and in general, pp.920–47. See as well the lengthy court opinion for GM's appeal of its antitrust case: *United States v. General Motors Corporation et al.*, 121 F.2d 376 (7th Cir. 1941).

38. See 'Government's Summation by Mr. Baldridge', pp.1866–7; and 'Testimony of William B. McClain', pp.245–57, Transcript of Record in the US Circuit Court of Appeals for the Seventh Circuit No. 7146, Box 1003, RG 276, NA, Chicago.

39. *United States v. General Motors Corporation et al.*, 121 F.2d 376, 395–6 (7th Cir. 1941). See also examples from the FTC investigation, such as J.J. Baney, 'Field Report on J.E. Harris', 19 Sept. 1938, Box 3107, RG 122, NA; and US Federal Trade Commission, 'Report on Motor Vehicle Industry', p.109.

40. See 'Government's Summation by Mr. Baldridge', pp.1873, 1880–81, Transcript of Record in the US Circuit Court of Appeals for the Seventh Circuit No.7146, Box 1003, RG 276, NA, Chicago.

41. See 'Opening Statement by Mr. Baldridge', p.89, Transcript of Record in the US Circuit Court of Appeals for the Seventh Circuit No.7146, Box 1003, RG 276, NA, Chicago. The FTC also gave an example of flexible plans for teachers who made payments when they received their salaries. US Federal Trade Commission, 'Report on Motor Vehicle Industry', p.950.

42. *United States v. General Motors Corporation et al.*, 121 F.2d 376, 397 (7th Cir. 1941).

43. See 'Government's Summation by Mr. Baldridge', pp.1896–7, Transcript of Record in the US Circuit Court of Appeals for the Seventh Circuit No.7146, Box 1003, RG 276, NA, Chicago.

44. In his autobiography, Sloan just noted that GMAC was investigated and that (at the time of the book's publication in 1964) dealers were free to choose their source of financing. Sloan, *My Years with General Motors*, pp.305–9; Hewitt, *Automobile Franchise Agreements*, pp.104–6.

45. H.L. Horton to W.E. Holler, 26 Jan. 1937, p.3, Box 3156, RG 122, NA.

46. B.G. Koether to C.F. Kettering, 17 June 1927, with H.G.W., Sales Section, 'The Manufacturer, the Dealer, and the Used Car', April 1927, p.11, File 87-11.4-1, Box 110, Charles F. Kettering Archives, Richard P. Scharchburg Archives, Kettering University, Flint, MI (hereafter KU). Koether told Kettering that the bulletin covered different aspects of the problem of used cars and had been written for 'internal distribution among our passenger car Divisions'. The FTC dated GM's recognition of the impact of used cars on new car sales to 1925. US Federal Trade Commission, 'Report on Motor Vehicle Industry', p.215.

47. US Federal Trade Commission, 'Report on Motor Vehicle Industry', pp.221–3.

48. Ibid., pp.92–3.

49. Hewitt, *Automobile Franchise Agreements*, pp.86–7.

50. U.S. Federal Trade Commission, 'Report on Motor Vehicle Industry', pp.92–4, 219.

51. Grant gave his instructions in a 1929 bulletin, 'Proposed Highway Safety Plan' quoted in ibid., p.94. Records in the FTC files are extensive on this topic. See, e.g., J.J. Baney, 'Field Report of C.M. Woodard', 26 and 28 July 1938, Box 3108, RG 122, NA.

52. US Federal Trade Commission, 'Report on Motor Vehicle Industry', p.96.

53. H.H. Carter, 'Report on Chevrolet Dealer Association', no date [1938], Box 3108; H.H. Carter, 'Field Report: Rudolph Kysela', 29 Aug. 1938, pp.1–4, Box 3108; J.J. Baney, 'Field Report of C.M. Woodard', pp.7–8, 26 and 28 July 1938, Box 3108, RG122, NA. The LA example and others were reported in US Federal Trade Commission, 'Report on Motor Vehicle Industry', pp.371–400, 1075. This point is noted in 'Consumer Negotiations', pp.107–8.

54. Alfred P. Sloan to C.S. Mott, 26 Jan. 1938, Charles S. Mott Collection, File 77-7.4-3.6, KU; Sloan, *My Years with General Motors*, pp.299–300; Macaulay, *Law and the Balance of Power*, p.16.

55. US Federal Trade Commission, 'Report on Motor Vehicle Industry', p.111, quote p.1077.

56. Sloan, *My Years with General Motors*, p.300; Macaulay, *Law and the Balance of Power*, p.71.

57. US Federal Trade Commission, 'Report on Motor Vehicle Industry', p.920.

58. Packs, for instance, came in money added to a dealers' loss reserve that exceeded what was needed to manage the risk of losses. Packs also came in the form of a 'dealer's bonus'. Ibid., p.932.

59. 'Testimony of Ira G. McCreery', pp.175–6, Transcript of Record in the U.S. Circuit Court of Appeals for the Seventh Circuit No. 7146, Box 1003, RG 276, NA, Chicago.

60. Alfred P. Sloan to C.S. Mott, 26 Jan. 1938, Charles S. Mott Collection, File 77-7.4-3.6, KU; Federal Trade Commission, 'Report on Motor Vehicle Industry', pp.932, 940–44, 1074, 1076.

61. US Federal Trade Commission, 'Report on Motor Vehicle Industry', pp.934, 941, 972.

62. Consumers also lost flexible payment plans that dealers had offered them, as noted above. Ibid., pp.933–44. *United States v. General Motors Corporation et al.*, 121 F.2d 376 (7th Cir. 1941).

63. N. Borden, *Advertising: Text and Cases* (Chicago, 1950), pp.525–8.

64. For the 1950s, see Macaulay, *Law and the Balance of Power*, pp.18–19. In 2000, two suits were filed charging racial discrimination in dealers' handling of credit. See Diana B. Henriques, 'New Front Opens in Effort to Fight Race Bias in Loans', *New York Times* (22 Oct. 2000), pp.A1, A26; Diana B. Henriques, 'Extra Costs on Car Loans Draw New Legal Attacks', *New York Times* (27 Oct. 2000), pp.A1, A23.

65. J.J. Baney, 'Field Report of C.M. Woodward', 26 and 28 July 1938, p.5, Box 3108; J. Baney, 'Field Report of J.E. Harris', pp.5, 8, 19 Sept. 1938, Box 3107, RG 122, NA. The FTC reported more than 90% of GM dealers made 'excessive allowances' on used cars (meaning offered a trade-in price in excess of the car's 'fair market value'). US Federal Trade Commission, 'Report on Motor Vehicle Industry', pp.240–41.

66. Dealers and management acknowledged the problem of gauging consumer demand in a market. See, e.g., J.J. Baney, 'Field Report for J.E. Harris', 19 Sept. 1938, p.5, Box 3107, RG 122, NA.

67. I discuss GM's estimates of consumer demand in 'Consumers, Information and Marketing Efficiency at GM', *Business and Economic History*, Vol.25 (Fall 1996), pp.189–90. H.G. Weaver, 'The Development of a Basic Purchasing Power Index by Counties', *Harvard Business Review*, Vol.4 (1926), pp.275–88. Also see Weaver's address to the Sales Executives Division of the American Management Association, 'To Fix Territorial Sales Quotas', *Automotive Industries* (17 June 1926), pp.1061–2; Sloan, *My Years with General Motors*, pp.136–7, 284–5.

68. 'William E. Holler Testimony', Transcript of Record for US Circuit Court of Appeals for the Seventh Circuit No.7146, Box 1003, RG 276, pp.1639–41, 26 April 1940, NA, Chicago.

69. William Holler to all Chevrolet Dealers, 10 Aug. 1939, and H.L. Horton to W.E. Holler, 26 Jan. 1937, pp.3–7, Box 3156, RG 122, NA.

70. The FTC reported higher fines of $35 on Chevies up to $200 on Cadillacs. H.H. Carter, 'Field Report: Rudolph Kysela', 29 Aug. 1938, p.5, Box 3107, RG 122, NA; 'G.M. III: How to Sell Automobiles', *Fortune*, Vol.19 (1939), p.105; Dicke, *Franchising in America*, p.65; US Federal Trade Commission, 'Report on Motor Vehicle Industry', pp.118–22.

71. Profits included owners' salaries, and the earnings translated into a 56% average return on net working capital for the years from 1933 to 1941. Bill Holler to C.S. Mott, 10 Aug. 1942, Charles S. Mott Collection, File 77-7.4-3.5, KU. Bedros Pashigian finds that GM dealers reported a 27% return on equity after taxes in 1940. B.P. Pashigian, *The Distribution of Automobiles, an Economic Analysis of the Franchise System* (Englewood Cliffs, NJ, 1961), pp.212–16; Sloan, *My Years with General Motors*, p.296.

72. I thank Philip Scranton for calling McDonald's memoir to my attention. McDonald, *A Ghost's Memoir*, pp.178–82, quotation on p.181.

73. McDonald guessed that a memo from 1921 with its specific reference to monopoly had been the source of trouble, but even then, he felt this did not qualify as a reason for 'suppression by GM'. McDonald, *A Ghost's Memoir*, pp.75–6, 151–5, 161–4, 181, quotation on p.161.

74. Sloan liked using the word 'science' to describe his approach to management. See, e.g., *My Years with General Motors*, p.132.

75. N.R. Lamoreaux, 'Reframing the Past: Thoughts about Business Leadership and Decision Making under Uncertainty', *Enterprise & Society*, Vol.2 (Dec. 2001), pp.632–59.

76. In 1934 a dealer council was established, but its members were appointed by GM management, as Sloan noted 'each year I chose a different panel of dealers'. In his analysis of manufacturer–dealer

relations, Stuart Macaulay observed that being appointed by GM the council's members did not
necessarily voice the views of their fellow dealers but 'told top management just what it wanted to
hear'. Regarding dealers' contracts, Sloan noted that in 1955, after a study of the situation,
management offered dealers the option of five-year sales agreements and allowed dealers to
'nominate' a person to take over the business on the dealer's death. Sloan did not offer an
accounting of the political context in which these changes took place. Macaulay noted that the five-
year contract was announced at the time the Senate had called GM executives to testify in hearings.
Macaulay, *Law and the Balance of Power*, pp.28–9, 53–4, 77–8, quotation on p.28; Sloan, *My
Years with General Motors*, pp.300, 309–11, quotation on p.291.
77. Sloan, *My Years with General Motors*, p.287.
78. Ibid., p.288.
79. Ibid., p.134.
80. See, e.g., note 76; Macaulay, *Law and the Balance of Power*.

Foreign Multinationals and Innovation in British Retailing, 1850–1962

ANDREW GODLEY
University of Reading

That foreign direct investment (FDI) largely benefits host economies has almost become a truism in modern economics as multinationals are mostly seen to introduce new technologies and organisational innovations into host countries. Recent research on FDI in British manufacturing concurs, for example, documenting almost 1,000 subsidiaries of foreign firms that had entered UK manufacturing by 1962, and mostly in relatively high-technology sectors.[1] FDI in UK manufacturing has therefore been composed overwhelmingly of relatively high productivity entrants, bringing new techniques and processes, and thus disproportionately responsible for productivity growth in the manufacturing sector overall. The message is clear. Without this inward investment by foreign multinationals witnessed over many decades, British manufacturing's sluggish performance since the late nineteenth century would have been considerably worse.[2]

Whether this was the case outside the manufacturing sector remains a mystery, for relatively little is known of foreign multinationals in the service sector.[3] It is widely accepted that new technologies were introduced by manufacturing multinationals, from canning to motor vehicles, and from electrical engineering to business machines, with important consequences for manufacturing productivity growth. But whether there was any kind of service sector equivalent, with commensurate gains to service sector productivity growth, is simply unknown.[4]

While the current state of knowledge makes it impractical to gauge the historical impact of FDI on all UK services, this essay presents the results of a research project that concentrates on Britain's largest service, retailing. It maps the relative importance of foreign entrants in British retailing from 1850 (before when any entrants are assumed to have been insignificant) up to 1962 (the year before the first census of foreign multinationals in the UK, which supersedes the methods used here).[5] This research has documented 118 subsidiaries of 99 foreign parent companies active in British retailing during this period. The methods of data collection and estimates of the survey's coverage are discussed in the appendix below.[6]

An earlier article has shown how the chronological development of FDI in British retailing closely followed the downward spread in purchasing power. Initially entrants were overwhelmingly luxury goods retailers in London's West

End, but by the end of the nineteenth century most new entrants were distributing durable goods to lower middle- and working-class households. During the inter-war period, most new entrants focused on mass marketing simple consumer goods.[7] While this suggests that the pattern of foreign entry into British retailing was particularly sensitive to income, what is of more concern here is whether these entrants were successful or not after entry. This essay therefore concentrates on assessing how significant foreign multinationals became in British retailing over the period. The next section outlines the patterns of entry in each retail trade. Then an initial explanation is offered, one that focuses on the vast majority of entrants during this period, foreign manufacturers most of whom needed some method of controlling their British distribution channels. Finally the essay compares the frankly unimpressive role of FDI as a method of importing innovations into British retailing with the remarkable upsurge of international retailing since the 1960s.

II

Perhaps the most revealing indicator of the foreign influence in British retailing would be market share. To the extent that foreign entrants gained market share in retailing, they must have overcome the disadvantages of foreignness (for example, higher costs of learning about local consumer preferences) through offsetting competitive advantages. It is these advantages, such as superior marketing skills or more efficient purchasing or logistics, that represent the retailing equivalent of, for instance, new production technology brought to British manufacturing by a foreign multinational, with all its attendant economic benefits.

While foreign entrants were present in British retailing from 1850 at the very latest, before 1885 they were essentially confined to a range of single-unit luxury goods boutiques in London's West End. While no doubt important for some customers, these entrants were insignificant in British retailing overall, and, as Table 1 illustrates, the first entrant of any significance was Singer, with its branch network already well developed by 1885. Moreover, little had changed by 1907, when the much bigger Singer retail organisation still accounted almost entirely for the foreign multinationals' market share of around one-quarter of one per cent of all British retailing.

After the First World War, foreign multinationals were increasingly active in the sector, their market share increasing to around 1.3 per cent in 1929 and 1939, before rising rapidly to around four per cent of the UK retail sector captured in the 1961 Census of Distribution. Despite this growth in market share, however, FDI cannot be said to have ever attained any great significance in British retailing overall throughout the period. It clearly lagged behind the ever growing importance of FDI in manufacturing.

By 1914 around one-half of one per cent of the British manufacturing workforce was employed by a subsidiary of a foreign multinational. This

TABLE 1
FOREIGN MULTINATIONALS' MARKET SHARE OF BRITISH RETAILING, 1885–61 (%)

TRADE	1885	1907	1929	1939	1961
Bakers				0.7	12.7
Butchers					
Dairies					
Fishmongers					
Green-grocers					
Grocers			5.3		
Self-service					42.2
Off-Licences			0.1	0.1	
FOOD	0.0	0.1	1.9	0.1	0.8
Footwear				1.8	2.7
Menswear					
Womenswear			0.1	0.3	0.2
Women's underwear[a]				10.0	10.0
CLOTHING	0.0	0.0	0.1	0.5	0.7
Booksellers/Stationers[b]					0.7
Confectioners					
Tobacconists					
Newsagents					
CTN	0.0	0.0	0.0	0.0	0.1
Sports Goods			0.4		
Chemists			6.8		0.6[c]
Furniture					
Ironmongers					
Jewellers			0.1	0.2	
Music sellers			0.1	0.1	
Sewing machines	90.0	90.0	90.0	75.0	40.0[d]
Variety Chain Stores			38.7	67.8	89.4
Department Stores					
Typewriters				50.0	50.0[e]
Petrol				0.2	12.0[f]
Vacuum Cleaners[g]			90.0	90.0	60.0
Cycle Dealers					
Elec. etc.					
Misc.					
OTHER	1.0	1.3	4.2	5.1[h]	14.3[i]
ALL RETAIL	0.15	0.24	1.30	1.35[h]	3.92[i]

Notes: a) Based on estimate of US corset and lingerie direct salesforce out of trade's total salesforce. b) Estimate of *Encyclopaedia Britannica*'s market share derived by their salesforce (200) out of trade's total salesforce. c) Estimate based on Max Factor's 105 concessions in department stores out of all branches. As concessions were smaller than a typical chemist goods branch, this is an overestimate. d) Singer's collapse in market share estimated from its much reduced post-war store count. e) Estimate of retail sales through typewriter manufacturers' own outlets only. f) Dixon, 'UK Petrol Case', p.384, shows that company controlled stations were around twice the size of the independents (tied or otherwise) in 1964, hence the estimated market share here is twice the share of total outlets. g) Estimate of combined market share of Electrolux and Hoover machines via own outlets and direct sales forces. After WW2, both companies increasingly began using independent dealers. h) Because variety chain store sales per branch in 1939 were around eight times higher than average, Woolworth's contribution to overall market share has been reweighted accordingly. i) Because variety chain store sales per branch in 1961 were fourteen times greater than average, Woolworth's contribution to overall market share has been reweighted accordingly. Also, company owned petrol stations were twice as large as independents, so the oil majors' contribution to overall market share has also been reweighted. Blank cells = zero. Note values less than 0.1 per cent counted as zero.

Source: Multinationals' share of total branch by retail trade, sector and overall from Appendix, Table A1 (except where indicated in the notes).

certainly does not indicate that foreign multinationals were especially significant in British manufacturing before World War One. Although, with an above average output per employee, a reasonable conclusion is that FDI was around three times more significant in British manufacturing than retailing (that is around three-quarters of one per cent compared to around one-quarter of one per cent output or market share in both sectors – both sectors incidentally dominated by the single entrant Singer). By 1963, however, seven per cent of British manufacturing workers worked for a foreign multinational, producing 10.6 per cent of manufacturing output. In the midst of the 'American Challenge', FDI in British manufacturing was assuming the level of overall significance that we are familiar with today. It was also by that stage still around three times more important than FDI in British retailing.[8] This overall relative insignificance of FDI in retailing notwithstanding, Table 1 also shows that some retail trades experienced a much greater foreign presence at certain times.

The largest sector in British retailing was, and remains, food retailing. The food sector included over 40 per cent of all outlets and sales over the period, with the grocery trade dominant.[9] This was also the sector that saw the beginnings of what Jefferys described as the 'revolution in the distributive trades', with the first multiples and co-operative societies both introducing some form of organisational innovation.[10]

The first foreign entrants into food retailing were meat distributors. T.C. Eastman, the pioneer of refrigerated shipping in the 1870s, negotiated a joint venture with the leading Scottish multiple butcher, John Bell, guaranteeing provincial outlets for his American beef. This enabled him to avoid having to sell at below-cost prices in an overstocked London market before the meat deteriorated. The eponymous chain soon became the largest multiple butchers in Britain, although Eastman's involvement appears to have been minimal; indeed, managerial control soon seems to have reversed direction, with the Bell family taking over Eastman's American interests.[11]

Despite much debate among foreign suppliers, apart from two small, abortive attempts by Antipodean frozen lamb interests and the Eastman joint venture, the door to British meat retailing was closed.[12] This represents a marked contrast with margarine, where the Dutch producers, Van den Berghs and Jurgens, made the first genuinely significant investments in British food retailing acquiring a string of grocery multiples from 1906 to 1927.

The development of a new hydrogenation process allowed cheaper vegetable fats to be used in place of animal fats from around 1900. The downside was that these techniques increased margarine's perishability and so reduced its shelf-life. Dutch producers, having already sunk large investments in establishing their brands, were reluctant to let independent retailers sell a below par product; the risk of destroying their brand reputations was too high. This therefore suddenly increased the importance of controlling their distribution channels and pushed Van den Berghs and Jurgens, as well as their principal British competitor, Maypole, to further vertical integration. By 1929, the two Dutch firms had merged and together controlled 4,000 British grocery stores, or over five per cent of the entire trade.[13] With the merger of Lever Brothers, Van den Berghs and Jurgens, the Dutch margarine interests drop out of Table 1 after 1929, as Allied Suppliers (Unilever's combined British grocery interests) was no longer a foreign-controlled company. The foreign share of British food retailing recovered only with the post-war growth of Garfield Weston's Associated British Foods.

Weston, a leading Canadian biscuit manufacturer, was convinced that the UK biscuit industry was overstocked with too many small producers, and so, in the depths of the 1930s Depression, he acquired several bakeries. He then simply rationalised production on to fewer sites and, with modern equipment, produced biscuits at half the cost and set about undercutting competitors.[14]

Many of these newly acquired bakers had small chains of tied retail outlets, and Weston kept them on as outlets for his bakery products. Their number increased dramatically after the war as Weston acquired further regional bakeries in the 1950s in his pursuit of economies of scale. As with the Dutch margarine producers, Weston's interest in retailing was nevertheless perfunctory.[15] He changed his mind, however, when he recognised that his Canadian retailing subsidiary had successfully developed the self-service supermarket format. Fine Fare was the vehicle chosen to import the format into Britain. From 1954 to 1961 the firm quickly expanded to a chain of 253 supermarkets, or over 40 per cent of the still fledgling British self-service grocery trade.[16] However, while Weston takes some credit for introducing the format, other grocers, such as Sainsburys and Tesco, proved rather more successful supermarket retailers than Fine Fare thereafter.[17]

In sum, therefore, whether it was in meat, margarine, or biscuits, the real significance of the foreign retailers in food retailing was even more muted than that suggested by the market shares in Table 1. There were no new innovations in food retailing introduced into Britain by these entrants. The big foreign investors, Van den Berghs, Jurgens, and ABF, were primarily interested in production and devoted little managerial time or attention to retailing. Outside these three entrants, the rest were failures. Weston's pioneering attempt to introduce the self-service supermarket format was the only foreign investment in the food sector that was primarily concerned with retailing and with introducing some sort of retail innovation.

Clothing was the second largest sector in British retailing throughout the period, with around one-fifth of all British retail sales and outlets. In contrast to the food trades, there were many more foreign entrants in clothing, but rarely of any prominence. This was largely because of the numerous but small luxury goods retailers. Beginning with L.T. Piver, a ladies' glove maker who opened a Regent Street shop in 1850, and Revillion Frères, a furrier with another West End branch that opened in 1869, a succession of mostly French artisans opened elite clothing outlets in London.

This group of luxury goods entrants also included many in non-clothing trades: Tiffany and Cartier in jewellery, the American-acquired Dunhill tobacconists, two Danish ceramists, Ipsen and Royal Copenhagen, as well as a Japanese art dealer, Yamanaka, among many others. Of the 118 firmly identified retail subsidiaries owned by foreign parents, 24 were luxury boutiques. None attained any great prominence in this period, however.

The significant inward investors in the clothing sector were actually clustered in the footwear trade. The Swiss firm, Bally, for example, wanted to increase its UK sales primarily through mail order, but acquired the small London Shoe chain in 1899 to give the firm more British presence. It soon acquired Dolcis, a larger chain, and then, after the Second World War, Russell & Bromley, so that in 1956, just before Dolcis was sold to the leading British footwear chain, Sears, Bally had almost 300 British retail branches. Along with Scholl (the US parent entered in 1924 and built up a chain of 100 outlets by 1939), Bata (the Czech parent entered in 1933 and quickly opened 200 stores by 1939), and several smaller ventures, foreign multinationals collectively owned around 400 branches in both 1939 and 1961.[18] This paled into relative unimportance when compared to the leading British retailers, however. Already by 1929 the two Sears subsidiaries, True-Form and Freeman, Hardy & Willis, along with Saxone, Barratt, and Mansfield, had nearly 3,000 branches between them.[19]

Similarly, in menswear and womenswear, the entrants that grew to some prominence, such as Etam (the Swiss parent entered in 1924 and by 1929 was the largest hosiery retailer in Britain with 40 branches), C&A (the Dutch parent entered in 1922 and was a leading ladies' outfitter by 1939), and Spirella (the US parent entered in 1913 and was the pioneer of the direct selling of ladies' corsets), were nevertheless very small when compared to the leading British clothing multiples, such as Burtons (333 and 595 branches in 1929 and 1939 respectively), Hepworths (around 300 by 1939), Prices Fifty Shilling Tailors (over 260 by 1939), Hipps (100), Alexandre (around 70).[20] The foreign entrants' market share in the broad clothing sector correspondingly never amounted to very much in this period.

The confectionery, tobacconists and newsagents sector included around one-fifth of all British shops over the period but was dominated by small single-unit firms. Outside the big stationers (W.H. Smith and John Menzies) with their railway station kiosks, and two tobacconists' chains (Findlays and Salmon & Gluckstein), there were almost no substantial multiples. There were, moreover, fewer foreign multinationals in this sector than any other; the *Encyclopaedia Britannica* has been included here with its 200-strong sales force in 1961.

The residual sector of British retailing included everything from hardware to music shops, from department stores to petrol stations. With the consumer goods retailed in this sector generally relatively income-elastic, these trades grew in importance as living standards rose.[21] In this environment of growing opportunities, several foreign manufacturers of consumer goods each opened a small number of retail outlets, but continued to distribute the vast majority of their imported goods via independent dealers. The former US baseball star-pitcher turned sports goods producer, A.G. Spalding, for instance, entered in

1899 and built a small chain of around five outlets, but the firm continued to sell most of its golf clubs, tennis rackets, and so on through independents. Ingersoll, the leading watch multiple with 30 branches in 1939, still sold the majority of its watches elsewhere; as did A.W. Faber his pencils, despite a solitary store in Queen Victoria Street, London. Remington, Underwood, and other typewriter manufacturers, as well as Steinway, Blüthner, and Bechstein, among piano manufacturers, all had just one or two retail outlets in central London to act as showcase locations for their products. While several trades therefore had a foreign presence, sales through these subsidiaries' own branches were less significant than through independent dealers.[22]

The retail trades where foreign multinationals attained genuine importance and a significant market share over the period were therefore restricted to sewing machines and variety chain stores, along with, although to a lesser extent, vacuum cleaners, chemist's goods, and petrol. As already noted, the first significant entrant was Singer, which opened its first shop in Glasgow in 1856. Its importance in British retailing, however, dates from the 1875 decision by the company's British agent to target the consumer market through company-owned outlets and a vast army of door-to-door salesmen rather than via independent dealers. This met with a rapid growth in demand, and Singer's UK sales quickly exceeded those of any other foreign market. The retail organisation grew from 20 branches in 1875, to 394 in 1885, to 625 in 1907, and finally to a peak of 900 branches and 6,000 employees by 1914. Almost half of all British households owned a Singer sewing machine by then, its monopoly of the British market being almost total.[23]

Next was Woolworths. Frank W. Woolworth opened his first British store in Liverpool in 1909, before also rolling out national coverage with extraordinary speed; 375 branches by 1929, 759 by 1939, 1,068 in 1961. Something similar to the variety chain store concept had long existed in Britain, but Woolworths' recipe for success was simple. Financial muscle in purchasing gave cost savings that were passed on in the form of a much wider range of products than competitors could sell under the fixed price formula. With much larger staffing per branch than all retail trades (bar department stores), Woolworths not only became the most important foreign multinational in British retailing (overtaking Singer during the 1920s), but became Britain's biggest retailer, employing well over 60,000 by 1961.[24]

Like Singer, Electrolux (Swedish parent entered in 1912) and Hoover (US parent entered in 1919) both used armies of door-to-door salesmen to distribute their vacuum cleaners. Both had some retail outlets (Hoover around 20 by 1939), but they focused almost exclusively on direct sales before the 1950s, and together enjoyed around 90 per cent of the rapidly growing British market for vacuum cleaners.[25]

Boots, the chemist's goods store, had come into American hands in 1920 when Jesse Boot's attempts to avoid passing the company to his son coincided with the expansionist dreams of Louis Liggett, the American entrepreneur who had built the Rexall chain. Liggett had struggled to establish his business in Britain, so the acquisition of Boots gave him the largest multiple chemists at a stroke. American techniques transformed much of Boots' management, but domestic expansion during the 1920s soon caught up with Liggett as he was forced to sell his British assets in 1933 to stave off bankruptcy.[26]

Finally, Esso, Mobil, Regent, PetroFina, and Total, together with the dominant British incumbents, Shell and BP, transformed the retailing of British petrol after the relaxation of post-war building restrictions in 1954. Esso had first experimented with company-owned stations in the 1930s, but petrol stations before the 1950s were overwhelmingly independents, typically stocking two different brands. The transformation came as a competitive scramble broke out in the late 1950s, when the oil companies attempted to reduce delivery costs, expand the range of oil products available, and increase the quality of service to consumers by purchasing sites and building their own stations.[27]

To draw this brief survey to a conclusion, these empirical results, summarised in Table 1, contribute to filling something of a gap in the history of FDI in the British economy. Despite its overall unimportance, some retail trades clearly witnessed dramatic change as a result of FDI. Whether it was the direct selling techniques of the sewing machine, corset, or vacuum cleaner salesmen, or Woolworths' variety chain store format, or the spread of producer-controlled petrol stations, some new retail techniques were introduced by these foreign multinationals. Nevertheless, this mapping of the foreign influence leaves many questions unanswered, and the next section attempts to fashion an explanation for the uneven impact of foreign multinationals in British retailing.

III

Despite its tendency to involve an ever higher share of scarce resources as economies mature, distribution has traditionally been seen by economists simply as a residual activity. Some chains or department stores may have exploited economies of scale or scope, but, according to the conventional view, overall the sector has been a drag on productivity growth.[28] This view clearly appears to be at odds with much of the historical narrative of the emergence of modern retailing, where the development of mass retailing is supposed to have led to considerable welfare benefits.[29] But such conflicting views arise probably because the theory of retailing remains by and large underdeveloped.

Most retail history has in fact simply assumed that increasing firm size arose from increasing economies in advertising, logistics, management, and so on, rather than any trend to monopolistic competition. But the economic theory of retailing needs to explain far more than the relationship between increasing concentration and increasing returns to scale. Indeed, while such economies may have been present in this period, their impact on concentration levels can hardly be described as revolutionary. Jefferys estimated that multiples accounted for between 12 and 14 per cent of all sales in 1930, for example; hardly a dominant form of organisation. Moreover, the large multiples, those firms that would be expected to benefit most from economies in distribution, accounted for far less.[30] In fact, any explanation of historic patterns of retail development needs to pay far less attention to any putative scale economies and far more to its most distinctive characteristic: its spatial specificity.

Retailing is an activity that is physically constrained by the location of consumption.[31] When the costs of personal transportation are high, consumers cannot easily switch from one shopping area to another. Because physical locations are imperfect substitutes for one another, imperfect competition in retail sites leads to a degree of market failure.[32] Incumbents, or first-movers, therefore have strong advantages over new entrants because spatially constrained consumers face significant switching costs.

Foreign multinationals were, by definition, late-comers into the already developed British high streets. Where these new entrants were successful, they must have held some strong advantages to oust the incumbents. As noted above, these may have been superior economies in the supply chain, such as in purchasing, or logistics, or other management functions. Or they may have developed superior merchandising skills elsewhere and so simply imported better advertising or display activities and so on to a receptive British audience. Or, following the classic account of the motives for FDI in manufacturing, they may have invested in dedicated distribution channels because of some combination of genuine productivity advantages over competitors, the importance of strong presence in the important UK market, and of high transaction costs inhibiting either market entry or growth.[33]

When we turn to the historical experience of British retailing, even the cursory review of the empirical results reported above reveals that most foreign entrants were not actually retailers but rather manufacturers.[34] Explaining the determinants of FDI in British retailing may therefore be sensitive not only to the economics of distribution but manufacturing also. In fact, the vast majority of entrants were foreign manufacturers investing in their British (and often other) distribution channels. This initial attempt to explain historic FDI in British retailing therefore begins by concentrating on the costs facing foreign manufacturers that so prompted them to invest in British retailing.

Foreign manufacturers were not directly interested in retailing, rather their concern was in properly marketing their products. For many consumer goods producers, marketing is essentially limited to brand building and advertising. But for some particular markets, as is explained below, peculiarities of consumer demand mean that producers and especially new entrants need to do more to communicate their brand's value to their target audience than simply run an advertising campaign. It is in these market segments that foreign entry into British retailing was especially concentrated.

Closer examination of all the foreign entrants into British retailing up to 1962 suggests that there were three different groups of manufacturer-led investments in response to the information problem outlined here. These included retail investments by foreign luxury goods producers, investments by foreign branded consumer goods producers in showcase outlets, and the creation of distribution channels by the foreign manufacturers of novel products. These were all manufacturers of products that faced very specific and unusual demand conditions, requiring unusual marketing solutions in whichever national market they happened to have targeted. A fourth group of manufacturer-led investments appears to follow more of the logic associated with strategic behaviour in oligopolistic markets. This leaves as a fifth and final group the small number of foreign retailers, perversely relegating them to some sort of small, residual group of entrants into British retailing.

Luxury goods retailers have long been recognised as an important sub-group of multinational retailers. They were almost invariably small-scale foreign artisans with boutiques in London and Paris, as well perhaps as one or two other major fashion centres. These were mostly manufacturers and they acquired dedicated retail outlets in these key markets because of the peculiarities of the demand for luxury goods. While luxury goods are normal goods, at the margin they experience a perverse demand curve because of what Leibenstein described as snob effects.[35] Instead of price rationing demand, for consumers of luxury goods an increase in price can signal an increase in its value – or snob appeal. At the margin, therefore, luxury producers can sell more when they *raise* prices.

While luxury goods incumbents may benefit initially, the outcome is an extremely unstable equilibrium, where high profits attract new entrants. The danger to the entire market arises, however, should the new entrants seek to gain market share through price competition. If snob factors remain an important component of total demand, cutting prices will *reduce* demand.

Luxury goods producers were therefore faced with an exaggerated form of the usual difficulty facing producers of branded consumer goods. While brands are expensive to build up, because of the high cost of communicating to consumers the additional value the brand is supposed to capture, price competition has the effect of exaggerating the reduction in brand value. The moves by luxury goods manufacturers into retailing are therefore best explained as attempts to gain full control over the distribution channels and so ensure that competition in the key British market was confined to differentiation strategies.

The second group consisted of those foreign producers of branded consumer goods, ranging from pianos to pencils, and from watches to typewriters, who did not face quite the potential catastrophe that price competition posed to luxury goods producers, but nevertheless needed to recoup their high sunk costs in brand development. They therefore needed to retain some control over the ability of independent retailers to engage in competitive practices that might diminish brand value, albeit to a far lesser extent than the luxury goods producers. The solution preferred by several foreign manufacturers was to open a single or a small number of outlets, around which much of their nation-wide marketing strategy focused. For piano manufacturers like Steinway and Bechstein, for example, advertising strategies based on artist endorsements and their plush

West End showrooms clearly differentiated their products from cheaper rivals and encouraged pre-sale demonstration. The brand value was thus clearly communicated. Independent retailers therefore risked confusing potential customers, and so losing sales, should they engage in price-cutting strategies. Similar examples include Spalding in sports goods, and Faber in pencils.

With the 24 entrants in the luxury trades and the 33 showcase retailers, almost half of all foreign entrants are best interpreted as attempts by foreign manufacturers of highly differentiated products to minimise the threat of price competition through these vertical restraints of one kind or another. While their profits might have been higher under this kind of monopolistic competition, the real incentive to producers was to underline product differentiation and so maintain consumer confidence in the brand. Whether it was pianos or watches, jewellery or *haute couture*, a notable feature of both luxury and showcase entrants was their virtual disappearance with the widespread adoption of resale price maintenance after the First World War.[36] Because producers could legally control retail prices, the primary incentive to invest in their own distribution channels disappeared.

Foreign manufacturers of novel consumer goods, such as sewing machines and vacuum cleaners, were interested in developing newly emerging markets. But independent retailers in these markets, with their incumbent advantages, faced few incentives to market and distribute novel products. Without direct access to the manufacturer's previous experience in other markets, or with less optimism than a novel product's manufacturer, independent retailers were always likely to be more cautious in marketing new products. Foreign manufacturers of novel products therefore faced high transaction costs in their international marketing and so a strong incentive to internalise their distribution channels. Where they had already solved such a dilemma in their home markets, they were able to establish similar dedicated distribution channels in Britain.[37]

Furthermore, producers of novel goods faced particular risks if they did not invest in distribution channels in newly emerging markets. This is because the demand for novel products moves through various stages as they enjoy a life cycle pattern of diffusion in a market. For producers of novel products, the key point is the transition from the introductory to the growth stages, when the increase in sales is dynamic, and total cumulative sales can be disproportionately important in a relatively short period (leading to the classic bell-shaped distribution of annual sales, or the 'S'-shaped curve for cumulative sales over time). Therefore, the optimal risk-averse strategy when transaction costs were high was to invest in their own distribution channels, and the optimal timing was at a relatively early stage.

It follows, of course, that once markets were mature, the manufacturers' dilemma was no longer present. First, independent retailers would by then have recognised the true nature of market demand, and so be eager to distribute the product, reducing transaction costs. Second, without another closely related product innovation, there was little possibility of another rapid take-off in sales to justify such costly retail investments. Not surprisingly, all these entrants disposed of their British retail organisations either shortly before or after the early 1960s, and their products were then distributed through independent retailers.

The fourth group of manufacturing-led investments comprised foreign producers of what were already well-developed and standardised goods, such as margarine, bread, chemists goods, and petrol, at the time of the initial investment in retailing. The case histories here suggest that while brand protection might have prompted some initial move, the bulk of investment in UK distribution channels was more a retaliatory response to competitor strategies in what were extremely concentrated industries.

Game-theoretic solutions to the competitive strategies in oligopolistic industries are complex to model, but a common result is that the ever present threat of retaliation both gives some stability to the eventual outcome and minimises the likelihood of price competition. Under such circumstances, if for whatever reason one producer pursues forwards integration, the others would follow regardless of any corporate competence or interest in retailing. Moreover, with competition limited to product differentiation and service, controlling distribution channels becomes ever more important.[38] As the earlier discussion of the meat and margarine sectors suggested, technological changes may have prompted initial entry. Increased perishability would have exposed producers to the risk of distributors acting opportunistically, and so increased transaction costs. Initial entry, however, triggered a competitive scramble into British retailing that either continued under its own momentum (as in margarine and petrol), or did not (as in meat).[39]

Out of the entire population, this leaves only 18 entrants that were foreign retailers. Moreover, once several short-lived and unsuccessful ventures are excluded, this group coalesces into Woolworths, C&A, Etam, Fortnum & Mason, Fine Fare, Safeway (entered 1962), and a few foreign voluntary grocery wholesalers, including Spar, Vivo, VG, and Centra. While Fortnums came into Weston's control almost by accident, and the voluntary grocers were really concerned with wholesaling, the others do represent attempts to introduce novel retail formats and other innovations. Whether it was the self-service supermarket, the expanded variety chain store, or the chains of ladies outfitters, these are the closest historic examples to the dominant type of retail entrants today. And yet, during this period, they were only a very small minority.[40]

IV

That FDI in British retailing was really very different than is the case in the recent past should now be obvious. In the recent past dozens of foreign retailers have entered in some years, nearly 200 in total between 1980 and 1994, for instance.[41] This compares with the very small number of foreign retailers included in the final group above that were entering up to 1962. In recent years, as absolute levels of FDI in retailing have shot up, the role played by manufacturers has been negligible.

The explanation of why these multinationals sought foreign retail outlets has focused primarily on understanding the principal demand constraints facing the entrants in each retail trade. Because retailing is an extremely heterogeneous sector, trying to shoehorn all entrants into a single explanatory framework would be injudicious. Rather, it has been shown here that as the nature of demand facing foreign producers varied, so the incentives facing foreign manufacturers to invest in retailing varied. For those that actually did establish retail outlets, whether it was to control the market better (as with luxury goods producers or the established and oligopolistic mass market distributors) or to invest in the brand (as with showcase retailers), or to build market share during the dynamic growth phase of the life cycle for novel products, the common denominator was the need to reach consumers directly. Foreign entrants were not unique in this; indeed perhaps the most celebrated cases during this period were in clothing with manufacturers Sears and Burtons pursuing vertical integration strategies.

In fact the somewhat chequered history of foreign multinationals in British retailing before the surge in the 1980s is perhaps best interpreted not as the early phase of the later and more mature phenomenon of international retailing (where retailers pursue internationalisation strategies), but more a sub-set of responses by producers to prevailing conditions in British retailing generally.[42] For the vast majority of consumer goods producers existing distribution channels were acceptable. For some, however, including our population of foreign multinationals documented here, they were not, and no doubt the minority of these actually pursued costly retail investments. And as the nature of British demand conditions and retailing have changed in recent years, so has the character of FDI in British high streets.[43]

APPENDIX I
ESTIMATING FOREIGN MULTINATIONALS' MARKET SHARE
IN BRITISH RETAILING, 1850–62

For the period before it is captured by official statistics, there is no obvious data nor any straightforward proxy for inward foreign direct investment (FDI) into the UK economy. The best estimates of FDI into British manufacturing are based on the proxy of the entry and exit of foreign companies' subsidiaries.[44] Apart from its sheer laboriousness, the principal disadvantage of this method is that it plainly fails to capture the flows of international investment. Nevertheless, while strictly speaking FDI is a capital flow, its interest as an economic activity comes from its ability to augment the value-adding activity of a host economy. This arises not simply through a flow of funds from economies X to Y, but from the impact of new technologies, forms of organisation, labour practices, and other innovations. In other words, multinationals are primarily of interest because of the role of their management.

Counting multinationals therefore has the decided advantage of identifying the population of entrants, enabling historians to focus on these firms and their impact on employment, market share, and a range of other firm- and industry-specific variables. In the absence of data on the capital invested, transforming the population of entrants into estimates of historic FDI depends upon weighting each entrant by some reasonably close proxy for total capital employed; perhaps employment, or perhaps sales. Securing credible firm-level estimates for even these variables remains extremely hazardous, however, and the current coverage of historic data is far from complete.

The counting methodology was also adopted to estimate historical FDI in British retailing, but, because it was possible to discover the number of branches for essentially all of the retail entrants over the period, the resulting population bears a far closer resemblance to total FDI in British retailing. This was possible because several key sources of data, such as various trade directories, included each firm's total number of branches or units. There is therefore considerable confidence in the completeness of the survey's coverage from around 1900 onwards.

For the earlier decades, the survey's coverage is likely to be less complete, although to what degree is frankly unknowable. This is, however, unlikely to be of any serious moment to the resulting population for two reasons. First, retailing was so undeveloped before 1900 that any foreign entrant of any size would, like Singer, have attracted considerable popular attention. Conversely, any missing entrants would therefore almost certainly have been small, single-unit subsidiaries, and thus relatively insignificant. Second, as documented above, foreign entrants before 1900 were clustered overwhelmingly in the luxury goods trade, based in London's West End. It follows that any missing entrants would also disproportionately have come from this sector. Yet historians have effectively mapped London's nineteenth-century retail trade, reducing the chances of our having overlooked entrants.[45] Moreover, even if we had missed ten per cent, 20 per cent, or more, of luxury goods entrants in the late nineteenth century, having full and complete information would not materially add to our understanding of the luxury trade's overall importance in the wider history of FDI in British retailing. In sum, even if our coverage of foreign entrants before 1900 omits several luxury goods boutiques, because this sector is already well represented, and because they were invariably only single-branch subsidiaries, their absence has only a marginal significance to the study of the wider population's impact in British retailing overall.

Focusing on the numbers of retail branches controlled by foreign parents also aids our attempt to estimate foreign multinationals' market share in the different retail trades. Ideally, market share would be calculated by comparing the foreign entrants' retail sales with total sales in each trade. Prior to the first *Census of Distribution* in 1950, however, there are no data on total sales in each retail trade, never mind any data on firm sales for the foreign entrants.[46] There are, however, a range of sources giving the total number of branches in each retail trade for a number of benchmark years before the census. Comparing the subsidiaries' branch counts with the total number of branches in each trade gives a reasonable indicator of the foreign multinationals' market share in British retailing over the period.

Before listing this information (in Table A1), it is important to consider whether the branch counts are a reasonable proxy for market share. One way of assessing this is to consider whether branch size varied significantly from one trade to another. If variation was high, then the branch count proxy would need significant modification before conclusions about overall market share could be drawn.

Two trades, department stores and variety chain stores, were atypical, with branch size and variation both much greater than in any other trade.[47] Elsewhere, however, and as Chart A1 shows, there was actually relatively little variation in mean branch size across retail trades.

Figure A1 shows that while the dispersion of sales per branch rose from 1938 to 1961 across most of British retailing, it nevertheless remained relatively low. The coefficient of variation in sales per branch across the trades included in the figure increased from only 0.30 in 1938, to 0.47 in 1950, to 0.73 in 1961. Moreover, and as the figure indicates, this increase was a by-product of restructuring in one trade only: dairies. The 1961 coefficient of variation for the rest remained at only 0.33. In other words, as long as its interpretation is sensitive to the structural change in specific trades (such as dairies), it seems reasonable to assume that for the pre-census period branch counts are a good proxy for market share for all trades outside department and variety chain stores.

Even with Weston's acquisition of Fortnum & Mason, the foreign entrants' total market share in department stores was negligible, so no adjustment has been necessary there. Variety chain stores have, however, had their branch counts reweighted by the ratio of this trade's employment (or sales) per branch to the employment (or sales) per branch across all retailing.

Table A1 therefore lists the total number of shops for each retail trade (or sector for the earlier years where a breakdown by trade is unavailable) in Britain and the total number of shops for all foreign multinationals in each retail trade. This provides the underlying data for Table 1, and represents the activities of the 118 documented subsidiaries of 99 foreign parents active in British retailing from 1850 to 1962.

FIGURE A1

DISPERSION IN SALES PER BRANCH ACROSS SELECTED RETAIL TRADES, 1938–61
(MEAN SALES PER UNIT ACROSS ALL RETAIL TRADES = 1.0)

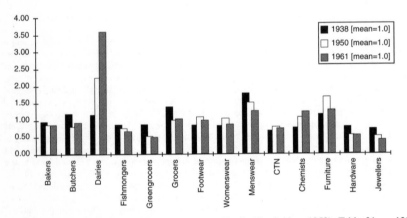

Source: J. Jefferys, *The Distribution of Consumer Goods* (Cambridge, 1950), Table 21, pp.120–22; *Censuses of Distribution, 1950 and 1961.*

TABLE A1
RETAIL BRANCHES IN BRITAIN, 1885–61 (ALL RETAIL TRADE AND FOREIGN CONTROLLED [MNE])

TRADE	1885 All	1885 MNE	1907 All	1907 MNE	1929 All	1929 MNE	1939 All	1939 MNE	1961 All	1961 MNE
1 Bakers					19,145		27,500	200	17,549	2,236
2 Butchers				1	42,070		38,900		44,248	
3 Dairies					16,648		14,800		6,580	
4 Fishmongers					8,390		9,400		7,857	
5 Green-grocers					26,465		28,000		42,070	
6 Grocers				85	65,603	3,482	80,000	0	149,308	1
7 Self-service									600	253
8 Off-Licences				5	7,383	5	9,800	10	9,000	
I. Food subtotal	130,000	0	137,000	91	185,704	3,487	208,400	210	276,852	2,490
9 Footwear				4	53,474	22	21,500	382	14,583	400
10 Menswear[a]				1	10,014		35,500		14,060	
11 Womenswear[b]		1		3	46,470	44	42,800	109	63,783	120
II. Clothing subtotal	60,000	1	72,800	8	109,958	66	99,800	491	92,426	620
12 Books/Stationers		1		1	20,580	1	27,650	1	6,284	
13 Confectioners				1	46,634	1	49,000		70,662	
14 Tobacconists					32,763	1	24,000			
15 Newsagents							28,750			
III. CTN[c] subtotal	40,000	1	60,600	2	99,977	3	129,400	1	76,946	0

TABLE A1 (Continued)

TRADE	1885		1907		1929		1939		1961	
	All	MNE	All	MNE	All	MNE	All	MNE	All	MNE
16 Sports Goods				2	1,245	5	1,400			2
17 Chemists & Photo		1		6	12,484	847	15,250	2	18,392	105
18 Furniture & Art				2	5,578	2	6,900	3	21,224	2
19 Ironmongers					20,218		13,500		24,830	
20 Jewellery & Watch		2		6	6,996	10	15,150	34	19,721	6
21 Music		3		9	3,779	4	3,100	2	n/a	1
22 Sewing machines		394		625	1,000^d	900	1,200	900	n/a	442
23 Variety Chain Stores					970	375	1,120	759	1,195	1,068
24 Department Stores									784	2
25 Typewriters				1	n/a	4	600	4	n/a	5
26 Petrol							22,500	39	34,400	2,060
27 Vacuum Cleaners							n/a	20		
28 Cycle Dealers				1			12,900			
29 Elec. etc. Dealers							39,100			
30 Misc.				7		21		22		8
IV. Other subtotal	40,000	400	50,900	659	52,170	2,258	132,720	1,785	120,546	3,744
TOTAL^e	270,000	402	321,300	760	447,809	5,814	570,320	2,469	566,770	6,903

Notes: a) Menswear includes Men's Outfitters and Hatters.
 b) Womenswear includes Drapers, Hosiers, Gown Shops, Ladies' Outfitters, and Ladies' Underwear.
 c) With such a large overlap between them, CTN trades varied from survey to survey more from classification problems than structural change. The subtotal gives a better indicator of overall change in the sector.
 d) Adjusted from the source to account for under-recorded independents.
 e) The total number of branches is an underestimate for all benchmark years except 1961. For 1885 and 1907 see below. For 1929 and 1939 the different sources used different classifications for the small shop and small category residual groups. They have been excluded here.
 n/a = not available. Blank cells = either zero or no data.

Sources: All retail trades:

 1885 and 1907: Crude estimates based on J. Jefferys, *Retail Trading in Britain, 1850–1950: A Study of Trends in Retailing with Special Reference to the Development of Co-operative, Multiple Shop and Department Store Methods of Trading* (Cambridge, 1954), Table 6 (sales by sector) and Table 4 (multiple branches), and assuming that the ratio of multiple branches to all branches was constant across all four sectors. 1885 is actually 1900, 1907 is actually 1910. Some kind of check on the totals comes from comparing them with the total of residential shops valued at £20 or over. These were 290,000 for 1899–1902 and 310,000 for 1909–1911 (see J. Jefferys, *The Distribution of Consumer Goods* (Cambridge, 1950), p.15n). These are clearly underestimates of all retail branches. P. Ford, 'Excessive competition in the retail trades: Changes in the number of shops, 1901–1931', *Economic Journal*, Vol.45 (1935), pp.501–8, estimated that there were around 600,000 retail outlets before 1914, for example. But these included market stalls and small corner shops. Such small outlets are not relevant here, where the focus is on the sectors foreign retailers may reasonably have been able to compete in. Moreover, given the tiny number of foreign entrants before 1914, the difference in total outlets makes no difference to the estimates of market share in Table 1.

 1929: US Department of Commerce, 'Chain Store Developments', 2.

 1939: *The Economist*, 27 April 1946; supplemented by Jefferys, *Distribution*, Table 21, pp.120–22, for additional trades. Despite slightly uneven coverage, these two sources gave remarkably similar results, with a correlation coefficient of 0.949 over the 22 trades common to both. Combining both to maximise coverage appears therefore reasonable.

 1961: *Census of Distribution, 1961*, Vol.1, Tables 1 and 2, pp.17–18. Except for Petrol, which was dropped from the 1961 census, and comes from D.F. Dixon, 'The development of the solus system of petrol distribution in the United Kingdom, 1950–1960', *Economica*, Vol.42 (1962), p.49; and except for Self-service, which was still a relatively insignificant branch of groceries. The Fine Fare estimate is from W.G. McClelland, *Studies in Retailing* (Oxford, 1963), p.23; and the total is from C. Davies, *Bread Men: How the Westons Built an International Food Empire* (Toronto, 1987), p.107.

 Multinational branches: For the 1885, 1907, 1939, and 1961 benchmark dates, see S. Fletcher and A. Godley, 'Foreign Direct Investment in British Retailing, 1850–1962', *Business History*, Vol.42 (2000), pp.43–62. 'Foreign Direct Investment', supplemented for the smaller subsidiaries by A. Godley, 'Foreign Multinationals in British Retailing, 1815–1962', paper presented at ABH Conference, 2001. End of award report, award no. R000234859', (ESRC 2000), which gives the full database listing. For 1929, see US Department of Commerce, *Chain Store Developments in Great Britain* (Washington, DC, 1930), pp.13–15, supplemented by Godley, 'Report'. Note that the miscellaneous category includes Goodyear tyre dealers, some leather goods retailers, and one or two others not elsewhere classified.

NOTES

The author thanks the ESRC for funding this research under grant R000222393; also Geoffrey Jones and, especially, the late Frances Bostock, to whom this essay is dedicated. The usual disclaimer nevertheless applies.

1. A. Godley, 'Pioneering Foreign Direct Investment in British Manufacturing', *Business History Review*, Vol.73 (1999), pp.394–429; G. Jones and F. Bostock, 'US Multinationals in British Manufacturing before 1962', *Business History Review*, Vol.70 (1996), pp.207–56; and F. Bostock and G. Jones, 'Foreign Multinationals in British Manufacturing, 1850–1962', *Business History*, Vol.36 (1994), pp.89–126; building on the pioneering work of J. Dunning, *American Investment in British Manufacturing Industry* (1998, orig. 1958); and M. Wilkins, *The Emergence of Multinational Enterprise* (Cambridge, MA, 1970), and idem, *The Maturing of Multinational Enterprise, 1914–1970* (Cambridge, MA, 1974). The standard definition of a multinational as an enterprise with value–adding activities in more than one nation is adopted here. See G. Jones, *The Evolution of International Business: An Introduction* (1996), pp.4–6.
2. N. Oulton, 'Labour Productivity and Foreign Ownership in the UK', National Institute of Economic and Social Research, Working Paper 82128 (1998), found that the productivity gap between the manufacturing subsidiaries of US parents and UK independents was 26% in the mid-1990s.
3. Jones, *Evolution*, pp.147–93, provides a summary. Prior to the development of North Sea oil, FDI in the primary sector was negligible.
4. On apparently sluggish service sector productivity growth in the UK, see S. Broadberry's three papers, 'Forging Ahead, Falling Behind and Catching-Up: A Sectoral Analysis of Anglo-American Productivity Differences, 1870–1990', *Research in Economic History*, Vol.17 (1997), pp.1–37; 'Anglo-German Productivity Differences, 1870–1900: A Sectoral Analysis', *European Review of Economic History*, Vol.1 (1997), pp.247–66; and 'How did the United States and Germany Overtake Britain? A Sectoral Analysis of Comparative Productivity Levels, 1870–1990', *Journal of Economic History*, Vol.52 (1998), pp.375–407. But deriving accurate estimates of service sector productivity is fraught with difficulties: see J. Triplett and B. Bosworth, 'Productivity in the Services Sector', in R. Stern (ed.), *Services in the International Economy* (London, 2000), and many historians have hitherto viewed some UK services as relatively dynamic: for example, see C. Lee, 'The Service Sector, Regional Specialisation and Economic Growth in the Victorian Economy', *Journal of Historical Geography*, Vol.10 (1984), pp.139–55; and W. Rubinstein, *Capitalism, Culture and Decline in Britain, 1750–1990* (London, 1993). Oulton nevertheless convincingly demonstrates a considerable service sector productivity gap between recent entrants and indigenous competitors, 'Labour Productivity', 8–10, and Appendix B.
5. S. Fletcher and A. Godley, 'Database of Foreign Multinationals in British Retailing, 1850–1962' (ESRC Data archive, University of Essex, 2000), hereafter Database, described in Fletcher and Godley, 'Business History as a Social Science: The Population of Foreign Multinationals in British Retailing, 1850–1994', in T. Slaven (ed.), *Business History, Theory and Practice* (Glasgow, 2000), pp.172–86. Board of Trade, *Census of Production, 1963*.
6. Summary results are given in A. Godley and S. Fletcher, 'International Retailers in Britain, 1850–1994', *Service Industries Journal*, Vol.21 (2001), pp.31–46.
7. S. Fletcher and A. Godley, 'Foreign Direct Investment in British Retailing, 1850–1962', *Business History*, Vol.42 (2000), pp.43–62. Subsequent research has identified an additional ten subsidiaries than listed there.
8. Godley, 'Pioneering', n.83; and B. Mitchell, *British Historical Statistics* (Cambridge, 1988), p.111 for the 1914 estimate. P. Dicken and P. Lloyd, 'Geographical Perspectives on United States Investment in the United Kingdom', *Environment and Planning A*, Vol.8 (1976), Table 2, p.691 for 1963. This has further risen to over one-quarter of manufacturing output and employment today, Jones, *Evolution*. The allusion is to J. Servan Schreiber, *The American Challenge* (London, 1967).
9. See Table A1, and J. Jefferys, *Retail Trading in Britain 1850–1950: A Study of Trends in Retailing with Special Reference to the Development of Co-Operative, Multiple Shop and Department Store Methods of Trading* (Cambridge, 1954), Table 85, p.453.
10. Jefferys, *Retail Trading*, p.6; J. Benson and G. Shaw (eds), *The Evolution of Retail Systems, c.1800–1914* (London, 1992).
11. The development of refrigerated rail trucks in 1876 reduced the problem of frozen meat's imminent perishability after landing, and so Eastman probably faced little incentive to increase his control of

the key British market. M. Yeager, *Competition and Regulation: The Development of Oligopoly in the Meat Packing Industry* (Greenwich, CT, 1981), pp.55–9; and M. Wilkins, *The History of Foreign Investment in the United States to 1914* (Cambridge, MA, 1989), pp.307–9.

12. J.T. Critchell and J. Raymond, *A History of the Frozen Meat Trade* (London, 1969, orig. 1912), pp.202–4.

13. P. Matthias, *Retailing Revolution: A History of Multiple Retailing in the Food Trades based upon the Allied Suppliers Group of Companies* (London, 1967); idem, 'Manufacturers and Retailing in the Food Trades: The Struggle over Margarine', in B. Supple (ed.), *Essays in British Business History* (Oxford, 1977); United States, Department of Commerce, *Chain Store Developments in Great Britain* (Washington, DC, 1930), p.14. And a much higher share of margarine outlets.

14. C. Davies, *Bread Men: How the Westons Built an International Food Empire* (Toronto, 1987), chapters 3–4; and W. Rukeyser, 'The $44-Billion Business Garfield Weston Built', *Fortune*, 1 June 1967.

15. Matthias, 'Struggle', p.143.

16. Davies, *Bread Men*, chapters 5–6.

17. B. Williams, *The Best Butter in the World: A History of Sainsbury's* (London, 1994); C. Morelli, 'Britain's Most Dynamic Sector? Competitive Advantage in Multiple Food Retailing', *Business and Economic History*, Vol.26 (1997), pp.770–81.

18. Database; A. Cekota, *Entrepreneur Extraordinary: A Biography of Tomas Bata* (Rome, 1968); and *Economist*, 10 April 1952, p.56, on Bata.

19. US Dept of Commerce, 'Chain Store Developments'; Jefferys, *Retail Trading*, pp.353ff.

20. K. Honeyman, *Well Suited: A History of the Leeds Clothing Industry, 1850–1990* (Oxford, 2000), chapter 3; A. Kershen, 'Morris Cohen and the Origins of the Women's Wholesale Clothing Industry in the East End', *Textile History*, Vol.28 (1997); P. Wilsher, 'C & A's £225 Million Family Shop', *Sunday Times*, 12 April 1964; and M. Pye, 'The Modernisation of old Aunty Etam', *Sunday Times*, 18 June 1972.

21. R. Stone *et al.*, *The Measurement of Consumers' Expenditure and Behaviour in the United Kingdom, 1920–1938* (Cambridge, 1953); M. Winstanley, 'Concentration and Competition in the Retail Sector, c.1800–1990', in M.W. Kirby and M. Rose (eds.), *Business Enterprise in Modern Britain from the Eighteenth to the Twentieth Century* (London, 1994).

22. US Dept of Commerce, 'Chain Store Developments', p.13; Jefferys, *Retail Trading*, p.416; J. Jefferys, *The Distribution of Consumer Goods* (Cambridge, 1950), pp.402–3; and W.A. Beeching, *Century of the Typewriter* (New York, 1974); C. Ehrlich, *The Piano: A History* (London, 1976); and Fletcher and Godley, 'Foreign Direct Investment'.

23. A. Godley, 'The Global Diffusion of the Sewing Machine, 1850–1914', *Research in Economic History*, Vol.20 (2001), pp.1–45; and idem, 'Selling the Sewing Machine around the World: Singer's Global Marketing Strategy', *Enterprise and Society* (forthcoming), together explain the importance and success of the direct sales force. On Singer more generally, see idem, 'Pioneering'; and idem, 'Singer in Britain: The Diffusion of Sewing Machine Technology and its Impact on the Clothing Industry in the UK, 1860–1905', *Textile History*, Vol.27 (1996), pp.59–76; additional Singer data come from the company archive at the State Historical Society of Wisconsin, Madison, Wisconsin. See 'Synopsis of Organization' (UK March 1906), Box 109, folder 2. The only other multiple in the trade was Jones Sewing Machine Co. Ltd., whose branch network Jefferys described as 'small' in 1900. By 1938 Jones had grown to 90 branches, one-tenth of Singer's total. See Jefferys, *Retail Trading*, p.401

24. J. Winkler, *Five and Ten: The Fabulous Life of F.W. Woolworth* (London, 1941); F.W. Woolworth & Co., *Woolworth's First 75 Years, 1879–1954* (London, 1954); F.W. Woolworth & Co. Ltd, Company Reports for 1950s; D. Jeremy, 'The Hundred Largest Employers in the United Kingdom, in Manufacturing and Non-Manufacturing Industries, in 1907, 1935 and 1955', *Business History*, Vol.33 (1990), pp.93–111; G. Shaw *et al.*, 'Structural and Spatial Trends in British Retailing: The Importance of Firm-level Studies', *Business History*, Vol.40 (1998), pp.79–93.

25. Jefferys, *Distribution*, pp.297–8; *Economist*, 17 March 1951, p.654; S. Bowden, and A. Offer, 'Household Appliances and the Use of Time: The United States and Britain since the 1920s', *Economic History Review*, Vol.47 (1994), pp.725–38. On Hoover, see P. Seikman, 'Hoover's Well-Vacuumed World', *Fortune*, June 1964; and *Business Week*, 19 Aug. 1972. On Electrolux, see Electrolux Ltd., *60 Years of Electrolux Quality 1927–1987* (Luton, 1987). By the early 1960s, Electrolux claimed 25% of the vacuum and 17% of the refrigerator market.

26. S. Merwin, *Rise and Fight Againe: The Story of a Life-Long Friend* (New York, 1935); S. Chapman, *Jesse Boot of Boots the Chemist* (London, 1974); F. Carstensen, 'Liggett, Louis',

American National Biography (New York and Oxford, 1999), Vol.13, pp.645–6; P. Whysall, 'Interwar Retail Internationalization: Boots under American Ownership', *International Review of Retail, Distribution and Consumer Research*, Vol.7 (1997).

27. D.F. Dixon, 'The Development of the Solus System of Petrol Distribution in the United Kingdom, 1950–1960', *Economica*, Vol.42 (1962), pp.40–52; and idem, 'Economic Effects of Exclusive Dealing and Ownership Control: The UK Petrol Case Revisited', *Antitrust Bulletin*, Vol.39 (1974), pp.375–90.

28. See e.g. W. Baumol, 'Macroeconomics of Unbalanced Growth: The Anatomy of Urban Crisis', *American Economic Review*, Vol.57 (1967), pp.415–26.

29. A.D. Chandler, Jr., *The Visible Hand: The Managerial Revolution in American Business* (Cambridge, MA, 1977); building on W.J. Baxter, *Chain Store Distribution and Management* (New York, 1928). For Britain, see Jefferys, *Retail Trading*; J. Jefferys and D. Knee, *Retailing in Europe: Present Structure and Future Trends* (London, 1962); and Benson and Shaw, *Evolution of Retail Systems*.

30. Jefferys, *Retail Trading*, Ts.18–19, pp.73–4. US Dept of Commerce, 'Chain Store Developments', shows that large chains accounted for only 7% of retail outlets.

31. The complication of mail order has never been significant and can be ignored.

32. Hence most retail theory comes from geographers. See Shaw *et al.*, 'Spatial and Structural Trends', for a review.

33. The allusion is of course to Dunning's OLI paradigm (Ownership, Location and Internalisation advantages) explaining FDI. See J. Dunning, *The Globalization of Business* (London, 1993), for example. P. Buckley and M. Casson, *The Future of the Multinational Enterprise* (London, 1976) is the classic on internalisation. Recent attempts by international retailing specialists to adopt internalisation theory have been decidedly mixed. See N. Alexander, *International Retailing* (Oxford, 1997) for a review.

34. N.A. Stacey and A. Wilson, *The Changing Pattern of Distribution* (Oxford, 1965), p.247, for a similar observation by contemporaries.

35. H. Leibenstein, 'Bandwagon Snob, and Veblen Effects in the Theory of Consumers' Demand', *Quarterly Journal of Economics*, Vol.64 (1950), pp.183–207. See S. Hollander, *Multinational Retailing* (East Lansing, MI, 1970) on luxury goods retailers' internationalisation.

36. B.S. Yamey, 'The Origins of Resale Price Maintenance: A Study of Three Branches of Retail Trade', *Economic Journal*, Vol.52 (1952), pp.522–65; and idem, *Resale Price Maintenance* (London, 1966).

37. Following a variant to the classic product cycle logic to internationalisation in manufacturing. See R. Vernon, 'International Investment and International Trade in the Product Cycle', *Quarterly Journal of Economics*, Vol.80 (1966), pp.190–207.

38. F.T. Knickerbocker, *Oligopolistic Reaction and the Multinational Enterprise* (Cambridge, MA, 1973), is the classic on multinationals' retaliatory strategies. The literature on Cournot and Bertrand equilibria and game-theoretic competitive strategies in oligopolies is vast. See B. Friedman, *Oligopoly Theory* (Cambridge, 1990), for a review.

39. L. Hannah, *The Rise of the Corporate Economy* (London, 2nd edn. 1983).

40. Davies, *Bread Men*, pp.66–7; Godley and Fletcher, 'International Retailing'.

41. A. Godley and S. Fletcher, 'Foreign Entry into UK Retailing, 1850–1994', *International Marketing Review*, Vol.17 (2000), pp.392–400.

42. A. Godley, 'What was New About the 1980s? International Retailing in Britain from 1850 to 1991', *International Review of Retail, Distribution and Consumer Research*, Vol.12 (2002), pp.29–37.

43. Ibid.

44. Godley, 'Pioneering'; Jones and Bostock, 'US Multinationals'; and Bostock and Jones, 'Foreign Multinationals'.

45. A. Adburgham, *Shopping in Style: London from the Restoration to Edwardian Elegance* (London, 1979).

46. Jefferys, *Distribution*, Table 21, pp.120–22, and idem, *Retail Trading*, Table 85, p.453, gives estimates of sales by value across a range of trades for 1900 to 1938 but at too great a level of aggregation for our purposes here.

47. Jefferys, *Retail Trading*, pp.59–63, and Table 15, average employment in each variety chain store branch in 1938 was eight times that of the average multiple branch. The *Census of Distribution, 1950*, shows that variety chain store sales per branch were 12 times that of the mean retail branch. Each department store's sales were 65 times greater than the typical branch, see Table 5, pp.32–41.

Building Knowledge about the Consumer: The Emergence of Market Research in the Motion Picture Industry

GERBEN BAKKER

London School of Economics and Political Science

The aim of marketing is to make selling superfluous. The aim is to know and understand the customer so well that the product or service fits ... and sells itself.

Peter F. Drucker[1]

Culver City, August 1944. Producer David O. Selznick is supervising the final changes to *The House of Dr Edwards*, the latest film by Alfred Hitchcock. Selznick has sunk nearly $1.7 million in the film and is determined to get it back. Feeling uncomfortable about the title, he contacts Audience Research, a market research firm, to test several titles among cinemagoers. While *Hidden Impulse* and *The Couch* register little interest, *Edwards* – Hitchcock's favourite – and, finally, *Spellbound*, ring a bell. Selznick notices that while men prefer *Edwards* to *Spellbound* by a 15 per cent margin, women prefer *Spellbound* to *Edwards* by 13 per cent. Since women 'bring men to the theatre much more than men bring women', and Hitchcock's name already guarantees a masculine appeal, he ignores Hitchcock and decides the ultimate title will be *Spellbound*.[2]

By the 1940s, adequate knowledge about consumer preferences had become essential for survival in the motion picture industry. Film companies had been among the first customers of market research firms using scientific research design and random sampling, which emerged in the 1930s.[3] Many films considered classics today were shaped by feedback from market research. Ever since the emergence of cinemas in the mid-1900s, the film industry had been obtaining detailed knowledge about the tastes, desires, and habits of consumers. While life-cycles of other products were measured in years, or at least a season, those of early films were measured in days. While many other industries launched new products infrequently, the film industry launched them constantly.

The short product life-cycle forced film producers to track changes in consumer preferences closely. They had to observe and record how customers reacted to their products, to quickly adapt products they were developing to changes in market tastes, and to apply effective marketing strategies. The short product life-cycle also meant that when a film company discovered an unsatisfied need, it could cater for it in a few weeks. The success of film producers was not primarily dependent upon technological innovation or scientific discovery, but on determining and meeting consumer tastes.[4]

Although several other consumer goods industries shared this characteristic, the early film industry was most like fashion goods industries. These industries had a similar, extreme sensitivity to changes in consumer preferences and also launched new products constantly. They therefore shared a need to obtain detailed knowledge about the consumer. In the 1870s, for example, the hat manufacturer John Jacob Astor employed an artist to sketch women's hats in the park, to help him determine the most popular fashions.[5] In the pottery and glassware industries, 'the ability to envision target audiences was essential for survival'.[6] These industries used 'fashion intermediaries', persons who observed shoppers browsing the shelves, or store managers who reported the latest tastes back to the manufacturer.[7]

Nevertheless, while fashion products lasted at least a season and were launched in batches, early films lasted a few weeks and were launched continuously. Second, the fashion industries could target market segments such as women, teenagers, or the middle class, while the film industry had to reach as many segments as possible, before television.[8] Third, motion picture companies incurred large sunk costs and only small marginal costs. While fashion companies could adjust their output if a product proved unpopular, and sell unpopular products at rock-bottom prices, film producers had already incurred most costs.

This article, then, examines how motion pictures changed from an industry that obtained knowledge about the consumer like a fashion goods industry, drawing on informal research by fashion intermediaries, into an industry that used modern scientific market research, like mass-producers of consumer goods. It investigates how changes in the industry structure affected market research, and how market information was used in business strategies. The research is relevant to marketing history generally, because it examines an early and avid user of market research. But the constant launch of new products enables the further study of many cases, like scientists studying fruit flies, so giving micro-level insight into the impact of market research on business strategies.[9]

The period covered ranges from the industry's beginnings in the 1890s until the late 1940s, when television, vertical disintegration, and the emerging youth culture changed the nature of market research. Using detailed primary sources, the focus will be on the US and Britain, because the former was the largest entertainment market in the world, the latter the largest in Europe, and because the former was a large exporter, the latter a large importer.[10] The section below discusses how the changing industry structure shaped the development of market research, the subsequent sections focus on two significant firms that brought market research to the motion picture industry: Sidney Bernstein's Granada Theatres and George Gallup's Audience Research.

II

In the late 1900s, several American firms conducted rudimentary market research. In 1908 J.G. Fredrik founded Business Course, a company collecting market information, and in 1910 Charles Coolidge Parlin set up a commercial research division at Curtis Publishing Company, investigating consumers' buying habits and several specific markets, such as farm implements and department stores. In 1913, the *Chicago Tribune* conducted a door-to-door market survey. Sears kept records of its customers' names, addresses, and buying habits, to which it tailored the set of catalogues it sent to them. In 1916, R.O. Eastman, Kellogg's advertising manager, founded the Eastman Research Bureau. One of his first clients, General Electric, commissioned an investigation into the public awareness of its Mazda trademark.[11]

Between the wars, market research became increasingly formal and systematic, using scientific sampling techniques.[12] Arthur C. Nielsen surveyed purchasing habits in drugstores, George Gallup set up the first formal Marketing Research Department, within the advertising firm Young & Rubicam.[13] Fenner & Beane and Merrill Lynch, which later merged, were the first brokerage firms to commission detailed research on customers and to change their business model accordingly.[14] In Britain, market research was less common. There were a few exceptions, such as the confectionary manufacturer Rowntree and health drink maker Horlicks.[15] But the subsidiaries of American firms, such as Vauxhall under General Motors,[16] and the London subsidiary of the US advertising agency J. Walter Thompson, were pioneers in Britain.[17]

The development of market research in the film industry followed a similar path. Films were capital goods sold or leased from producer to distributor to the exhibitor, which used them to provide a consumer service. Changes in the contractual relationship between these three strata, changes in technology and organisation, and an increase in sunk costs all affected the ways in which film companies obtained knowledge about the consumers. During the industry's formative years, little market research was done. Producers made their films by trial and error, as costs were low, revenues limited, and regular customers such as cinemas hardly existed. Film viewing was an inexpensive, brief, and haphazard activity; viewers saw many films in borrowed venues such as fairground tents, music halls, and theatres. Showmen sold each other a supply of copies varying in quality and quantity through local networks. Film production was a low-cost and eclectic activity involving many movies of different types and lengths, which were directly sold by producers to showmen.

The emergence of the first cinemas, which seated a few hundred people, revolutionised the industry's technology and organisation. Cinemas needed a reliable and continuous supply of films, whose audience interest could be anticipated. Producers and emerging distributors had little interest in market research because they sold film copies by the foot for a largely undifferentiated price. Although a successful title, despite rampant piracy, sold many more copies, producers saw little of the additional marginal revenue generated by each copy in cinemas. This produced marginal profit only for cinema owners. Therefore, the latter were the first to do informal market research, mainly by audience observation and sales analysis. Carl Laemmle began his career conducting audience studies in Chicago for Hale's Tours, a 'Nickelodeon' operator. 'For two days [Laemmle] counted the attendance of what went in to see Hale's Tours pictures. When he got through he had an accurate notion of what kind of people went to see the pictures, what hours of the day they found the time to do it in, and how many of them there were per hour and per day.'[18] Likewise, when Adolph Zukor opened a Nickelodeon in New York, he carefully studied customers' responses: 'I spent a good deal of time watching the faces of the audience, even turning around to do so. A movie audience is very sensitive. With a little experience I could see, hear and "feel" the reaction to each melodrama and comedy. Boredom was registered – even without comments or groans – as clearly as laughter demonstrated pleasure.'[19] Years later, Laemmle would found Universal and Zukor Paramount.

This emergence of cinemas was followed by another technological-cum-organisational change: the emergence of film distribution networks in the late 1900s. These film 'exchanges' concentrated information from exhibitors and sent it back to the producer. Industry observer Benjamin Hampton noted:

> [The film exchange system] established a route of communication from audience through exhibitor to distributor and producer, enabling the nickelodeon patrons to make their wishes known to the makers of pictures. If spectators enjoyed a film and applauded it, the nickelodeon owner scurried around and tried to get more like it, and if they grumbled as they left the show he passed on the complaints to the exchange, and the exchange told the manufacturer.[20]

This elementary feedback system was similar to the use of intermediaries in many fashion goods industries.[21]

First, cinemas and then these distribution networks together led to a third change in the industry. Around 1910 fictional films of 1,000 feet (15 minutes) became a standard; later, between 1915 and 1917, the feature film itself. In contrast to other formats such as news, sports, or travelogues, fictional films could be planned and budgeted in advance, enabling a reliable supply to cinemas.[22] This change was reinforced by a synchronous change in the industry's contractual relationships: films started to be rented. This meant a higher share of marginal revenue flowed to distributors and producers, and so increased their incentive to craft successful films. Film companies devised strategies to lure consumers, first building their reputation and adopting trademarks, and then through stars, serials, and famous stories. Nevertheless, these strategies were essentially intuitive, based more on trial and error than quantitative market research.[23]

The research commissioned by a major US producer-distributor, probably Paramount Pictures, marks the transition from a simple and intuitive approach to the modern market research. In 1916, Paramount decided to advertise its trademark and pictures directly to consumers and hired an advertising agency. Stopping short of directly polling consumers, the agency sent questionnaires to exhibitors, asking which family member they thought decided on film and cinema, and which magazines they thought they read. The subsequent advertising campaign was based on the outcome: it addressed women and used fan magazines and women's weeklies such as *Ladies Home Journal*.[24]

Another contractual change was the use of long-term, 'seven-year', contracts with stars.[25] Combined with the short 'shelf-life' of films, this gave producers an incentive to measure their stars' popularity.[26] Most consumers saw a film only once, making market research more feasible on production inputs that could be re-used, such as stars, story types, genres, and formats. Film companies therefore increasingly used stars and stories to brand their films. Because films are made by teams, the research could also be used to assess each input's contribution to sales.[27] From 1915 onwards the *Motion Picture Herald* held an annual poll among exhibitors on 'box office potential' of stars, presenting the results as a rank order. It was widely read throughout the industry, and probably provided a compass as to which stars to contract.[28] Fan magazines had organised reader polls in the US as early as 1909, but their accuracy was doubtful because readers sent in postcards, which affected representativeness and enabled manipulation.[29]

Initially the fictional film was a cost-saving technology, cheaper to produce than other formats. Paradoxically, when it became industry standard, production costs increased, and continued to increase until the late 1940s. Because rising sunk costs increased the risk, they gave producers a further incentive for market research.[30] Synchronously, the lag between a film's production and release rose, from a few days in the early 1910s, to a few weeks in the early 1920s, to a month or more in the 1940s. This not only meant that interest costs further increased production costs, but also that the feedback obtained through sales analysis and consumer response became ever more delayed. A company could already be busy producing several subsequent pictures when it received the market feedback from the previous film. Only better knowledge about the market could make up for the lag-related risk.

During the 1920s, renting for a fixed fee was replaced by renting on a percentage basis. This made even more of cinemas' marginal revenues translate into distributors' and producers' marginal profits, further increasing their incentive for market research.[31] Analysis of four-yearly samples of films from 1914 to 1964 shows that producers did indeed respond quickly to changes in consumer sentiment: during the Depression, films portraying big business and wealth positively gave way to films criticising big business and being slightly more inclusive towards women and minorities. Despite their reliance on Wall Street capital and a draconian Production Code, the studios had to adapt their films to consumer preferences or go under.[32]

Clearly studios became ever more reliant on accurate knowledge of their consumers' preferences. But modern market research techniques were built only slowly. The earliest systematic consumer surveys were not done by companies, but by scholars and social organisations concerned about the effects of cinema attendance, especially on children. A German study of 1909 was followed by many more, such as the Payne Fund studies in the US and the Mass Observation studies in the UK in the 1930s.[33] Several of these surveys were published in the American *Film Daily Year Book*.

One of the first companies to undertake primitive market research was Universal, beginning in 1922. Laemmle had advanced from Nickelodeon owner to president of this Hollywood studio, but had not forgotten the importance of knowing his customers. He ran a signed weekly advertisement in the *Saturday Evening Post*, asking readers to state their favourite stars and to answer some questions. In a 1928 advertisement, for example, Universal asked whether respondents liked happy endings, and if Universal should retain unhappy endings when turning books or plays into films. Once, Laemmle even placed a job advertisement for a 'Master Psychologist' who could 'analyse plot-situations' and 'forecast public reaction'. Reportedly, Universal received 100 letters a day and built a substantial mailing list, from which it selected 300 people whom it consulted frequently.[34]

Another form of primitive market research was fan mail analysis. Film studios kept track of fan mail because it gave them a rough indication of stars' appeal.[35] In the 1930s, all major Hollywood studios had fan mail departments. Each received between 18,000 and 45,000 letters or postcards a month, which were tabulated by star and the fan's estimated age, gender, and location. The department heads claimed they could 'tell when a new actor or actress has "clicked" with the public from the kind of fan letters which begin to come into the studio: letters asking why the player was not given bigger roles'.[36]

Yet another way to obtain knowledge about the market was the 'preview', the test-screening before release. These started as informal events for studio personnel or nearby Los Angeles cinemagoers. Producer Harry Rapf of Warner Brothers, for example, would frequently change films after consulting a panel consisting of his driver, carpenters, electricians, the studio barber, a hospital intern, the gate keeper, the masseur, and their wives and children.[37] During the 1920s, previews became more serious, as studios paid attention to theatre location, audience composition, and observation method. Irvin Thalberg at MGM used a first cut like a first draft. He always changed his pictures, reshooting whole scenes and doing numerous subsequent previews until he was satisfied.[38] Selznick had a similar approach: when at the first preview of *King Kong*, the ape's pursuers were attacked by huge slimy insects and snakes and graphically eaten alive, 'the screaming on the screen was matched ... by the screaming of the audience ..., a great many of whom left; those who stayed kept up a buzz of conversation for the next few minutes making it difficult to keep up with the continuing story'. The scene was removed, leaving the special effects expert heartbroken.[39] World Wide Pictures, which distributed foreign pictures in the US and Canada, used previews in New York to set its rental rates, because it was difficult to predict the box office appeal of foreign movies, and because pictures were not rented in large blocks, which would have limited the effect of flops.[40]

In addition to previews and early market research, sales analysis remained an important tool in building knowledge about consumer preferences in the 1920s and 1930s. For the major studios, which produced large film portfolios during a year, launching a portfolio over a season could serve as a substitute for costly and impractical market research, as failures and successes could cancel each other.[41] During the 1930s, Warner Brothers, for example, carefully tracked the box office revenue of its films and adjusted its star portfolio accordingly.[42] In 1939, for instance, producer Samuel Goldwyn, after studying the financial returns of Merle Oberon's pictures, cancelled her contract.[43] Although the constant product launches made sales analysis a handy tool, the increasing lag between production and release gradually reduced its usefulness.

The integration of production and distribution in the late 1920s made market research even more important. After a merger wave, eight major Hollywood producer-distributors remained. The five major ones also owned cinema circuits, each in a different US region. This meant that a yet higher share of the marginal revenues in distribution and exhibition would translate into producers' profits, further increasing their incentive for market research.

The emerging majors also integrated vertically internationally. They set up foreign distribution subsidiaries rather than sell rights to local distributors, maximising the rents they could capture from their copyrights and guaranteeing strategic access to screen-time. This increased the incentive to make pictures appealing to foreign audiences. Sales analysis had been important for assessing the international appeal of future films. The Danish Nordisk company, for example, a large European film company in the 1910s, focused nearly exclusively on export markets, because of the small Danish market. It relentlessly cut its films to the needs of different markets. For the same film it often filmed a happy ending for Western markets, and a sad, dramatic ending for Eastern European markets.[44] Likewise, in the 1930s, low-budget US westerns were often more popular outside the US. United Artists, for example, bought a series of six Rex Bell movies specifically for export.[45] But, for a long time, sales analysis was almost the only way of gaining information on foreign markets, because most were too small to warrant elaborate consumer polls, and many even too small to send representatives.[46]

Overall, therefore, the changes in contractual relationships, technology, and rising sunk costs encouraged film companies to invest in ever more reliable estimates of consumer demand. In the early decades these were mostly informal and intuitive. Increasingly more reliable techniques were devised, such as surveys, previews, and sales analysis. But all these were precursors to the modern 'scientific' market research that emerged in the 1930s. A turning point was probably the pricing of *Gone with the Wind* in early 1939. A Gallup poll commissioned by newspapers had shown the film's potential audience was 55 million – the largest ever for a picture. With this information, Selznick, the producer, was able to convince a reluctant MGM, the distributor, that higher prices were viable. The picture was 'roadshown' at a price range of $0.75–$2.20.

Key cities received a 'double exhibition format', with one luxury, high-priced theatre, and a second venue showing for $0.75–$1.10, when an average cinema ticket cost $0.25. This novel pricing strategy substantially increased profits.[47]

Soon after, independent market research firms emerged. The two major ones were Audience Research and the Motion Picture Research Bureau (MPRB).[48] The former worked for several studios, the latter exclusively for MGM. Smaller firms included the Roper Organization, Research Services, and the Opinion Research Corporation, all of which probably also conducted market research for other industries.[49] In Britain, the detailed polls of Granada Theatres foreshadowed the advent of modern market research. All the firms segmented the market by age, gender, income, and location.[50]

This new market research was closely connected to methods developed for the radio industry. P.F. Lazarsfeld, who ran the Bureau of Applied Social Research at Columbia University, primarily researched radio audiences, for example, but at times diverted to motion pictures. Although his research was largely academic, he looked for clues applicable to companies' business strategies, in contrast to the earlier social studies. He showed, for example, that word-of-mouth recommendation was the key for rapidly reaching high brand-awareness, because it made the picture sell itself. This word-of-mouth recommendation could best be influenced by what Lazarsfeld called taste leaders: socially active, frequent filmgoers under 25, who also read magazines and listened to radio extensively, who were in the same social class as those they tended to advise. Crucially, taste leaders could be influenced by studio publicity or advertising.[51]

The link with the radio industry was also important for the development of new, more 'scientific' preview techniques, which tracked audience interest scene-by-scene. The Motion Picture Research Bureau used the Cirlin Reactograph and the Lazarsfeld-Stanton Program Analyzer, originally designed to measure radio listening habits.[52] Audience Research used the Preview Jury System.[53] One of its employees, Albert Sindlinger, was a former cinema owner who had bugged cinema restrooms to discover patrons' tastes. Sindlinger developed the Teldox system to preview plays, and, reportedly, out of eight plays likely to succeed according to Teldox results, seven were successful on Broadway, and, out of 17 likely to fail, 16 actually failed.[54]

III

In Britain, by the late 1930s, media market research was increasing. In 1936, the BBC started the Listeners Research Department and Gallup founded the British Institute of Public Opinion, which also surveyed media consumption.[55] Granada Theatres, a London cinema-circuit, had already started polling its customers in the late 1920s. Founded during the 1910s as Bernstein Theatres, it was managed by Sidney L. Bernstein. In 1928, Bernstein sold a 51 per cent stake to the Gaumont-British circuit for a reported £250,000, but continued to manage his circuit separately.[56] With the proceeds he bought more cinemas. In 1934, capital and reserves were £300,000 and profits £31,500.[57] In 1936, Granada sold nearly 11 million tickets, 1.2 per cent of all British admissions.[58] Its cinemas grew from ten in the late 1920s to 34 in 1939 to 56 by 1949.[59]

Bernstein's influence in the industry reached far beyond his circuit's size. A respected industry figure, he passionately supported British films, founded the Film Society, published policy pamphlets and cultivated contacts with US studio heads.[60] He was a local Labour councillor, served as the film advisor of the Ministry of Information, and from 1944 was Head of the Psychological Warfare Division.[61] He arranged agreements on US film imports, supervised propaganda films, and asked Hitchcock to produce a film on the German concentration camps.[62] After the war, Bernstein and Hitchcock founded Transatlantic Productions, which produced two films. When in 1955 the major British circuits refused to show Charlie Chaplin's British-produced *A King in New York*, because of his alleged communist sympathies, Bernstein distributed his friend's film, something which he advertised widely.[63] Shortly afterwards he launched one of the first commercial television stations, Granada, which eventually pushed his cinemas to the background.[64]

Granada gathered information about its customers in several ways. Initially, each cinema manager wrote a monthly, later weekly, report to the head office, which mapped audience responses and suggested improvements. Their reports were largely based on intuition and anecdote, such as 'Increased receipts largely due to bad weather. Patrons show a definite dislike for Western films, more because of their bad quality than their type. The appearance of Elman and his band proved a big draw on May 23rd',[65] or:

> Willesden found "Dinner at Eight" rather a disappointment. Its entertainment value was neither simple enough nor direct enough for them. The Beery-Harlow-Lowe stuff could have been built into a feature which would most likely have eclipsed "Dinner at Eight" at the box office. These top-heavy all-star shows, however, never seem to make any bulges in our cash records.[66]

Between 1927 and 1955, Granada carried out eight questionnaires among customers of 10 to 12 cinemas in and around London.[67] These added a direct channel to the consumer. In 1934, for example, the survey covered 11 cinemas totalling 16,575 seats.[68] Granada also separately polled celebrities from politics, clergy, peerage, arts, and business. The questions focused on cinema-going habits (which cinemas did consumers visit, how often, and why) and on film preferences (favourite genres, story types, stars, directors, formats, sound, single/double feature).[69]

Granada segmented its customers by sex, age, and 'class', which was derived from the cinemas' neighbourhoods (Table 1). These were divided between 'poor' and 'petty-bourgeois', with two labelled 'county + poor + rural' and 'county'.[70] Most cinemas were in the 'richer' neighbourhoods. Granada probably found segmenting important because each single cross-tabulation was expensive and slow before computers. The substantial differences in stars' popularity across segments indicates that segmenting made sense. In the 1932 poll, Granada researchers found that British films were more popular in the countryside than in suburban London, 'perhaps because the English province is more insular, more cut off from the life of other countries, as reflected in the assumptions and the background of other films; to understand the background of an American film requires no doubt a cosmopolitanism which is, even by a shade, more lacking in the country side.'[71]

Granada also found that popularity of stars varied substantially across segments. Clark Gable, for example, was liked nearly twice as much by women than by men, and most by women below 21 and richer customers (Table 1). Two actors of roughly similar overall appeal often served different segments. In contrast to Gable, George Arliss was liked almost equally among the sexes and poorer and richer segments, for example. Only his popularity across age groups varied, highest among consumers above 40. The combination of popularity in a segment with its size enabled a studio to estimate the likely size of a star's market. The popularity of George Arliss and Norma Shearer among older consumers, for example, gave little incentive to book more of their films, because older consumers hardly ever watched films.

Bernstein asked his friend Angus McPhail, of the scenario department of Gainsborough Pictures and later Gaumont-British's film production subsidiary, to comment on the questionnaires. McPhail wrote lengthy reports. In 1927 he noted:

> The first section [celebrity responses] is ... of comparatively little value to exhibitors, renters or producing companies. The second section, on the other hand, is of immense practical value from beginning to end. The questioners are all normal patrons of normal cinemas in normal neighbourhoods. Their answers are free of the snobbery and self-importance of the answers to the first section; and they are frank and unbiased because they are not dictated by the necessity for circumspection.[72]

The researchers liberally speculated about the causes of differences in star-popularity. On the 1934 questionnaire, for example, they noted:

> Gracie Fields draws about all her popularity from among the older patrons, and Jean Harlow from among the younger. ... More men than women for Marlene Dietrich, more women than men for Greta Garbo. This is the same as in 1932. ... The Garbo–Dietrich comparison is exceedingly interesting. Though one might have guessed that Garbo would have all the women and Dietrich all the men. Garbo is the better dressed. In exposing herself she usually exposes the whole figure in relation with some gown. Dietrich on the contrary is continually exposing these particularly and conventionally

TABLE 1

POPULARITY AND MARKET SEGMENTED BY INCOME AND AGE FOR TOP-3 MOVIE STARS, AROUND LONDON, 1934

	Name	All	Income			Male (age)				Female (age)			
			Poor	Middle	Rich	<21	21–40	40–60	>60	<21	21–40	40–60	>60
Popularity	Arliss	11	10	11	11	9	11	15	14	9	9	15	13
	Gable	7	6	6	7	5	5	3	6	12	8	4	5
	Beery	5	6	4	5	7	9	7	4	3	3	4	2
	Shearer	12	10	10	13	9	12	11	13	11	14	12	15
	Dressler	10	11	10	9	9	11	11	12	7	9	13	10
	Garbo	7	6	6	8	5	6	6	5	8	8	7	6
Market	Arliss	100	15	19	66	12	19	8	1	16	24	17	3
	Gable	100	14	17	70	10	14	2	1	35	30	7	2
	Beery	100	18	15	67	18	32	8	1	13	18	9	1
	Shearer	100	14	16	70	10	19	5	1	19	32	12	3
	Dressler	100	19	20	61	12	22	6	1	15	26	15	2
	Garbo	100	15	17	69	9	17	5	1	24	31	12	2

Notes: Top-3 male and female stars are given. Full star names: George Arliss, Clark Gable, Wallace Beery, Norma Shearer, Mary Dressler, Greta Garbo. 'Popularity' refers to the percentage of respondents which named the star as favourite. 'Market' refers to the percentage of all responses for a star in a particular segment.

Source: Sidney L. Bernstein Collection, British Film Institute, London.

decorative parts usually used as a weapon in the nineteenth century music hall. Dietrich with these tricks and her general attitude is obviously interested in the men she plays with. While the women fans – unconsciously or otherwise – have recognised as homo-sexual Garbo's boredom with all her men opposites.[73]

In 1936, Granada asked the National Institute of Industrial Psychology to assess the responses to the Bernstein questionnaire. A.M. Lester wrote that questions did not always distinguish between audience segments.[74] A question on best starting times, for example, was unusable, because the most frequently named time was halfway through the evening, which would certainly keep away customers who only could go early or late. Lester advised changing the questions to obtain definite information for producing or booking films.[75] 'Market research ... should aim at providing information which will assist actual policy decisions. This may sound an obvious platitude, but it is extremely easy to find oneself inserting a lot of questions whose answers come under the heading rather more of general interest than specific information.'[76]

This observation begs the question which role the questionnaire played in Bernstein's business strategy. The surveys' large samples and detailed cross-tabulations must have cost Granada dearly. Costs of the 1946 questionnaire amounted to £3,379, and Granada's mail room was severely disrupted by incoming responses.[77] A 1950s critical report alleged that Granada failed to distinguish between four main purposes: 'to obtain general publicity for the company; to give the audience the feeling of being attentively watched by management; to obtain information useful in running the circuit; to provide data which can be used as "ammunition for negotiation", e.g. advertising, double features.' The author thought Granada hardly used the questionnaire for management decisions or film booking. On specific questions, such as on non-smoking nights, no action had been taken, although that would have generated 'lots of publicity' while inaction jeopardised customers' goodwill.[78]

The prime purpose of the questionnaires was to generate publicity. Granada widely distributed press releases, and many articles appeared, liberally mentioning Bernstein and Granada.[79] In its craving for publicity, Granada sometimes overstated the number of respondents. In 1927, for example, it boasted 250,000 respondents, while unpublished tabulations show only 1,200.[80] The celebrity survey was probably done solely for publicity and Bernstein's reputation, because it showed that celebrities hardly ever watched films. Another industry figurehead, Alexander Korda, manager of London Film Productions, also published a questionnaire – in the *Daily Mail* – so general it could only have served publicity purposes.[81]

A second purpose was to yield ammunition for Bernstein's industry campaigns. A fervent supporter of British films, he always inserted questions about the topic. The accompanying letter to the 1928 questionnaire stated: 'The future of films, and particularly of British films, is in the balance just now. This

questionnaire is an attempt on our part to help swing the balance the right way.'
The questions were just as biased: 'Do you consider that an abundant supply of
representative British pictures is essential for the propagation of – (a) British
ideals? (b) British business ethics?'[82] Questions on the double feature and
Sunday openings probably also served industry campaigns.[83] In 1950, Granada
solicited questions for a planned questionnaire from British producers: 'We feel
that the Bernstein Questionnaire can be a powerful influence in the "Bigger
Business Drive". ... From [the questionnaire] can be diagnosed the general
nature of the complaint, along with an indication of the shape of the cure.'[84]

But the questionnaires were also used to estimate a film's likely market size. For
instance, it is probable that Granada and Gaumont-British staff used the
questionnaire for film booking. Staff had to assess prospective films' audience
appeals, either as a first feature, or as a second feature in a double-feature
programme, and so wrote a short report evaluating the film's quality and market
after viewing.[85] On *Feathered Serpent*, for example, the viewer noted: 'Edgar
Wallace story, with the usual red herrings. Narration at times obscure, and the acting
lacks conviction. Author's name is best bet, and can possibly be used as support for
the smallest theatres.' And on *Courageous*: 'Sentimental drama. Slender story, but
helped by the good performances given by Barbara Stanwyck & Frank Morgan, and
by Ricardo Cortez & Lyle Talbot in minor roles. This will perhaps have most appeal
for the women and better class patrons. Do not think we should feature this.' Given
the many references to gender, age, location, and social class of the potential
audience, the Questionnaire's findings on audience structure probably helped with
booking. Bernstein acknowledged this in a letter to respondents: 'The information
thus gathered, which is unobtainable by any other means, will prove of immense
value in the arrangement of film programs calculated to appeal to the majority of
patrons.'[86] Bernstein staged live entertainment in each cinema one week a year,
organised 'amateur art competitions', introduced the cheap 'Children's Matinee',
and numerous other innovations, all no doubt focused on luring specific audience
segments into his cinemas.[87]

Furthermore, the Questionnaire provided control data against which to check
the viability of new cinema sites. Whenever Bernstein considered a site he would
send in market researchers with questionnaires on tastes, occupations, and
cinema-going habits. If promising, Bernstein would submit a bid.[88] Bernstein's
knack of site research would later surface in his choice of Manchester for his
television station: 'I looked at two maps. One showed population density. The
other showed rainfall.'[89]

Finally, the questionnaires were probably used by Gainsborough and
Gaumont-British for producing or acquiring new films, literary properties, and
screenplays.[90] Bernstein almost certainly used his own knowledge about the
market while producing *Rope* and *Under Capricorn* for Alfred Hitchcock in the
late 1940s. For instance, when Bankers Trust refused to finance *Rope* because
James Stewart had dropped in the star ratings, Bernstein nevertheless pressed
ahead and was proved right by the film's profits.[91]

   Whilst the Bernstein Questionnaire clearly generated useful publicity, it was
also a serious attempt to gain knowledge about the consumer. It was an advanced
example of 'pre-scientific' market research, carried out over a long period, with
effort and enthusiasm. By the early 1940s, however, Bernstein was evidently
aware of the reliable survey methods others were using. In July 1942, when
visiting the US for the Ministry of Information, he was summoned by the British
Embassy about *Mrs Miniver*, a film about an Englishwoman in war-time. It sold
1.5 million tickets in ten weeks, but the Embassy thought it gave a shocking and
distorted picture of Britain. Bernstein rang up Gallup, who conducted a survey
showing that respondents who had seen *Mrs Miniver* or two other pro-British
movies were 'seventeen percent more favourable towards Britain in their
feelings than those who had not', which helped Bernstein appease the Embassy.[92]
Equally, when Hugh Trevor-Roper, who examined Hitler's bunker, sent him the
draft of *Last Days of Hitler*, Bernstein asked Audience Research to examine the
American public's attitude towards a film version.[93] Finally, hand-written notes
for an article, possibly by Bernstein, raise several technical issues about
sampling methods and questionnaire design, showing that the Questionnaire
did not exclusively serve publicity purposes or Bernstein's industry campaigns.[94]
It was the principal forerunner of modern market research in the British
film industry.

                                          IV

In the US, media research had developed considerably since the late 1920s.
Gallup actually started his career analysing newspaper reading habits. His
findings that the picture page and comics were most widely read led to a
substantial increase in advertisements using comic strips.[95] In 1935, he founded
his illustrious polling firm, the American Institute of Public Opinion (AIPO).
Gallup included film-related questions in the polls, possibly using them as a shop
window to interest film companies.[96] In early 1940, Gallup set up Audience
Research. George Schaefer, president of Radio-Keith-Orpheum (RKO), a major
studio, offered an exclusive contract for the first year.[97] Gallup later called
Audience Research's work in the 1940s 'some of the best research that I've ever
seen or ever had part in'.[98]
   The firm was located in Princeton, New Jersey, along with AIPO. David
Ogilvy, who later founded the advertising agency Ogilvy & Mather, was its first
director. It had 50 to 60 employees, who did research design, tabulation, and
analysis, but used the 1,000 or so AIPO interviewers for field interviews,
enabling Gallup to achieve economies of scope.[99] In 1941, Audience Research
also started research for other film producers. By 1946, it had 14 regular
customers, among which were at least half the Hollywood majors.[100] Besides
commissioned work, many industry executives subscribed to Audience
Research's *Continuing Audit of Marquee Values*, which measured stars'
popularity every few months.

Audience Research challenged prevailing industry notions. It found that the Motion Picture Producers and Distributors of America systematically overstated the number of admissions at 82 million a week. Audience Research showed they were only 54 million, and corroborated this with states' tax data. It also showed the grand majority of picture-goers were poor and young: 65 per cent were under 30, and 19-year-olds went the most frequently. Gallup advised studios to lure older and richer consumers, but also to make big budget movies for the 19–25 age group and carry along as much other segments as possible, or to make low-budget movies for specific age groups.[101]

Since its only major competitor used a similar approach, Audience Research's methods were typical.[102] Careful to obtain representative samples, it carried out non-commissioned surveys on general cinema-going habits against which to test particular cases. Some questionnaires contained 200 questions, taking over an hour to ask.[103] Audience Research carefully designed the questions and inserted control questions. Film titles were a key determinant of success, and Audience Research tested the popularity of alternative titles against two controls out of a secret list of 40 highly popular titles.[104] Gallup explained: 'Audience Research cannot tell a producer whether or not a story is worth $20,000, $100,000, or $500,000, but Audience Research can point out that this story starts with initial interest equal to, greater than or less than other properties which were sold for $20,000, $100,000 or $500,000.'[105]

Another method Audience Research perfected was the preview. Using its 'Preview Jury System', it supplied 100 people closely resembling the cinema-going population with a Hopkins Electric Televoting Machine, a telephone dial that could be pulled into five positions: 'like very much', 'like', 'neutral', 'dull', 'very dull'. The dials connected to a central 'seismograph', which plotted a line on paper, to be compared with the film sequences. After recuts or reshoots, a new sample audience would see the film, as many times as necessary. The first cut was often longer than intended, enabling the deleting of entire unpopular scenes.[106]

Exploiting its large data library, Audience Research started to offer forecasts of total US box office revenue (apparently, *after* the picture's initial opening).[107] It boasted that these never 'missed the mark more than 3 percent'. Figure 1 shows how it used market research data for the forecasts.[108] The top line traces the general public interest, measured with the question whether they would want to see the picture. The other three lines show 'penetration', which is measured with questions testing the respondents' knowledge of the picture and their plans to see it.[109] The picture was clearly more popular in New York. During its release, the national publicity campaign increased penetration in not-shown areas. Audience Research calculated its box office forecasts from the difference between market-want-to-see and the not-shown-penetration using a secret 'simple mathematical formula', taking into account demographics, entry prices, and geographical differences. The studio confirmed that the forecast had been correct within a three per cent margin.[110]

FIGURE 1
AWARENESS AMONG VARIOUS GROUPINGS OF US CONSUMERS OF A MAJOR
MOTION PICTURE RELEASED IN FEBRUARY 1946, DECEMBER 1945–APRIL 1946

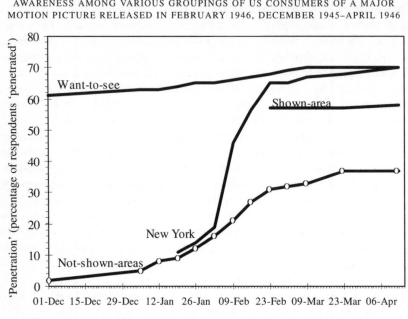

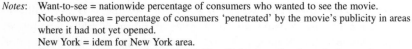

Notes: Want-to-see = nationwide percentage of consumers who wanted to see the movie.
         Not-shown-area = percentage of consumers 'penetrated' by the movie's publicity in areas
         where it had not yet opened.
         New York = idem for New York area.
         Shown-area = idem for regions outside New York where the picture had opened.
Source: Audience Research, Inc.

In a similar manner to Granada, Audience Research segmented the market
into sex, age, and income. In Table 2 considerable differences show between
income levels: James Stewart was 11 percentage points more popular among the
richest consumers than among the poorest, while Lana Turner differed only a few
percentage points. Additional segmentation by city size seemed to matter, since
substantial differences were found: Clark Gable was ten percentage points more
popular in small cities than in large ones. Just as with Bernstein's Questionnaires,
the data showed considerable differences between popularity in a segment and
the percentage of the star's market in that segment, because of differing cinema-
going habits and segment sizes.[111] Of the richest consumers, for example, 51 per
cent wanted to see a movie starring Gable, but altogether they constituted just 14
per cent of Gable's market, while the 57 per cent poorest Gable fans constituted
34 per cent.

The method of measuring the star 'want-to-see' factor over short periods, as
shown in Figure 2, was new. Previously polls were held roughly yearly. It
foreshadowed how consumer goods companies would track brand awareness.
Star popularity fluctuated: Lana Turner was a rising star, Gable was consistently

TABLE 2

POPULARITY AND MARKET SEGMENTED BY INCOME AND AGE FOR THREE MOVIE STARS, US, 1940–42

	Name	All	Income ($ per week)				Male (age)			Female (age)			Cities (1,000s inh.)		
			<25	25–35	35–60	>60	12–17	18–30	>30	12–17	18–30	>30	<10	10–100	>100
Popularity	Gable	50	57	49	52	51	43	53	43	54	55	56	65	58	54
	Stewart	42	34	42	43	45	36	41	38	41	44	43	46	45	40
	Turner	25	22	24	25	26	27	29	14	42	25	11	32	35	25
							Age (all)								
Market	Gable	100	34	20	32	14	18	41	41		n.a.			n.a.	
	Stewart	100	27	22	35	16	18	40	42						
	Turner	100	29	21	34	15	30	46	24						

Notes: Full star names: Clark Gable, James Stewart, Lana Turner. 'Popularity' refers to the percentage of respondents which named the star as favourite. 'Market' refers to the percentage of all responses for a star in a particular segment.

Source: Audience Research, Inc.

a top star, while Stewart's popularity was high but volatile.[112] The increases in Gable's popularity roughly coincided with his releases, suggesting that while producers used Gable partially for the brand-awareness of his name, each use (film) subsequently increased or maintained that awareness in what seems to have been a self-reinforcing process.

Audience Research applied the survey data to formulate specific policies for studios. After carefully examining the market for minor RKO actors, for example, it advised who to develop. 'On the basis of this experimental study we would nominate Dorothy Comingore, Ruth Warrick, Edmund O'Brien and Jack Briggs as most likely to become big ticket-sellers.'[113] It also advised that 'any star who makes fewer than three pictures a year is liable to do serious damage to his or her power to sell tickets'.[114] Similarly, Audience Research found that Myrna Loy and William Powell together would sell substantially more tickets than each separately, although most other combinations scored lower than their weakest constituent, 'a powerful argument against the indiscriminate piling up of high-priced talent in one picture'.[115] Further, Gallup personally observed that while 52 per cent of film consumers were under 25, only about 20 per cent of RKO stars were. He advised: 'Perhaps it would be good business for RKO to concentrate on building up one or more personalities in this age group.'[116] Audience Research also looked at whether consumers cared if a star was a communist: two-thirds did not.[117]

FIGURE 2
POPULARITY OF CLARK GABLE, JAMES STEWART AND LANA TURNER IN THE US,
APRIL 1940–OCTOBER 1942

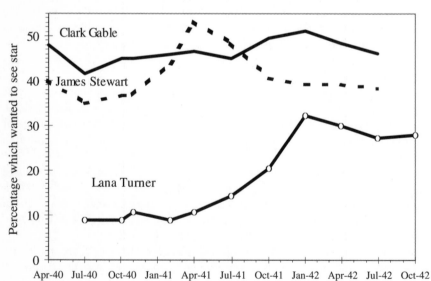

Source: Audience Research, Inc.

The question remains how Audience Research's clients used its advice. Since they were paying, they must have regarded the research as valuable. For RKO, market research was part of the new management's strategy after it emerged out of bankruptcy in 1939. The strategy certainly coincided with a successful period between 1942 and 1947.[118] Gallup's advice to choose between producing expensively for the lowest common denominator or cheaply for specific segments was taken in full: while RKO turned out big-budget features aimed at a younger audience, it also created a unit producing low-cost films based on pre-tested titles, to be heavily promoted by theatre owners. The unit's first production, *Cat People*, a horror film, cost $80,000 and grossed over 1 million dollars. Other films were *I Walked with a Zombie*, *The Body Snatcher* and *The Curse of the Cat People*.[119]

Because there were so little reliable industry data on cinema-going habits, this was an important product of Audience Research. After Selznick had experienced the usefulness of research for pricing *Gone with the Wind*, he subsequently proposed to have Gallup poll the picture's best starting time.[120] His colleague Goldwyn asked Audience Research to measure interest in the double feature, to have ammunition for his campaign against it. A substantial minority, 43 per cent, preferred double features, making studio executives conclude that abolishing them would alienate this segment.[121] Another study queried New York cinema-goers about their television watching habits, showing that 70 per cent had seen at least one television programme.[122] Comparing statistics of RKO audiences to the population, Audience Research showed RKO that its audience was above industry average among the over-30s, but below among younger consumers. RKO pictures were also liked above average among richest consumers, and below among others. Similarly, RKO pictures performed averagely well in cities of over 500,000 inhabitants, but underperformed in smaller cities. Audience Research concluded: 'RKO pictures ... are least successful with the economic segments in which the greatest number of ticket-buyers are found.'[123]

Title tests constituted another important category that shaped business decisions of customers. When Disney wanted to expand its audience to adults, it asked Audience Research to check which titles evoked memories of childhood. *Uncle Remus*, for example, was changed to *Song of the South*, a title more popular among adults.[124] Similarly, RKO found that *I'm Still Alive*, the title for an action adventure, scored high, but aroused unwanted associations: most respondents expected a farce or comedy.[125] When Selznick wanted to film *Jane Eyre*, Ogilvy reported that the title and concept tested lower than for any other film. Even a stellar cast – Ronald Colman and Joan Fontaine – increased the 'want-to-see' factor only marginally. The scene remembered most, the burning of Thornfield Hall, was only indirectly represented, and respondents even remembered scenes not in the novel. Despite this, Selznick went ahead, although he included the fire scene, which was not in the original screenplay.[126]

Yet another category of information, star ratings, was also important to studio executives. Many subscribed to the *Continuing Audit of Marquee Values*, leading a journalist to observe:

> Many a player already knows the feeling of walking into a producer's office only to have him open that secret drawer, look down a column of figures and say "Sorry, you're not the type." It becomes quickly obvious then that when the doorbell ringer for some research outfit asked a few hundred Mrs. Doakeses, "Would you go see a picture starring Maisie Glutz?" too many had said *"No"*.[127]

Greta Garbo had such an experience when attempting a come-back in 1947, after five years off-screen. Having already done wardrobe tests, she was set aside when producer Walter Wanger could not obtain finance on her name.[128] The new era of market research was also exemplified by Goldwyn in 1947: eight years earlier he threw out Merle Oberon after careful sales analysis, now he dumped Teresa Wright after examining her latest marquee ratings.[129]

Previews constituted another important product of Audience Research. Gallup was astonished how Selznick interpreted a preview-graph: 'Selznick used to just put a ruler on this graph and then have his people cut out the valleys.'[130] The blunt approach showed with the preview of *The Paradine Case* in 1947, when Gallup's figures demonstrated that while support star Louis Jourdan excited moviegoers, his colleague Alida Valli did not. Selznick cut out as much of her appearance as possible.[131] His colleague Goldwyn also received unfavourable preview results of *Enchantment*: the audience found the film 'confusing' and 'slow-moving'. Goldwyn, however, boldly released the film unchanged, claiming its difference was its strength. It turned out otherwise.[132]

Finally, information on advertising effectiveness was an important product. Audience Research warned one client not to advertise a classical music score, although the preview audiences liked it, because it would put people off. Likewise, the firm found sexual connotations counterproductive: most respondents said they had discovered that pictures advertised in that way did not live up to expectations. When a picture which was prominently advertised by female anatomy opened disastrously, Gallup advised the studio to use crime-themed advertisements instead.[133] Audience Research even previewed a picture that had already opened successfully, to help its client decide about additional advertising. It found an additional $75,000 expenditure would yield at least double in net revenue.[134] Another study concluded that 58 per cent variation in popularity between pictures related to advertising outlays.[135] Gallup personally met RKO executives to discuss advertising strategies. They asked him to develop a standard advertising procedure for all pictures. Gallup ensured that 'we are now in a position to draw conclusions which will enable you to increase the net effectiveness of your paid advertising by *at least one hundred percent*'.[136] Audience Research found reviews influenced revenue only slightly, and that the 'want-to-see' factor could be increased most cheaply by using famous stars and stories.[137]

V

Culver City, February 1946. *Spellbound* has opened successfully in the large cities. Yet Selznick has a problem: it underperforms in small-town markets. After tests, Audience Research concludes that the star-centred graphics of the advertisements are 'too sophisticated for towns under 50,000 in population'. The firm prescribes advertisements telling the story. An obstinate Selznick, however, blames United Artists' uninspired sales effort instead. But when Oklahoma reviewers call the film 'heavy psychological going' and 'another Alfred Hitchcock thriller with a lot of psychoanalytical stuff', market research wins over Selznick's emotions and he turns a potential disaster into an Oklahoma hit by advertising the story: 'WOMEN will be strangely moved, fascinated ... men will be intimately intrigued, thrilled ... by this bold woman who risks everything in one reckless experiment to unlock the fearful secret in the heart of a man ... a man suspected of murder!'[138]

The sophisticated way in which Selznick exploited knowledge about the consumer underlines how far market research had taken the film industry. Initially, the ways film companies built knowledge about the consumer resembled those of fashion goods industries. In half a century, however, changes in technology, contracts and costs caused market research to resemble that of mass-distribution industries. On the technological-cum-organisational level, the emergence of cinemas, film exchanges, and eventually the carefully planned feature film, increased the incentives for conducting careful, scientific market research. The widening lag between production and release reduced the utility of sales analysis, the only proprietary source of useful market information. On the contractual level, the change from selling films to fixed-fee renting and then to percentage-based renting, combined with increasing vertical integration, further increased the profit incentive for market research.

By the late 1930s, therefore, the growing need for market information quickly made film companies adopt newly available research techniques. Granada and Audience Research were first-movers. Granada held its surveys irregularly and analysed all responses to its printed questionnaires, which focused on cinema-going habits and stars' popularity. It did not aim to make profits with each individual question, but mainly wanted to obtain publicity, ammunition for industry campaigns, and information useful for site purchase and film booking. Audience Research employed much more sophisticated methods. It polled frequently, using interviewers, scientific sampling and research design, and control data. It obtained information on advertising effectiveness, stars and titles, predicted box office revenue, and tested films' appeal in previews. It claimed it could respond to clients' questions in three days and aimed to supply information which directly translated into clients' profits.

The film industry was a pioneer in understanding the segmentation of its market. However, while fashion firms could focus on specific segments, film companies had to reach as wide an audience as possible. They analysed market segments to make sure films appealed across as many as possible, not to produce films aimed at specific segments. Only after the period examined here, when television made screen-time less scarce, could film companies afford to target specific segments, while television took over the focus on the lowest common denominator. By the 1950s, the emergence of a younger, more educated, affluent audience further changed the fragmenting market, while Hollywood's forced divesture of cinemas and the out-sourcing of film production affected the incentive for market research. The subsequent decline of seven-year star contracts diminished the value of star ratings. This fragmenting, unstable market probably made expensive nationwide representative sampling less cost-effective. Specialised firms such as Audience Research and MPRB closed during the 1950s, but research was continued by general market research firms and inside the studios. Gallup's AIPO, for example, was still working for Hollywood in the 1970s. By the 1960s, most Hollywood studios had a vice-president for market research.[139]

Today, techniques such as metered previews and statistical box office forecasting have become commonplace. Nearly all films are previewed, and every Sunday night Hollywood's computers are humming to predict final US box office revenues for the weekend's releases. Television adopted the ratings techniques pioneered by radio and film companies. Film studios also pioneered the continuous tracking of brand awareness, of their stars. Advertising agencies have been keen users of these methods. Young & Rubicam, of which Gallup was a vice-president, and Ogilvy & Mather, which Ogilvy set up after his work at Audience Research, have stretched the techniques to the limit. The surveys by Bernstein's Granada Theatres stood on the threshold of this era of modern market research, the work of Gallup's Audience Research marked its advent.

NOTES

The author thanks Andrew Godley, Paul Johnson, Tim Leunig, Jaime Reis, Robert Sklar and the anonymous referees for comments and suggestions. The author also benefited from seminars by professors Al Lieberman and Samuel C. Craig on entertainment marketing and the international entertainment business at the NYU Stern School of Business. Janet Moat and Saffron Parker of the British Film Institute provided invaluable help with sources. The research for this article has been partially made possible by European Union Marie Curie Fellowship HPMF-CT-2001-01273.

1. *Management: Tasks, Responsibilities, Practices* (New York, 1973), pp.64–5, as quoted in P. Kotler and G. Armstrong, *Principles of Marketing* (Englewood Cliffs, 6th edn. 1994), p.5.
2. L.J. Leff, *Hitchcock and Selznick: The Rich and Strange Collaboration of Alfred Hitchcock and David O. Selznick in Hollywood* (London, 1987), pp.160–61, 167; R. Haver, *David O. Selznick's Hollywood* (London, 1980), pp.347–8.
3. L.C. Lockley, 'Notes on the History of Marketing Research', *Journal of Marketing*, Vol.14 (1950), p.736.
4. R. Fitzgerald, 'Rowntree and Market Strategy, 1897–1939', *Business and Economic History*, Vol.18 (1989), pp.45–58, 56–7, makes this observation for consumer goods industries in general.
5. P.M. Chisnall, *Marketing Research* (New York, 5th edn. 1997), p.7.
6. R.L. Blaszczyk, *Imagining Consumers: Design and Innovation from Wedgwood to Corning* (Baltimore, 2000), p.1.

7. Ibid., pp.9–10, 12, 38, 105. Similar configurations existed in the clothing industry. For a historical analysis of the economics of this industry and the role of fashion see A. Godley, 'Immigrant Entrepreneurs and the Emergence of London's East End as an Industrial District', *London Journal*, Vol.21 (1996), pp.38–45; idem, *Jewish Immigrant Entrepreneurship in New York and London, 1880–1914: Enterprise and Culture* (Basingstoke, 2001), pp.90–108.

8. See below.

9. P.N. Golder, 'Historical Method in Marketing Research with New Evidence on Long-term Market Share Stability', *Journal of Marketing Research*, Vol.37 (2000), pp.156–72, calls for more historical studies on market research.

10. A historical introduction on France is L. Creton, 'Marketing et Stratégies dans le Secteur Cinématographique. Une Mise en Perspective des Pratiques du Cinéma Français', in P.-J. Benghozi and C. Delage (eds.), *Une Histoire Economique du Cinéma Français (1895–1995): Regards Franco-Américains* (Paris, 1997), pp.229–64.

11. P. Larson, *The Naked Consumer: How Our Private Lives Become Public Commodities* (New York, 1994, orig. edn. 1992), pp.19–20; Chisnall, *Marketing*, pp.7–8.

12. Lockley, 'History', p.736.

13. Larson, *Naked Consumer*, pp.19–20.

14. E.J. Perkins, *Wall Street to Main Street: Charles E. Merrill and Middle-Class Investors* (Cambridge, 1999), pp.7, 121, 148.

15. Fitzgerald, 'Rowntree'; V. Ward, 'Marketing Convenience Goods between the Wars', in G. Jones and N. Morgan (eds.), *Adding Value: Brands and Marketing in Food and Drink* (London, 1994), pp.259–90.

16. R. Church, 'Mass Marketing Motor Cars in Britain Before 1950: The Missing Dimension', in R.S. Tedlow and G. Jones (eds.), *The Rise and Fall of Mass Marketing* (London, 1993), pp.36–57.

17. T.A.B. Corley, 'Consumer Marketing in Britain, 1914–1960', *Business History*, Vol.29 (1987), pp.65–83. The National Institute of Industrial Psychology (NIIP) also carried out 'market studies', 14 in total between 1929 and 1935. For a study on corsets for Berlei (UK) Ltd., for example, researchers interviewed a representative sample of 1,000 middle- and upper-class women. 'NIIP Reports (Abstracts)', Section 7, File 10, NIIP Archives, London; ibid., Report 577.

18. T. Ramsaye, *A Million and One Nights* (New York, 1926), p.450, as quoted in B.A. Austin, 'The Motion Picture Audience: A Neglected Aspect of Film Research', in idem (ed.), *The Film Audience: An International Bibliography of Research* (Metuchen and London, 1983), pp.xvii–xlii, xxi.

19. A. Zukor with D. Kramer, *The Public is Never Wrong* (New York, 1953), p.42, as quoted in S. Ohmer, 'Measuring Desire: George Gallup and the Origins of Market Research in Hollywood' (unpublished Ph.D. thesis, New York University, 1997), p.1.

20. Ibid., p.46, as quoted in Austin, 'Motion Picture Audience', p.21.

21. Blaszczyk, *Imagining Consumers*, e.g., pp.12, 38, 105.

22. G. Bakker, 'Stars and Stories: How Films Became Branded Products', *Enterprise and Society*, Vol.2 (2001), pp.461–502.

23. Ibid.

24. 'Baldwin Pictures Corporation: Producer and Distributor – Motion Pictures', in H.T. Lewis (ed.), *Cases on the Motion Picture Industry* (New York, 1930), pp.435–43. The companies' real names were kept secret.

25. J.M. Gaines, *Contested Culture: The Image, the Voice and the Law* (London, 1991), pp.148–59. Stars were production inputs (used as brands to brand films), not products sold or leased to distributors and cinemas.

26. Contrary to other products, after launch films immediately moved into the growth and maturity phases, which could hardly be distinguished, reaching their highest box office revenues shortly after opening. Sales promotion therefore started before product launch, and was intensive. If the film was successful, it was increased to maximise revenue, if it flopped it was stopped. Profit was only reached late in the product life-cycle, if ever. In the end phase profitability did not decline, because most costs were fixed and sunk, so ex-post any sale would improve profitability. In the end phase, sales promotion was limited because revenues were. R.H. Cochrane, 'Advertising Motion Pictures', in J.P. Kennedy (ed.), *The Story of the Films* (Chicago, 1927), pp.233–62. Cf. R.E. Caves, *Creative Industries: Contracts between Art and Commerce* (Cambridge, MA, 2000).

27. Bakker, 'Stars and Stories'.

28. *La Cinématographie Française* held a comparable French poll from 1936 to 1938.

29. *Moving Picture World*, 1909; cf. the 1930s British polls in *Picturegoer*.

30. Bakker, 'Stars and Stories', pp.466–7.

31. Generally with a fixed sum as 'minimum guarantee'.

32. L. May, *The Big Tomorrow: Hollywood and the Politics of the American Way* (Chicago, 2000).

33. E.g., H. Blumer, *Movies, Delinquency and Crime* (New York, 1933); J. Richards and D. Sheridan, *Mass-Observation at the Movies* (London, 1987).

34. *The Saturday Evening Post*, 21 July 1921; 'Universal Pictures Corporation. Producer and Distributor – Motion Pictures – Merchandise Analysis', in Lewis (ed.), *Cases*, pp.132–7.

35. From the early 1910s, the French Gaumont company counted fan letters. Its star Renée Navarre received 300 to 400 letters daily. I. Aimone, 'Un Statut pour les Acteurs, 1910–1920', in Benghozi (ed.), *Cinéma Français*, pp.81–92.

36. L.C. Rosten, *Hollywood* (New York, 1941), pp.409–13.

37. B.B. Hampton, *A History of the Movies* (New York, 1931), pp.311–12.

38. T. Schatz, *The Genius of the System: Hollywood Filmmaking in the Studio Era* (London, 1988).

39. Haver, *Selznick's Hollywood*, p.113.

40. 'World Wide Pictures, Incorporated – Distributor – Motion Pictures – Unit of Sale – Pricing', in H.T. Lewis (ed.), *Cases on the Motion Picture Industry: With Commentaries* (New York, 1930), pp.288–94.

41. Sometimes one failure endangered a studio, such as *Heaven's Gate* (1981), which practically bankrupted United Artists, forcing a merger with MGM. A portfolio strategy analysis is J. Sedgwick and M. Pokorny, 'The Risk Environment of Film Making: Warner Brothers in the Inter-War Years', *Explorations in Economic History*, Vol.35 (1998), pp.196–220.

42. J. Sedgwick and M. Pokorny, 'Stardom and the Profitability of Film Making: Warner Bros. in the 1930s', *Journal of Cultural Economics*, Vol.25 (2001), pp.157–84.

43. A.S. Berg, *Goldwyn: A Biography* (New York, 1989), p.334.

44. K. Brownlow and D. Gill, *The Other Hollywood* (TV documentary, London, 1997).

45. R. Vasey, *The World according to Hollywood, 1918–39* (Madison, 1997), p.161.

46. It was actually the US government which started to survey foreign markets. In the 1910s, it asked consuls to write short reports on foreign film industries, published in the *Commerce Reports*. In the 1920s it set up a dedicated Motion Picture Division inside the Bureau of Foreign and Domestic Commerce. The Division tried to gather as much basic quantitative information as possible, such as number of cinema seats, average rental rates, market shares, import, exports, and invested capital.

47. S. Ohmer, 'The Science of Pleasure: George Gallup and Audience Research in Hollywood', in M. Stokes and R. Maltby (eds.), *Identifying Hollywood's Audiences: Cultural Identity and the Movies* (London, 1999), pp.61–80, at 66; Memo to Al Lichtman, vice-president MGM, 20 Oct. 1939, 'not sent', printed in David O. Selznick, *Memo from David O. Selznick* (New York, 1972), pp.223–7.

48. T. Schatz, *Boom and Bust: The American Cinema in the 1940s* (New York, 1997), pp.68–71.

49. H. Golden, 'Hollywood Takes to the Polls: RKO Enlists Dr. Gallup for Public Pulse-Feeling on Pix Preferences', *Variety*, 8 Jan. 1941, pp.29,45.

50. Ward, 'Convenience Goods', shows that in 1930s Britain, Horlicks also identified specific market segments.

51. This concept came close to the 'opinion leader', a commonplace in later days. P.F. Lazarsfeld, 'Audience Research in the Movie Field', in 'The Motion Picture Industry', *Annals of the American Academy of Political and Social Sciences*, Vol.254 (Nov. 1947), pp.160–68. Lazarsfeld also found heavy radio listeners were heavy movie-goers and vice versa. P.F. Lazarsfeld and P. Kendall, *Radio Listening in America* (New York, 1948). Cf. I. Jarvie, *Towards a Sociology of Cinema* (London, 1970), p.308.

52. L. Handel, *Hollywood Looks at its Audience* (Urbana, 1950); T.S. Simonet, 'Industry', *Film Comment*, Vol.14 No.1 (1978), pp.72–3.

53. See below.

54. Simonet, 'Industry'; G. Seldes, *The Great Audience* (New York, 1950), p.222. It is unclear whether Teldox was tested reliably and independently.

55. Chesnall, *Marketing*, p.9.

56. C. Moorehead, *Sidney Bernstein: A Biography* (London, 1984); A. Eyles, *The Granada Theatres* (London, 1998).

57. According to company publicity, ibid., p.111. However, a letter from Gaumont British Picture Corporation Ltd. to Sidney L. Bernstein, 17 April 1930, File D, Box(B)22A, Sidney L. Bernstein Collection (SLB), mentions £404,000 as the 'capital value theatres for insurance purposes' of eight cinemas; in 1934 at least 11 existed.

58. Ibid., p.122. Granada's cinemas being first-run and in London, market share in revenue was probably higher.

59. Ibid., p.137.

60. Ibid.; Moorehead, *Bernstein*; 'Bernstein, Sidney Lewis' in D. Jeremy and G. Tweedale, *Dictionary of Twentieth Century British Business Leaders* (London, 1994), pp.15–16; S.L. Bernstein, *A Memorandum on the Scarcity of the Film Supply together with a Scheme to Assist British Film Production* (London, 1939).

61. Attached to the Supreme Headquarters Allied Expeditionary Force. Jeremy, *Dictionary*; Moorehead, *Bernstein*, pp.84–5. As council member, he accomplished theatre space and equipment for all local schools.

62. E. Sussex, 'The Fate of F3080', *Sight and Sound*, Vol.53 No.2 (1984), pp.92–7.

63. Eyles, *Granada*, pp.165–6.

64. M. Davis *et al.*, *Granada: The First 25 Years* (London, 1981). Under Bernstein, Granada produced several lasting television programmes, such as *Coronation Street*, *What the Papers Say* and *World in Action*. Bernstein was made a life peer in 1969 and became Baron Bernstein of Leigh. Jeremy, *Dictionary*.

65. File 'Theatre monthly reports, 1934', SLB, B47, Rialto Leytonstone, May 1930.

66. File 'Theatre weekly reports, 1934', SLB, B47.

67. *Box Office*, 4 Feb. 1956, p.40.

68. 1934 survey, SLB, BBQ1.

69. A 1950 report criticised the method: 120,000 questionnaires distributed, 20,000 returns tabulated, when 2,000 would have sufficed, and longevity created a self-selected sample. G.R.T., 'Some Observations on the Bernstein Questionnaire', 5 Oct. 1950, SLB, BBQ2, p.5.

70. J.P. Mayer carried market segmentation further. Attendance frequency by income, education, and occupation showed that the lower the income and education, the higher the cinema attendance. Munitions workers went 3.4 times a month, agricultural workers only 1.0 times. J.P. Mayer, *British Cinemas and their Audiences: Sociological Studies* (London, 1948), pp.269–71.

71. 'Report on 1932 survey', File 1932, BBQ2, SLB, p.18.

72. A. McPhail, 'Analysis of Replies', File 1927/1928, BBQ1, SLB.

73. 'Report on 1932 survey'. Handel also addressed this issue, which was apparently important for marketing. 'A Study to Determine the Drawing Power of Male and Female Stars upon Movie-Goers of their own Sex', *International Journal of Opinion and Attitude Research*, Vol.2 (1948), pp.215–20. Cf. Jarvie, *Sociology of Cinema*, p.283.

74. Letter A.M. Lester, NIIP, to Edward Porter, Bernstein Theatres Ltd., 3 Feb. 1936, BBQ2, SLB.

75. Letter A.M. Lester, John Haddon & Co. Ltd., Incorporated Practitioners in Advertising, to Ewart Hodgson, Granada Theatres Ltd, 29 April 1940, BBQ3, SLB. Lester had left NIIP, but still advised Granada.

76. Ibid.

77. 'Expenditure on questionnaire 1946', BBQ2, SLB. Previous questionnaires' costs must have been substantial: although size and scope of NIIP's 'market studies' were probably smaller, costs were a fraction of Granada's – if previous costs were comparable to the 1946 questionnaire (which cost £2,299 1933 pounds). In 1933, market studies for Southall Barclay (manufacturing chemists), Wright (soap) and John Cotton (tobacco) cost £90, £188 and £25, largely consisting of wages. Account book, Costs of investigations 1933, NIIP, Section 7 File 14.

78. G.R.T., 'Some Observations', pp.4, 8, 17.

79. E.g.: 'The Most Popular Film Stars', *Daily Chronicle*, 3 April 1929, p.5; 'A Kinema Ballot', *Manchester Guardian*, 3 April 1929; 'A Kinema Ballot', *Daily Film Renter*, 3 April 1929. Eyles, *Granada*, also concludes the polls served publicity (p.114).

80. File 1927, BBQ2, SLB; R. Ford, 'What One Public Says It Likes. Comments on the Bernstein Questionnaire', *Sight and Sound* (Summer 1937), p.70, reports 160,000 respondents.

81. L. Wood, *British Film, 1927–1939* (London, 1986), p.135.

82. 1928 Questionnaire, BBQ1, SLB.

83. Ibid., pp.121–2. Cf. S. Street, *British Cinema in Documents* (London, 2000), pp.125–33.

84. Undated letter, c.1950, File D, BBQ7, SLB. Bernstein prepared a similar letter for US producers,

offering help with the 'many points puzzling you about film-going habits in the British Isles'.

85. The 1927 Cinematograph Act forbade block-booking and blind-selling in the UK.
86. Standard letter for 1937 questionnaire; Eyles, *Granada*, p.113.
87. The questionnaires probably helped Bernstein with planning these happenings. One question, for example, asked whether customers liked an organ solo, and how long it should last, helping Bernstein to assess if the distinguished organists he contracted were worth the money.
88. Moorehead, *Bernstein*, p.104.
89. Eyles, *Granada*, p.174. Granada Television continued the tradition of the Bernstein Questionnaire in its Viewership Survey.
90. Because Gaumont-British archives have not been traced, verification is impossible.
91. The drop was caused by Stewart's Air Force job. Fortunately for Bernstein, Stewart waived his fee for a percentage, eventually earning three times as much. Moorehead, *Granada*, p.175.
92. Moorehead, *Granada*, pp.141–2.
93. Ibid., p.177.
94. 'Kine Weekly', unsigned, undated, c.1946, File E, BBQ3, SLB. Granada also corresponded with the British Institute of Public Opinion (BIPO) about carrying out the 1946 Questionnaire for Granada, but nothing came of it. Letter Henry Durant, BIPO to Ewart Hogson, Granada Theatres, 6 Aug. 1946, File B, BBQ5, SLB.
95. Even sports pieces, love columns, and obituaries received more attention than news and political pages; Ohmer, 'Science of Pleasure', p.63. On Gallup and Audience Research Inc. see also S. Ohmer, 'Measuring Desire: George Gallup and Audience Research in Hollywood', *Journal of Film and Video*, Vol.43 (1991), pp.3–28; S. Kelley, 'Gallup Goes Hollywood: Motion Picture Audience Research in the 1940's' (unpublished MA thesis, University of Texas at Austin, 1989).
96. Ohmer, 'Measuring Desire'; 'Gallup Has Plan for Measuring Grosses with "Research Insurance"', *Motion Picture Herald*, 26 July 1941, pp.33–4. Cf. T. Schatz, *Boom and Bust*, pp.68–71.
97. 'Gallup's Pan On Pix Adv.', *Variety*, 14 Aug. 1940, pp.5, 19; Golden, 'Polls'.
98. Simonet, 'Industry'.
99. Ibid.
100. W.R. Weaver, 'Audience Research to Key Services to New Auction Sales Policy', *Motion Picture Herald*, 17 Aug. 1946, pp.28–9.
101. 'Measuring Grosses'.
102. See above.
103. 'Measuring Grosses'.
104. W.R. Weaver, 'Audience Research Answers the Question of What's in a Name', *Motion Picture Herald*, 27 July 1946, p.39.
105. 'The British Cinema at the Gallup', *Documentary News Letter*, June–July 1947, p.99.
106. W.R. Weaver, 'Studios Use Audience Research to Learn What Pleases Customers', *Motion Picture Herald*, 20 July 1946, p.37. Except for one year, MGM was under exclusive contract to Handel. Simonet, 'Industry'.
107. This statistical method compared the growth pattern of a picture's box office revenue during its first few days of release to similar data for numerous other films previously released. A large 'data library' was needed for this and probably substantial computing power. Nowadays, this way of box office forecasting has become a routine practice among the Hollywood studios.
108. Weaver, 'Sales Policy'. Results verified by Weaver.
109. AR, 'New York City Motion Picture Market Study' (Princeton, 1940), p.27.
110. Weaver, 'Sales Policy'.
111. Despite using interviews instead of questionnaires and a list rather than open questioning.
112. Kotler, *Principles of Marketing*, pp.522–5, distinguishes six different life-cycles for personalities: the standard path (going gradually to a steady peak), the sudden peak (e.g. Neil Armstrong), the come-back, the comet, the two phases, and the wave.
113. Audience Research (AR), 'RKO Stock and Contract Players', Report(R)62, 26 March 1941,
114. AR, 'How Many Pictures Should a Star Make Every Year?', R142, 22 Jan. 1942.
115. AR, 'Marquee Value of Teams', R80, 28 May 1941.
116. [sentence underlined by Gallup] G. Gallup, 'Demand for Stars under 25', R52, 24 Feb. 1941.
117. AR, 'Communism and Hollywood', R25, 10 Sept. 1940.
118. R. Haver, 'The RKO Years', *American Film*, Vol.3 No.2 (1977), pp.28–34.
119. Ibid., p.30; RKO ledgers state $147,000 and $525,000 as *Cat People*'s cost and world-wide

rentals. R.B. Jewell, 'A History of RKO Radio Pictures, 1928–1942' (unpublished PhD. thesis, University of Southern California, 1978), p.764.
120. Selznick, 'Memo to Al Lichtman'.
121. 'Goldwyn-gallup Survey Reports 57% Against Duals, 43% In Favor', *Motion Picture Herald*, 10 Aug. 1940, p.21; Gallup's Pan, 'If 43% of Pop. Still Want Dual's Now's No Time to End 'Em', *Variety*, 14 Aug. 1940, p.5.
122. Berg, *Goldwyn*, p.432.
123. AR, 'Publicity Penetration', R122, 19 Nov. 1941.
124. Ohmer, 'Science of Pleasure', p.71.
125. AR, 'Titles for Stunt Man Story', R17, 11 July 1940. Nevertheless RKO kept the title.
126. J. Sconce, 'Narrative Authority and Social Narrativity: The Cinematic Reconstruction of Bronte's Jane Eyre', in *The Studio System* (New Brunswick, 1994), pp.140–62, at 150–52.
127. 'Audience Research Blues', *Variety*, 8 May 1946, pp.5, 25, italics original.
128. Berg, *Goldwyn*, p.431.
129. Ibid., p.444.
130. Simonet, 'Industry'.
131. Gallup found the film's problem was that it appealed to older consumers, who were infrequent cinema-goers. Leff, *Hitchcock*, p.263.
132. Berg, *Goldwyn*, p.443.
133. Weaver, 'Sales Policy'.
134. Ibid.
135. AR, 'Market Study', p.27. Cf. AR, R78, 18 Dec. 1941; R82, 22 Jan. 1941.
136. AR, 'Advertising', R100, 22 Aug. 1941, italics original.
137. AR, 'Market Study', pp.83–6: 'Review Ratings and Box Office'; cf. Bakker, 'Stars and Stories', pp.493, g6–8.
138. Selznick's capitals. Leff, *Hitchcock*, p.170.
139. Simonet, 'Industry'.

'Times Change and We Change with Them': The German Advertising Industry in the Third Reich – Between Professional Self-Interest and Political Repression

HARTMUT BERGHOFF
Universität Göttingen

Prominent West German advertisers who had worked under the Nazis looked back on the Third Reich with highly ambivalent feelings. In 1981 Harry Damrow, former Hoechst advertising chief and a leading member of post-war professional bodies in the advertising industry, wrote in his memoirs: 'In politics, National Socialism operated with lies and half-truths. In commercial advertising, however, it re-established clarity and truth and a level playing field for all.'[1] Similarly, in 1972 the head of German Coca-Cola's advertising department judged that advertising in 1933 had been prepared 'to sacrifice certain freedoms for the sake of creating a salutary order in which this hitherto unruly industry could thrive'.[2]

This essay looks at the German advertising industry between 1933 and 1939. It focuses on the aims and methods as well as the successes and limits of the regime's regulation of advertising. In particular, it analyses the advertising industry's suppression, adaptation, and self-assertion. Finally, it takes up the ongoing discussion of the regime's modernising impact on German society.[3] Did the dictatorship have a dynamic or a retarding effect beyond 1945?

II
THE GERMAN ADVERTISING INDUSTRY BEFORE 1933

The bringing into line of advertising was among the first steps undertaken by the National Socialist regime and was welcomed by the greater part of the industry, which saw in the new government's intervention the solution to their business' chronic problems. These political measures and the advertisers' response are only comprehensible against the background of the advertising business during the Weimar years. Applicable here is Peukert's phrase, 'crisis years of classic modernity'.[4] Technical progress allowed for new advertising media such as radio, films, and electric lights; market research made its first inroads; the dazzling American model and the use of more scientific advertising methods opened new horizons for the advertisers; the beginnings of a systematic training were now in evidence. In the mass society of the late 1920s, with its rapidly changing fashion and styles, advertising had increasing influence on the consumer.[5]

On the other hand, advertising sales during the runaway inflation were less than half that of pre-war levels. By 1929 the gap had closed, but with the Great Depression the industry suffered a renewed setback. Many businessmen still considered advertising a superfluous luxury. In the economic crisis, advertising was a prime target of cost-cutting measures. Advertisers were either not hired or placed in subordinate positions. In 1928 the trade journal *Die Reklame* complained that many businesses 'are still even today not convinced of the necessity of systematic advertising'. In Germany the incorporation of the advertiser 'in the businessman's hierarchy as well as in the life of society' caused 'severe difficulties'.[6]

It was not only in the economic sphere that the advertising industry came up against stiff resistance. It was attacked by cultural critics on both the Right and the Left. Younger advertisers had poor prospects for the future in a career that garnered little prestige. Only very slowly, in the 1920s, did the industry become more professional and receive the concomitant social recognition. This was in stark contrast to advertisers in the USA and Great Britain, who had gained kudos for their engagement with propaganda during the First World War. American and British advertising federations were able to attract presidents and prime ministers as keynote speakers for their annual conferences. In 1924 Harvard University began awarding a prize for the best advertising campaign of the year. The Metropolitan Museum of Art had an official liaison with the advertising industry. In Germany such things were yet inconceivable.[7]

In the educated German middle class (*Bildungsbürgertum*), the word *Reklame* (advertising) was still a term of derision. German economists still regarded advertising as an unproductive squandering of resources.[8] It is hardly surprising, then, to discover that German advertisers nursed an inferiority complex and harboured social-climbing ambitions. Not until 1929 were they able to bring the World Advertising Congress to Germany for the first time. By doing so, they hoped to exchange their 'Cinderella status' for that of an 'equal partner'[9] with Germany's other well-respected economic sectors. The German advertising federation functionary, Johannes Schmiedchen, proclaimed a 'great advertising crusade', calling for an 'offensive against public opinion' and 'the correcting of numerous misperceptions and prejudices'.[10]

Until 1933 the regulation of advertising by the state concentrated exclusively on grave abuses. The 1909 law against unfair practice prohibited misleading, mendacious and immoral advertisements. Several federal laws permitted local authorities to tax and also delimit advertising in public venues, but as a whole, German advertising was distinguished by a lack of legal restrictions. Given such leeway (the 1909 law could be applied only upon petition), German advertisers were able to operate within a relatively *laissez-faire* atmosphere.

But it was precisely the lack of legal supervision that was the chief problem in the self-perception of this harassed industry, as Damrow's introductory statement demonstrates. The complaint that the advertising industry's terrain was 'stony and weed-ridden'[11] reflected the lack of stringent standards and generally accepted terms of business. Neither in line-width or paper size, in price lists or discount rates, did anything like a consensus reign. An unsound system of graduated bonuses and the uncontrolled proliferation of trade fairs burdened the work of the advertising firms without any concomitant increase in turnover. The fudged sales figures of the newspapers was an additional deception perpetrated at the expense of the client. The splintered, fractious, and ineffectual advertising federations failed in such elementary professional tasks as the setting up of standardised training courses and protection against plagiarism, which explains the subsequent demands for the founding of a college of advertising and an 'advertising document centre'.[12] This lack of professional standards led the industry press to judge it a dilettantish free-for-all – 'Anyone who can string a few words together believes he can write advertising copy', calls himself an 'advertising expert'[13] – and helped thereby to ruin the reputation of the entire industry.

Time and again the trade periodicals pilloried the notoriously low standard of professional ethics, the excesses of many of the advertisements, and the wilful misleading of consumers.[14] Such conduct undermined all efforts at professional upgrading. German advertisers admired the 'Truth in Advertising Campaign' waged by US advertisers to boost their industry's respectability, but at the same time the American style was not welcomed unreservedly. Reception of pace-setting American advertising in Germany oscillated between naive admiration and desperate attempts at limiting its influence. Occasionally there would be calls for an indigenous 'German advertising'. Behind these calls lurked the fear of eventual domination by those large American firms that were pushing into the German market.[15]

The economic crisis and the industry's plight help explain the widespread desire for the state's strong ordering hand. In addition, advertisers admired the modern campaign style of the Nazis. No other political party made greater use of the strategies of commercial advertising. Hitler and Goebbels knew well the manipulative effects of advertising and systematically availed themselves of its methods for political propaganda.[16] From the perspective of advertisers, the National Socialists were a progressive party which, it was hoped, would show understanding for the concerns of the advertising industry. Therefore, in March 1933, the professional journal *Seidels Reklame* happily greeted the founding of the Propaganda Ministry and the extension of its competence to the sphere of advertising, for now its 'cultural and economic importance has found official recognition'.[17] As a result of this fundamental accommodation with the regime, the advertising federations were integrated into the new order with little real resistance. Younger members of the German Advertising Association (Deutschen Reklame-Verband – DRV), who were suffering most under the effects of the Great Depression, ousted the older group of directors. On 30 April 1933, in a public display of allegiance to the regime, the DRV staged a mass rally with the motto 'German Advertising for German Workmanship'.[18]

In its May issue, the DRV put a portrait of Hitler on the cover of its official organ and saluted the man who 'is Germany's greatest advertiser, selfless in duty and whom we are all beholden follow. From now on, advertising must accord with his vision'. Inside were quotations from Hitler stressing the importance of advertising as well as a paean to Goebbels, the 'Führer's Herald' who 'embodies the advertising ideals of the nation'. The article hoped that he would reshape commercial advertising so that it 'can unconditionally serve the Propaganda Ministry'.[19] Kow-towing to the new rulers and professional ambition went hand in hand.

Advertisers' expectations of the new state were focused on three central concerns. First, that the regime should use its authority to bring order out of the advertising industry chaos. Second, it was hoped that the industry's public esteem would increase through its participation in the state publicity campaigns. Third, that criticism of and interference with the advertising industry would desist. 'Above all, we hope that advertising will be freed from unnecessary red tape.'[20] But the National Socialist regime had other plans.

III
THE REGIME'S POWER-POLITICAL TACTICS

The monopolisation and strict control of advertising content was part of the regime's general media policy. Its understanding of the political potency of mass communication and the need for instruments of manipulation led the regime to monopolise radio, press, publishing, art, and advertising. In contrast to the 'individualistic' advertising of the 'Weimar system', the basic principle now would be 'the common good placed before individual interest' so that the advertising business would have a closer relationship with 'the whole of the German people'. Already in March 1933, in the first statement emanating from the Propaganda Ministry concerning advertising, the industry was exhorted to support the 'heroic struggle' of the German people 'and the formation of the state, culture, and economy in accordance with the inner German essence'.[21]

Closely intertwined with this educational mission was the comprehensive registration and filtering of all members of the industry. By virtue of new admissions and the annexation of other federations, in May 1933 DRV membership stood at 7,000; in 1929 it had been 4,000. In the summer of 1933 the DRV disbanded and joined, to a man, the newly established National Socialist Federation of German Advertisers (Nationalsozialistische Reichsfachschaft Deutscher Werbefachleute – NSRDW). This organisation encompassed all those employees or freelancers whose chief professional interest was advertising and who practised it in either a direct or advisory capacity. Because professional activity was predicated on NSRDW membership, by 1939 this compulsory organisation had swollen to 17,000. The NSRDW, which was at first subordinate to the Reich Culture Chamber

(Reichskulturkammer – RKK), was in 1936 placed under the purview of the Advertising Council for the German Economy.

For those engaged in advertising for third parties (such as cinema owners and the like) there were several separate organisations controlled by the RKK, the Reichsgruppen of the Ministry of Economics, and the Advertising Council. However, all of these were constrained to report to the Advertising Council for final approval.

The third group integrated (in 1935) into the Association of Media Salesmen (Reichsverband der Deutschen Werbungsmittler), which as of 1938 was directly responsible to the Advertising Council, consisted of media salesmen who negotiated advertising contracts for others mostly in the area of print ads. Admission was strictly regulated because as of 1934 the largest agency, Allgemeine Anzeigen GmbH (Ala), was part of the business empire of Nazi press magnate Max Amann.

The fourth group consisted of those firms advertising their own products. These were organised primarily by the Ministry of Economics' Reichsgruppen and other subordinate federations. The Advertising Alliance (Reklameschutz-bund, established 1920), to which belonged several of the most famous manufacturers of brand-name articles, was renamed as the Reich Federation of Advertisers (Reichsverband der Werbungtreibenden). This link to the commercial sector fell likewise under the jurisdiction of the Advertising Council. After 1936, as proxy to the Advertising Council, the Reich Federation of Advertisers fielded individual questions from businesses which were unclear as to the permissibility of certain texts and design formats. Membership here was voluntary.[22]

Because the Reichsgruppen and the federations functioned as connecting rods, the actions of the Advertising Council were felt only in an indirect way by the majority of the 'self-advertising' concerns. On the first day of November 1933 they had been granted general permission to carry out commercial advertising – a permission that in individual cases could be peremptorily rescinded. The lion's share of total advertising revenue fell to this loosely controlled group. According to expert estimates, in 1936 this revenue amounted to between one and 1.5 billion Reichsmarks, only 220 million of which was recorded in the books of the Advertising Council, that is, at most one-fifth of the real total. In 1935 the Advertising Council counted 50,000 people who were chiefly employed in the advertising industry, this compared with practically an entire German economy – ranging from craftsmen to big concerns – that was geared to self-advertising. The total figure of just 6,000 registered employees of firms advertising their own products indicates that the overwhelming majority of advertising contracts were granted to persons who were not formally registered with the Advertising Council.[23]

Within the industry itself, the Nazi system, through its comprehensive registration of advertisers by the NSRDW, helped to realise German advertising's long-standing desire for organisational unification. At the same time, both registration and reorganisation served to ostracise the industry's unwanted members. The articulated plan in 1933 to 'cleanse the German advertising industry of all harmful pests' meant the exclusion of all those having no relationship 'to Germanness, be it in outlook or in race'. Subsumed under this rubric were Jewish and foreign colleagues, political opponents, the artistic avant-garde, as well as those less tractable advertisers who persisted in so-called 'alien business practices'. As a result of their opportunism, as well as their self-willed centralisation and deformation, the advertising federations were able to 'cleanse' themselves. According to NSRDW statutes, applications for membership could be rejected if the 'applicant is personally unreliable or otherwise unsuitable'.[24] With this general clause, a *de facto* professional ban could be imposed on political opponents or foreigners. Only in special cases could foreign agencies receive permission to operate in Germany, and by 1937 they had been completely excluded from the business; foreign ad placements were likewise banished; the number of media salesmen shrunk from 250 in 1933 to 208 in 1937, chiefly a consequence of 'Aryanisation'. While as late as 1938 it was still possible for individual Jews to work in the advertising industry by dint of special permissions, all of these were withdrawn on 1 January 1939.[25]

The Nazi state's involvement with the advertising industry began relatively early, inaugurated by the 'Commercial Advertising Law' of 12 September 1933. In the period that followed, the industry became tightly corseted with regulations and strictures that were a far cry from the fragmentary and ineffectual law of the past. The Advertising Council was created as a special regulatory body that levied a two per cent tax on all turnover from 'third party' advertising; those advertising their own products were exempt from the fees. The Advertising Council was simply the long arm of the Propaganda Ministry. Goebbels appointed the members of the governing board as well as the president and secretary. All of these positions were occupied by ministerial bureaucrats or party careerists. By contrast, members of the Advertising Council's expert committees (named by the president) consisted primarily of representatives from commercial advertising firms and their clients. This interaction of commercial and state actors enabled the Advertising Council to operate with a relatively small staff, and between 1933 and 1941 it grew from 89 to only 189 persons. That despite its small size it was able to exercise an intensive regulatory function had much to do with the delegation of its various tasks to the associations of individual trades, industries, crafts, and above all to the federations of the advertising industry, all of whom contributed to the creation of new advertising laws.[26]

In many respects the Advertising Council resembled other trade associations, which after 1933 mutated into hybrid organisations that were at the same time both government offices and lobby groups. The main differences consisted in the greater penetration of the Advertising Council's leadership with ministerial bureaucrats and party functionaries, and in its direct subordination to the Propaganda Ministry, which had asserted itself over rival claims of the Ministry of Economics.

The intervention of the Advertising Council was intended to be totalitarian. Its competence extended from trade fairs and exhibitions to all other advertising events. In fact, it created a closed shop. Without its consent, no one could work in the industry. Without necessarily having to attend to any of the quotidian minutiae, the Advertising Council was an all-powerful body whose decisions were subject to neither appeal nor judicial review. Numerous edicts, decrees, and guidelines were issued covering all sorts of matters ranging from price structuring to paper format to word choice for advertisements.

However, this state intervention suffered in practice from the fact that many of the affected parties were unable to penetrate the thicket of rules and regulations. In 1936 one businessman even dared criticise the Advertising Council publicly. The printed address began with praise. No German government had been 'a greater friend of advertising' than Adolf Hitler's, yet legal uncertainty still reigned. Moreover, the industry had been 'disrupted' and 'inhibited' by the Advertising Council.

> [Its regulations,] in their officialese, are confusing and complicated ... They can only be understood by those who have sufficient time and energy to invest in an in-depth study. This is time and energy that businessmen can ill afford, especially if they are manager and advertiser in one person, quite frequently the case with smaller enterprises.[27]

Although the Advertising Council declared that advertising law was never to become a 'secret code', in 1938 it needed 266 single-space pages to compile 'just a part' of the current guidelines.[28]

These guidelines were consistently violated, and the Advertising Council made equally consistent use of its power to revoke licences or the threat to do so. There was no end of reprimands and other disciplinary action undertaken against the 'stubborn and careless'. Towards the end of the 1930s the Advertising Council adopted a harder line, issuing more warnings and revoking more licences. Another major problem was overlapping jurisdictions.[29] 'Rulings' of the Advertising Council partially contradicted Reich and state law as well as decrees concerning trade federations.

The toughest measures, and the ones most easily enforced, were those prohibiting certain advertising media. For instance, as of 1 January 1936 the radio was decreed commercial-free. Goebbels assigned radio the task of being an instrument of government policy and an entertainment medium. With a stroke of the pen the National Socialist regime put paid to that most modern of advertising media. Already banned in 1934 was 'foreign advertisement' in travel and business guides, in plant publications and company circulars, as well as in cinema programmes, telephone books, and free papers – all of these consisting chiefly or exclusively of advertisements. During the war there emerged numerous other prohibitions and restrictions.

IV

ECONOMIC POLICY AND PROFESSIONAL GOALS

The regime's interest in harnessing capitalist dynamism and the advertising industry's long-held wish for a uniform regulatory system led to a partial convergence of both the state's and the advertisers' goals. The Advertising Council's actions frequently matched the industry's old demands for reform, which boiled down to the creation of binding standards to eliminate chronic abuses. With the elaborate motto, 'Respect for the German racial community, tactfulness vis-à-vis competitors, truth and even-handedness in dealing with the consumer',[30] the Advertising Council assisted the industry in attaining a unified orderliness whose cornerstones were the setting of prices and discount rates, and the laying down of clear business conditions. In internal conflicts the Advertising Council served as the industry's clearing house – and in this way helped to propagate its own standards. 'Out of the melée has emerged a common effort to achieve the best possible performance.'[31] In comparison to the Weimar period, when disputes could only be adjudicated via the courts, there was now a simple and swift way of dealing with internal conflicts. On the other hand, Damrow's judgement of 'a level playing field for all' is a remarkable example of selective perception because the industry was no longer open to 'all' and the 'clear rules' were part of a totalitarian drive to suppress competition and create a politically regulated economy.

The rule of fixed, uniform prices was designed to remove the handicap borne by small advertising clients. The notion of 'integrity' also manifested itself in the newly created and closely monitored duty to declare the exact circulation of publications. In a similar way, the prohibition of 'ostentatious' and 'disparaging' advertisements was an attempt to elevate professional standards and win the confidence of the public. At least in the area of comparative advertising, precise limits were set and the worst excesses curtailed. In 1935 the Advertising Council forbade 'product plugs', insisting that a strict line be drawn between advertisement and editorial content. In order to increase market transparency, further norms were established in the area of column and line formats. So as to 'protect the public against dishonest, unclear, misleading and purposely deceptive advertising', testimonials and recommendations (often apocryphal) were only to be used with the 'written permission of the person to which it is attributed'. Unauthorised advertising that featured prominent politicians and athletes was also outlawed. The same was true of false assertions, particularly in advertisements for pharmaceuticals. The promiscuous increase in the number of trade fairs was brought to an end in 1934 through issuance of licences by the Advertising Council. Accordingly, their number sank from 634 in 1934 to 191 three years later.[32]

In the area of outdoor advertising there was likewise the establishment of sliding price and discount scales, as well as requiring that posters and placards conformed to the standards of the German Institute for Standardisation (Deutsches Institut für Normung – DIN). Advertising columns, billboards, and other posting areas had to meet minimum size requirements. Furthermore, only one billboard business per city was allowed, a ruling that worked chiefly to the detriment of Jews. One billboard for every 1,000 inhabitants was officially permitted, yet this limit was always exceeded. 'Random posting' was strictly forbidden. Seeking to circumscribe competition and closely monitor standards, these regulations appear to have been smoothly implemented.

With few exceptions, advertising in the countryside and along roads was no longer tolerated. In urban settings, defacing the cityscape was also to be avoided.[33] Furthermore, there were diverse restrictions due to laws protecting historic buildings and monuments. However, outdoor advertising long remained a contentious area, due on the one hand to the confusing quality of the Advertising Council's directives, and on the other to the various local and state statutes conflicting with these directives. In some regions there were frequent clashes with local heritage defenders and authorities which prohibited outdoor advertising as such. In these cases, the Advertising Council would speak out for 'freedom in advertising' and try to assert this freedom with the help of the Interior Ministry in Berlin.[34]

In addition, the Advertising Council began to promote professionalisation of the industry. The restrictions placed on advertisers was a protectionist shield against outsiders and foreigners, while at the same time serving to increase the industry's homogeneity. The prohibition against price wars protected small, uncompetitive firms. In order to expand the job market, an attempt was made to discourage 'self-advertisers', who had been the targets of much recent polemic. 'Who is not familiar with the imperious … entrepreneur, high-handedly dictating the form and content of his advertising … without consideration for those things that only the professional can be truly expert in'.[35]

In 1936 an abiding dream of the industry was realised with the founding of the College of Advertising (Reichswerbeschule). This Berlin-based pedagogical arm of the NSRDW provided continuing education and vocational training for young advertisers. Its unique diploma allowed holders to become members of the NSRDW and to practise their profession, as well as giving them the right to supervise apprentices. Taking the academic professions as its model, the long-term aspiration of the NSRDW was to make entry into its ranks the sole privilege of those holding the requisite degree. But initially it stressed its continued readiness – probably due to the Institute's limited capacity of 85 full-time students (1940) – to accept members without 'special educational preparation'.[36]

Furthermore, the Advertising Council desired to increase advertising sales. This goal was in opposition to certain fundamental tenets of the National Socialist economic system. Market regulatories and cartels, restrictions on investment, raw material shortages, as well as the growing burden of state consumption, all reduced the need for advertising and made for very limited growth. According to the Advertising Council, this 'unpleasant situation' called for campaigns explicating the usefulness of advertising, as well as promoting collective action in the form of common-cause advertising for entire industries.[37]

TABLE 1
ECONOMIC INDICATORS AND ADVERTISING INDICES

	Economic Indicators (volumes)			Advertising Indices		
	Industrial Production	Consumer Goods Production	Real GDP	Turnover Newspaper Ads	Turnover Ads in Journals	Fee Intake of the Advertising Council
1934	100	100	100	100	100	100
1935	115	98	112	105	110	117
1936	129	105	125	113	126	125
1937	141	111	139	124	138	125
1938	151	116	152	135	147	126
1939	159	116	181	–	–	148
1940	154	110	210	–	–	52
1941	158	112	239	–	–	60
1942	159	100	253	–	–	33
1943	180	105	269	–	–	38
1944	176	100	246	–	–	27

Sources: D. Reinhardt, *Von der Reklame zum Marketing: Geschichte der Wirtschaftswerbung in Deutschland* (Berlin, 1993), pp.143 and 201; A. Ritschl and M. Spoerer, 'Das Bruttosozialprodukt in Deutschland nach den amtlichen Volkseinkommens- und Sozialproduktsstatistiken 1901–1995', *Jahrbuch für Wirtschaftsgeschichte* 1997/II, pp.51–2; D. Petzina *et al.*, *Sozialgeschichtliches Arbeitsbuch III: Materialien zur Statistik des Deutschen Reiches 1914–1945* (Munich, 1978), pp.61 and 78.

In order to gauge the success of these efforts, Table 1 takes 1934 as its point of departure and compares general economic parameters and those of the advertising industry. Advertising volume was measured by the turnover of print advertisements and the intake of the Advertising Council, which was based on a tax levied on all advertising for clients. In most years these figures failed even to keep up with industrial production and the Gross National Product. In 1936, according to an estimate of the Advertising Council, sales were about one-third below those of 1929.[38] It is obvious, on the other hand, that the advertising indices outpaced consumer goods production. This observation can probably be explained by the fact that advertising turnover fell extremely low during the Great Depression and had more opportunity to regain ground.[39] In the Second World War, advertising volume drastically trailed industrial production and GNP indices.

In other words: commercial advertising did not gain in importance. Rather, turnover was stifled by the regime. Had it been operating in a more free-market economy, these sales figures would no doubt have ridden the coattails of the economic upswing that Nazi Germany was experiencing in these years. Instead, advertising rapidly lost any standing it might have acquired to that point, and the industry's rather unimpressive recovery following the Great Depression shows why the Advertising Council was so often on the defensive. It was surrounded by hostile adversaries. From their initial seizure of power, an attitude of anti-modernism had reigned among the National Socialists, and this included the suppression of advertising. The consumer goods industry, one of the main customers of the advertising business, was restricted in many ways by Nazi economic policy. With the Four-Year Plan of 1936 and the outbreak of war in 1939, impatience with advertising grew: it seemed to offer little to a nation gearing for war and then fighting for its very existence. Also, in view of the favourable economy and the surplus in demand, businessmen were not exactly eager to engage professional advertisers. The preservers of historic buildings and monuments unceasingly attacked the advertising industry. The Advertising Council met these attacks and entrepreneurial reticence with the authority of a state organ, but could only point to limited success. It concentrated its arguments on the economic importance of advertising, that is, on its creation of jobs and the general economic impetus it lent, as well as on its cultural-political and educational tasks. Another argument occasionally forwarded was one that in the late period of the Federal Republic would emerge as a leitmotif of commercial advertising's self-justification: 'Advertising is art', declared Heinrich Hunke, named in 1939 as second president of the Advertising Council.[40]

The Advertising Council suffered clear defeats not only in striving for greater sales but also in the struggle against advertising restrictions from the side of cartels, industry federations, and the professions. The latitude afforded outdoor advertising was far less than that during the Weimar years. After 1939 nothing could be done about new restrictions on advertising following the shortages of the war economy, apart from delaying their application. Still, advertising survived until 1944, even if sales after 1939 (Table 1) plummeted. In order to fight the wartime 'advertising fatigue', the Advertising Council invested a great deal into a campaign called 'Continue to Advertise!' Moreover, ideas were floated by which the advertising industry could serve the war economy by acting as an indispensable manipulator for the ruling powers.

V

TOWARDS 'GERMANIC ADVERTISING':
CULTURAL-POLITICAL GUIDELINES

Problems with government control of advertising were most visible when intervention was motivated by ideology, especially in the cultural-political realm. At first there was the struggle against so-called 'Nazi kitsch'. The advertising business has always shamelessly appropriated the latest trends. This can be seen as either a lack of scruples or a salubrious flexibility, but it is in any case an essential trait. The motto, 'Times change and we change with them', was first formulated in early 1933 when there was an onslaught of swastikas and Hitler portraits being used in advertisements. Exploitation and tastelessness knew no bounds. Aprons and scrub brushes adorned with swastikas flooded the market, as well as playing cards ornamented with the heads of top Nazis. Butchers decorated their front windows with busts of the Führer carved from pig lard, and bakers cut swastikas into their dough. The catchphrase, 'It is the

Führer's desire', was used for virtually every product. Sales representatives donned Stormtrooper uniforms in order to impress their clients.[41]

From the standpoint of the new regime, this was a dangerous development, for it trivialised National Socialism's central symbols and even made them to look silly. Therefore, Goebbels, who has been described as a 'brand technician', acted quickly and decisively. In an act similar to securing a trademark, on 19 May 1933 he promulgated the 'Law to Protect National Symbols', in which he gave the NSDAP and the state exclusive rights to their national emblems. As a rule, their usage was forbidden for advertising purposes. Likewise prohibited was their decorative use on products or solely to boost sales. The police were permitted to seize without warrant any items that excited their suspicion, with an official judgement only then to follow. In 1933 there was a campaign in the industry press against those 'cheap marketing strategies at the expense of the Volk's [German people's] most sacred feelings',[42] and that summer an exhibition was held showing negative examples of advertisements using national motifs.

The legal situation was again somewhat confusing. In contrast to its general guidelines, the actual law of 19 May 1933 did not *completely* forbid advertising's use of Nazi symbols, but simply outlawed injuries to their 'dignity'. It was left unclear what that might entail. The NSDRW simply transmitted the text of the new law and asked that ideas be forwarded as to what 'dignified' and 'undignified' advertising might constitute. Various wings of the administration contradicted one another on the issue.[43] But, generally speaking, after 1933 advertisers exercised increasing restraint in their use of regime symbols and did so without direct reference to the party. The grotesque excesses of early 1933 largely vanished, though because the regulations were in many cases still being ignored they had to be repeated on occasion. Advertisers were finally learning the art of suggestion: for example, showing marching columns without national emblems. On the whole, however, the regime's brand-name strategy proved a success.

This was not necessarily true of the regime's – especially in its early stages – attempts at Germanifying the industry. It demanded the replacement of 'Jewish advertising' with 'German advertising', which, according to the Advertising Council, should no longer imitate foreign models and should be German 'in attitude and expression'. The industry press asserted: 'Public taste changes from day to day; the taste of the *Volk* remains immutable over the ages.' This taste was 'an outgrowth of the racial blood ... Let us jettison public taste and festoon the bow of our ship with a new escutcheon – the taste of the Volk'.[44] Practical examples of 'true German feeling' were then cited. Accompanying illustrations were of a mountain idyll that advertised a Black Forest scarf factory, and of wearers of traditional costume who hand-washed their linen in a tub and used exclusively Sunlight Soap from the British Lever concern. The texts were in the recommended 'urdeutsch' Gothic script, which it was hoped would drive out 'undeutsche' Latin type such as the Roman.

As a matter of fact, after 1933 advertisements were increasingly printed in Gothic lettering, which, because of the decelerated reading speed, signified a step backward in the area of graphics. Although Gothic never became the advertising standard, it was frequently employed to demonstrate a proper national 'attitude'. Mistrust of foreign firms may have been the compelling factor in Lever's decision to use Gothic for its German advertisements.

The use of antiquated type, the resuscitation of medieval imagery, the depictions of serried ranks of marching men, the 'völkisch' and martial motifs of 'Blut-und-Boden' paintings devoted to the glorification of a kind of rustic heroism – these were all typical of an advertising industry that aimed at political correctness. Moreover, a fondness for the supposedly apolitical world of consumerism was one of the prime features of the 'divided consciousness' of society under National Socialism. And advertising certainly catered to this split-level psyche. The diversion afforded by advertising, and the illusion of normality it helped create, served in the long term to stabilise the regime. Foreign advertising was closely observed even during the war, leading to a precarious tightrope act: 'It is certainly not necessary for us to ape foreign models, but we will never dispute the fact that there is ... a good deal ... that can be learned from them'.[45]

The frequently used comic strips of American advertising never gained much ground in Germany before the 1950s. Their American success – according to the German advertising industry press – was owing to the lower educational level and 'naïveté of the American'. An 'uncritical adoption of this form of ad ... is to be in all cases avoided'. There was an authentic German form of picture-advertisement that was recommended as 'something different'.[46] The cited examples distinguished themselves from the American cartoons only in their rhymed captions, their Gothic print, and their banal and simple-minded design.

With the battle cry, 'Eliminate Foreignness!', the Advertising Council worked to Germanise the language of advertising. Using as a model similar campaigns employed during the First World War, product terms were Germanified. Many of the suggestions were so abstruse that they never caught on, like the designation for perfume ('Riechwasser', literally 'smell water') or whisky ('Rauchbrand', 'smoked brandy'). In 1938 the textile industry received a 'Germanification list', with 152 terms such as 'Mischung' ('mixture') instead of 'Melange', or 'Aufschlag' ('lapel') instead of 'Revers'. These linguistic contortions in the name of purity were a disadvantage at international trade fairs. They confused both sellers and clients and thus met with resistance, frequently successful.[47] Attempts to change and manipulate language is a feature of all dictatorships. The Nazis often employed disingenuous language to distort their political and criminal intentions and to create a new perception. Victor Klemperer referred to the new German created by the regime as 'lingua tertii imperii'.

There were similar ambivalences in the Nazi's agenda concerning women. According to the regime's perception, an 'alien' female type had established itself in advertising under 'Jewish-Marxist leadership'. One encountered 'everywhere film stars and made-up dolls with shaved eyebrows ... in flirty poses ... not a trace of German essence. The German woman takes care of herself, but she is not "touched up" with razor blades and lipstick and powder'. Advertising should remain true to 'German customs', and instead of actresses, it should portray 'the housewife in her natural surroundings'. 'For instance, after doing the dishes in the kitchen, showing how she applies X-Creme to her hands.'[48]

In fact, after 1933 many firms placed advertisements with blue-eyed peasant women and mothers whose blond hair and high foreheads must have pleased racial fanatics. At the same time, the fashionable woman did not die out. Cigarette advertising turned a deaf ear to the Reich Surgeon General's admonition that 'the German woman does not smoke', regularly depicting women who did indeed smoke. Their hedonistic style and fashionable clothes and haircuts were in direct opposition to the government's express wishes. The forced attempt to introduce 'German' fashions ended in an embarrassing fiasco. Even in the Third Reich, it was international fashion which set the tone – or, more precisely, Parisian fashion.

The design guidelines of the Advertising Council were riddled with fuzzy notions about 'German feeling', 'German style', 'dignity', and 'honesty'.49 Even if the advertisers wanted to abide by the Advertising Council's instructions, they were stymied by the translation of these vague concepts into real terms. The industry periodicals pretended to see marked differences in advertising styles before and after 1933, but even in the highly selective examples they adduced to buttress this notion, what was most striking were the similarities.[50] The criterion of 'Germanic advertising' remained cryptic and ill-defined. And where the new guidelines took hold, in advertisements with Gothic lettering and Germanised terms, the results were old-fashioned and tedious. But the pressure to Germanify decreased over time as the first phase of the Third Reich ebbed and with it the initial wave of cultural agitation. All in all, the regime was unable to establish a distinct National Socialist advertising style.

VI

ADVERTISING AS AN INSTRUMENT OF REGULATING CONSUMPTION

From the very beginning, the National Socialist state regarded advertising as a means for 'controlling demand with a velvet touch', which would thus 'supplement' the pressure applied in the fight against the chronic currency and raw materials shortages. Already in 1933 the government had proclaimed:

> It is infuriating that even in this era of exchange controls ... 20,000 Marks worth of French lipstick and perfume cross the border into Germany every day. Advertising must step into the breach ... It must ... ceaselessly exhort the German consumer to buy German! ... The German compulsion ... to

worship all that is foreign must be shown for what it is ... a sickness contributing to German unemployment.[51]

The first area of concern was the advertisement of German goods so as to create greater demand at home and help lift Germany out of the Depression. The common-cause advertising of regions and industries, which replaced advertisements by individual companies – promoted by the Advertising Council as a means to counteract the 'individualism' of the Weimar period – was primarily concerned with helping ailing regions or industries back on their feet. For example, via trade federations, campaigns were organised for German wine and milk. There was hardly an industry, from handicrafts to tourism, from energy to transport, that did not participate in the drive.

Soon after the announcement of the 'New Plan' of 1934, which established a more *dirigiste* style of foreign trade, traditional advertising was augmented by a push for the conservation of resources, consumer belt-tightening, and the utilisation of ersatz materials. In 1934/35 the phase of a broad stimulation of demand in order to reduce unemployment ended. The new motto was: it is 'no longer permitted ... to create a demand greater than that which actually exists'.52 Within the framework of the preparations for war, this new common-cause advertising took on the colour of consumer manipulation. Advancing the theoretical tools for this propaganda were economists from the Nuremberg Institute for Economic Research and Nuremberg's Society for Consumer Research. Later Economic Minister of the Federal Republic, Ludwig Erhard, judged the old capitalist advertising to be 'an end in itself' and 'fun and games' for egotistical entrepreneurs. Their uncoordinated manipulations, as well as the 'moods of the consumer', had led to an 'upsetting of the market' and to impediments placed in the path of rational economic planning. Common-cause advertising, on the other hand, was 'a superior form of advertising'. In the new state, advertising had a 'supra-economic task' vis-à-vis the customer: to 'lead and ... not ... lead astray'.53

This consumer control in the guise of common-cause advertising and under the direction of the Advertising Council and the subordinate Reich Committee for Economic Enlightenment (Reichsausschuß für Volkswirtschaftliche Aufklärung – RVA) was to be a model for the future. But the 1936 campaign 'Don't Let Your Food Spoil', almost simultaneous with the Four-Year Plan, can be viewed as a prototype. Slogans such as 'Eat more fish' were designed to reduce dependence on food imports, and the topic of 'consumer control' dominated advertising periodicals. Already by the beginning of the year the following principle had been formulated: 'Advertising has become an instrument of state politics in the economic sphere. Its task is to steer the customer to buy in a way that benefits the commonweal. The ideal of consumer politics is the tractable customer'. Although such a concept gained rapidly in prestige as of 1936, until 1939 purely commercial advertising and the new 'enlightenment' in the framework of the Four-Year Plan led parallel lives. Even in early 1939, 'German Advertising' was still trying to close the 'gap' between state 'enlightenment' and private advertising.[54]

It was only with the outbreak of war that a comprehensive change took place. The dramatic collapse in advertising sales during the first months of the war and the immediate demands for a general advertising prohibition eroded resistance to state regulation of the industry. At the same time, the state increased its pressure. The final result was a palpable reduction in the volume of advertisement. Between 1939 and 1940 the Advertising Council's revenue fell by almost two-thirds. The compromise struck between the war economy and advertising resulted in a 'completely new alignment'. Commercial advertising in the sense of creating demand and 'whetting appetites' was no longer 'appropriate'. As an alternative, three forms of wartime advertising were propagated:[55] 1. 'Consumer control' to promote ersatz products; 2. 'Enlightened advertising' to promote greater understanding of the war economy, for example rationing and energy-saving and fibre-friendly methods of washing clothes; 3. 'Frugality advertising' to systematically shrink demand for and the sales of certain products in order to cover up shortages and reduce them through voluntary austerity programmes.

The regime's hopes of stabilising supply failed because of the desperate shortage of raw materials and currency and the inherent shortcomings of the war economy advertising concept. For one, the consumer was not easily manipulated. For another, the new style of advertising offered entrepreneurs sufficient scope to pursue their vested interest in whipping up demand. In practice, the 'new' advertising styles were not much different from conventional commercial advertising. In addition, the economy saw no point in working systematically against its own commercial interests. Even the Advertising Council had to concede that entrepreneurs 'who for decades have used advertising to create demand cannot adapt to a new form of advertising overnight'. Advertisers' typical *modus operandi* was to fulfil conditions of the Advertising Council out of a sense of duty while still creating or even heightening demand for certain products – much confusion reigning as to what was and was not a scarcity.[56]

Advertising in the consumer-control style finally succumbed to the same loss of credibility from which the political propaganda suffered. The contradictions between message and reality were simply too crass. If secret police's reports on the people's mood are any gauge, then anxiety concerning the supply situation never abated. Consumers knew very well that ersatz materials were of lower quality and that mere thrift could not end the shortages. The call to moderate one's consumption with empty shop windows lining the street had as cynical a ring to it as the call to fight on in a militarily hopeless situation. The regime's illusion that it could skilfully manipulate the consumer and thus eliminate or neutralise certain insoluble problems of the German war economy proved to be as megalomanical as the quest for German global hegemony.

Until the very end of the war, advertising volume was reduced by restrictive governmental measures, the growing paper shortage, and the drafting of advertising personnel. Consequently, the revenue of the Advertising Council in 1944 was 27 per cent what it was in 1934 and 18 per cent what it was in 1939. In 1943 the most important advertising periodicals had to stop publication altogether. As of 1944 the Advertising Council's circular was defunct. By the end of the year, advertising was virtually non-existent.

VII
CONCLUSION

The National Socialist state recognised the power-political significance of advertising relatively early and imposed upon it a totalitarian set of rules. The effectiveness of this authoritarian takeover was from the very beginning thwarted by the regime's strategy of 'self-administration of the economy', which provided ample opportunity for lobbying and the safeguarding of vested interests. In lieu of a sufficiently large apparatus, systematic pre-censoring of all advertisement was impossible. The effectiveness of the regulations was also limited by the vagueness of the cultural-political guidelines. In the end, the technocratic ideal of an easily manipulated consumer proved itself a chimera.

The advertising industry welcomed the Nazi takeover for two reasons. First, the Nazis were ardent users of all kinds of modern advertising techniques and thus seemed to be natural allies. Secondly, they promised and seemed able to solve the structural problems of the industry. However, the advertising industry's expectations that the Nazi regime would upgrade its professional standing were not fulfilled. Accommodation with the Third Reich helped bestow upon advertising the compulsory standards it had so long desired. But the price paid was not merely the exclusion of Jewish and foreign colleagues, for the hopes of a liberation from 'unnecessary red tape' proved to be illusory. The dream of a dynamic upswing within an established framework permitting individual advertisers room to manoeuvre turned out to be a bureaucratic nightmare with meagre economic results. The regime pushed producer goods to the detriment of the consumer goods industry. Despite the industry's eager support for the regime, it grew much more slowly than the economy as a whole. The state's intervention amounted to a step-by-step transformation of the advertisement from a private sales instrument to one placed in the service of a war economy. Instead of sales promotion, advertising was now to promote sacrifices and rationing in the cause of wartime economic mobilisation. By the end of the National Socialist era, perversion, self-denial, and decay were the hallmarks of German advertising.

What were the long-term consequences for German advertising? Did National Socialist policy have a retarding or progressive impact? Leading members of the profession regarded the experience of a unified organisational structure and strict regulations as pointing the way to the future. After 1945 they complained more loudly of the 'disorder' and 'excesses' of the Weimar period than they did of their status under the Nazis. As in many cases, they had been part of the Nazi system of advertising, in which industrial lobbying and political regulation had become bedfellows, they tried to exonerate themselves by stressing the regime's 'beneficial and constructive interventions' in their industry and separating them from the evil character of the regime as a whole. Thus they managed to stay in the industry and its lobbying organisations after 1945. Moreover, the technical standardisation initiated by the Third Reich was carried into the Federal Republic, as well as the nascent professionalisation strategy, particularly in the area of education. For all that, the industry failed to establish a professional degree, and to this day advertising remains a relatively open field. Even if advertisers' confidence had grown as a result of their close working relationship with the National Socialist state, in the early years of the Federal Republic reservations about the industry were still very strong – although there was simultaneously a disproportionate growth in advertising sales relative to GNP.

If these modernising factors are balanced with the retarding effects of Nazi advertising policy, it is clear that on the whole stagnation and regression predominated. The cultural-political guidelines of the regime pointed backward into the past, especially in the preference for old German lettering and 'ideals', as well as the ludicrous Germanification campaign. Advertising was completely banished from that most modern of media – the radio; also forbidden were pioneering methods such as the use of sports stars and the publication of free newspapers; and the expulsion of Jewish and foreign advertisers robbed the industry of many of its most creative minds. Given the Advertising Council's farrago of complex restrictions, often it was safest simply to stick with conventional and unexciting advertising campaigns. Advertising sales eventually lagged behind general economic development – that is to say, commercial advertising decreased in relative importance. In other words, there is no reason to interpret the fate of the industry as an example of economic modernisation.

The artificial preservation of small business structures, the protectionist stance towards foreign competition, and the elimination of price competition hindered the formation of competitive big businesses. That explains, among other things, why after 1945 American agencies were able to establish themselves so easily in the Federal Republic and take over German firms.57 That future model of the full-service agency never had a chance under the National Socialist regime, if only because of the forced and inflexible subdivision of the advertising profession. Under such circumstances, the gap between antiquated German advertising and the American style could only widen. The 'modernization' of the advertising industry in the Third Reich remained partial at best; regression was the rule.

NOTES

1. H. Damrow, *Ich war kein geheimer Verführer* (Rheinzabern, 1981), p.47.
2. H. Strauf, 'Werbung im Wandel seit 1945 als Standort für den Ausblick', in C. Hundhausen (ed.), *Werbung im Wandel 1945–1995* (Essen, 1972), p.4.
3. For summaries, see C. Dipper, 'Modernisierung des Nationalsozialismus', *Neue Politische*

Literatur, Vol.36 (1991), pp.450–56; N. Frei, 'Wie modern war der Nationalsozialismus?' *Geschichte und Gesellschaft*, Vol.19 (1993), pp.367–87; H. Mommsen, 'Nationalsozialismus als vorgetäuschte Modernisierung', in idem (ed.), *Der Nationalsozialismus und die deutsche Gesellschaft* (Reinbek, 1991), pp.405–27; H. Berghoff, 'Did Hitler Create a New German Society? Continuities and Changes in German Social History before and after 1933', in P. Panayi (ed.), *Weimar and Nazi Germany: Continuities and Discontinuities* (London, 2001), pp.74–104.

4. D.J.K. Peukert, *Die Weimarer Republik: Krisenjahre der klassischen Moderne* (Frankfurt/M., 1987), p.266. See also pp.166–90.

5. D. Reinhardt, *Von der Reklame zum Marketing: Geschichte der Wirtschaftswerbung in Deutschland* (Berlin, 1993), pp.441–5.

6. *Seidels Reklame* (*SR*) 1928, p.306.

7. See R. Marchand, *Advertising the American Dream: Making Way for Modernity, 1920–1940* (Berkeley, CA, 1985), p.8; U. Westphal, *Werbung im Dritten Reich* (Berlin, 1989), p.18.

8. See F. Redlich, *Reklame: Begriff-Geschichte-Theorie* (Stuttgart, 1935), pp.177–205; C. Wischermann, 'Grenzenlose Werbung? Die gesellschaftliche Akzeptanz der Werbewelt im 20. Jahrhundert', in C. Wischermann and P. Borscheid (eds.), *Bilderwelten des Alltags* (Stuttgart, 1995), p.377.

9. *SR* 1929, p.343.

10. Ibid., p.347. The convention received a certain acknowledgement by an official reception of the German government and an inaugural speech by Foreign Minister Stresemann. Chancellor Müller and President Hindenburg, however, did not take the opportunity to welcome the large number of foreign advertising specialists.

11. *Deutsche Werbung* (*DW*) 1933, p.303.

12. *SR* 1929, p.346; 1930, p.134. For the internal conflicts see *SR* 1928, p.306.

13. *SR* 1930, p.337.

14. See *SR* 1930, p.134.

15. See D. Schindelbeck, '"Asbach Uralt" und "Soziale Marktwirtschaft". Zur Kulturgeschichte der Werbeagentur in Deutschland am Beispiel von Hanns W. Brose (1899–1971)', *Zeitschrift für Unternehmensgeschichte*, Vol.40 (1995), p.236.

16. See *DW* 1932, p.269; P. Longerich, 'Nationalsozialistische Propaganda', in K.D. Bracher *et al.* (eds.), *Deutschland 1933–1945: Neue Studien zur nationalsozialistischen Herrschaft* (Düsseldorf, 1992), pp.291–6; Westphal, *Werbung*, pp.26–7.

17. *SR* 1933, p.77. Prior to 1933, the advertising industry's journals had been politically neutral.

18. *DW* 1933, pp.236–7; *SR* 1933, pp.112, 145 and 304–29; Reinhardt, *Reklame*, pp.137–9. The older functionaries had to step down but stayed in the profession in most cases unless they were persecuted for racist reasons.

19. *DW* 1933, pp.299 and 302.

20. *SR* 1933, p.77. At the same time, the new ministry received a long list with suggestions and wishes of the advertising profession.

21. *SR* 1933, p.110b.

22. See *SR* 1938, p.136; Reinhardt, *Reklame*, pp.132–3.

23. The council's rules did apply to them just the same; *DW* 1936, p.539; R. Riedemann, *Was ist erlaubt – was ist verboten? Werberecht von A bis Z* (Reutlingen, 1938), p.171.

24. *SR* 1933, p.183; *DW* 1933, p.320; *DW* 1933, p.320; *Wirtschaftwerbung. Amtliches Organ des Werberates* (*WW*) 1936, p.2.

25. See Reinhardt, *Reklame*, pp.114–18; Westphal, *Werbung*, pp.67–9 and 97–108; *SR* 1939, p.417; *WW* 1938, pp.11–12.

26. Reinhardt, *Reklame*, pp.141–5.

27. *DW* 1936, pp.537–8.

28. *SR* 1936, p.3; Riedemann, *Was ist erlaubt*, p.7.

29. *SR* 1937, p.348; *WW* 1940, p.5. Statistics regarding the council's sanctions were kept secret. Individual cases, however, were regularly published with the name and full address of the delinquents. *SR* 1939, pp.82–3.

30. *WW* 1937, p.84.

31. *SR* 1936, p.160.

32. See *WW* 1935, p.6 (quotation); *SR* 1934, pp.475–6 (quotation); *SR* 1938, p.6.

33. *SR* 1934, pp.201–4.

34. See *DW* 1939, pp.412–15; *WW* 1938, pp.73–6; Reinhardt, *Reklame*, pp.384–6.

35. *SR* 1936, p.342.
36. *WW* 1936, p.36. See also Westphal, *Werbung*, pp.90–96; Reinhardt, *Reklame*, p.140.
37. *WW* 1935, p.11.
38. H. Hunke, *Die neue Wirtschaftswerbung: Eine Grundlegung der deutschen Werbepolitik* (Hamburg, 1938), p.50.
39. Unfortunately my sources did not allow me to choose a different base year.
40. *DW* 1939, p.159.
41. Vgl. *SR* 1933, p.6 (quotation); *WW* 1934, pp.44–5, 66, 133 and 149; *WW* 1935, pp.36 and 39; H. Berghoff, 'Konsumgüterindustrie im Nationalsozialismus: Marketing im Spannungsfeld von Profit- und Regimeinteressen', *Archiv für Sozialgeschichte*, Vol.36 (1996), pp.304–8; Westphal, *Werbung*, pp.44–50.
42. *DR* 1933, p.420.
43. H. Berghoff, *Zwischen Kleinstadt und Weltmarkt: Hohner und die Harmonika 1857–1961. Unternehmensgeschichte als Gesellschaftsgeschichte* (Paderborn, 1997), pp.383–4.
44. Quoted by Riedemann, *Was ist erlaubt*, p.190; *SR* 1934, p.381.
45. *SR* 1934, p.408; H.D. Schäfer, *Das gespaltene Bewußtsein: Über deutsche Kultur und Lebenswirklichkeit 1933–1945* (Munich, 1981), pp.114–62.
46. *SR* 1937, p.7.
47. *SR* 1939, p.83 (quote); *WW* 1936, pp.80–81; *WW* 1938, pp.91–2 and 97–8; Westphal, *Werbung*, pp.50–53.
48. *WW* 1933, pp.392–3.
49. *DW* 1933, p.310.
50. *SR* 1936, pp.106–10 and 158–60.
51. Hunke, *Die neue Wirtschaftswerbung*, p.55; *DW* 1933, p.316. For a general survey, H. Berghoff, 'Enticement and Deprivation: The Regulation of Consumption in Pre-war Nazi Germany', in M. Daunton and M. Hilton (eds.), *The Politics of Consumption: Material Culture and Citizenship in Europe and America* (Oxford, 2001), pp.165–84.
52. *SR* 1935, p.81.
53. L. Erhard, 'Werbung und Konsumforschung', *Die Deutsche Fertigware*, Vol.7 (1935), Part A, pp.41–8. At the same time Erhard rejected the idea of dictating consumption patterns by the state.
54. *SR* 1936, p.25. See also *SR* 1936, p.341; 1939, pp.82, 266 and 406; *DW* 1939, p.6. More details in H. Berghoff, 'Von der "Reklame" zur Verbrauchslenkung. Werbung im nationalsozialistischen Deutschland', in idem (ed.), *Konsumpolitik: Die Regulierung des privaten Verbrauchs im 20. Jahrhundert* (Göttingen, 1999), pp.77-112.
55. *SR* 1939, p.406; *DW* 1940, p.72.
56. *WW* 1942, pp.266 and 293–4.
57. H. Schröter, 'Die Amerikanisierung der Werbung in der Bundesrepublik Deutschland', *Jahrbuch für Wirtschaftsgeschichte*, Vol.1 (1997), pp.93–115.

Abstracts

Madame Tussaud and the Business of Wax: Marketing to the Middle Classes, *by Pamela Pilbeam*

This essay explores the unique development of the Tussaud Wax Exhibition in the first half of the nineteenth century. Madame Tussaud was trained in the art and display of wax figures by Philippe Curtius in Paris. In 1802 she embarked on a wax tour of Britain, and never left. At a personal level her odyssey was amazing. When she arrived, in her 40s, she knew no one and was alone, apart from her tiny child. She had an interesting collection of wax figures, but little money and spoke no English. She ran a travelling wax show until 1835, when she settled in London. In her own lifetime her Baker Street Exhibition became the leading tourist attraction in the capital. This article explains how she was able to capture and hold a share of the bourgeois entertainment market and make her wax exhibition a 'national institution'.

Purposive Strategy or Serendipity? Development and Diversification in Three Consumer Product Companies, 1918–39: J. & J. Colman, Reckitt & Sons, and Lever Bros./Unilever, *by Roy Church and Christine Clark*

Combining the neo-classical model of imperfect competition approximating to the markets in which the three firms competed with the resource-oriented and agency concepts of Edith Penrose, this essay describes, analyses and compares the evolution of the product development policies of three leading British consumer goods companies between the world wars. Historical profiles of the size, structural, and organisational features, and of the managerial resources within each firm are compared, as is the process by which searches were instituted through committees charged with the task of product diversification and development. An assessment of the progress, outcomes, and relative success of such policies reveals the contingent nature of the process. The conclusion that serendipity as well as rational purposive strategy contributed to the patterns of product diversification offers a novel interpretation of one vital but neglected dimension of the business process.

Closing the Deal: GM's Marketing Dilemma and its Franchised Dealers, 1921–41, *by Sally Clarke*

If marketing enticed consumers into a car dealer's showroom, consumers' activities in buying automobiles – trading in their old vehicle, selecting new features and frills, and financing their purchases on instalments – created sources of tension between buyers and sellers, not only consumers and dealers but also dealers and manufacturers. Among automobile companies, General Motors led the field in its techniques for marketing cars and relying on franchised dealers to sell them. GM's CEO, Alfred P. Sloan, Jr., offered a narrative of dealer relations in his classic study, *My Years with General Motors*. Sloan explained his methods for systematically evaluating dealers' performance so as to sustain a network of healthy retailers as well as the firm's efficiency in co-ordinating production with demand. Although Sloan did not point to the conflicts between buyers and sellers in market transactions, federal regulators did. Their investigations invite an alternative narrative to Sloan's account, focusing on how management used their dealer network to cope with the tensions inherent in marketing automobiles. This perspective draws our attention to the nature of corporate power as seen in the firm's method of distribution; the question of distrust in market exchanges; and the role of the state in shaping car sales and market transactions.

Foreign Multinationals and Innovation in British Retailing, 1850–1962, *by Andrew Godley*

This essay draws on the first systematic study of foreign direct investment in British retailing up to the 1960s. It shows that while foreign multinationals were unimportant in British retailing overall, they dominated some retail trades. Moreover, these retail entrants were mostly not by retailers but by manufacturers. Their motives varied but were mostly seemingly related to their need to control distribution channels and build brands. Foreign retailers *per se* were actually relatively rare and mostly unsuccessful. In contrast to British manufacturing, therefore, foreign innovations were not by and large introduced into British retailing by multinational enterprises. The article then explains why these foreign manufacturers of branded consumer goods pursued international marketing strategies that involved investing in costly retail outlets.

Building Knowledge about the Consumer: The Emergence of Market Research in the Motion Picture Industry, *by Gerben Bakker*

The way film companies obtained knowledge about the consumer resembled that of fashion industries. Initially, intermediaries analysed sales and observed customers while they consumed the service. As the film industry developed between the 1890s and the 1940s, however, its gathering of information increasingly began to resemble the market research of mass-distribution industries. Technological and contractual changes, as well as a rise in sunk costs, affected the way market research was done. By the late 1930s, film companies' increasing need for market information quickly made them adopt the newly

available market research techniques. This essay traces this evolution showing
how market research techniques were systematised and developed. The surveys
by the British Granada Theatres cinema chain stood on the threshold of the era
of modern market research, while the work of George Gallup's Audience
Research of the US marked its advent.

**'Times Change and We Change with Them': The German Advertising
Industry in the Third Reich – Between Professional Self-Interest and
Political Repression,** *by Hartmut Berghoff*

In 1933 the German advertising industry welcomed the Nazi regime because it
promised to overcome the Great Depression and to improve the trade's
organisation and social status. Hitler's government immediately subjected
advertising to comprehensive political regulation, which was not in every case
efficient or practical. This essay examines the aims and methods of the regime's
measures and the industry's responses, which alternated between opportunism
and assertion of its self-interest. Although in the years 1933–39 a number of
long-standing professional problems were solved, the industry incurred a high
price, namely the arbitrary intervention of a racist and to some extent anti-
capitalistic dictatorship chiefly interested in preparing and waging war.

Index

Books of Related Interest

Business Institutions and Behaviour in Australia

David Merrett, *University of Melbourne* (Ed)

> *'an interesting collection of papers succeeds in its aim of providing
> a sample of work done by Australian business historians and
> placing it in a context for overseas scholars.'*
> **Asia Pacific Business Review**

This volume breaks new ground in the historical study of Australian
business institutions and practices. It places the rise of big business in
Australia in a comparative context through a study of its 100 largest firms in
the first six and a half decades of the twentieth century. Unlike many of the
wealthy economies of the northern hemisphere, Australia's lists of the 100
largest firms were dominated up to World War II by those from the resource
and service industries. The high levels of foreign direct investment in the
resources and manufacturing industries is also highlighted. Other chapters
employ modern theories of the firm to explore business behaviour in more
depth than has been the case in previous writings in Australian business
history. This collection presents important new research findings and signals
new directions for future research.

168 pages 2000
0 7146 4994 5 cloth
0 7146 8055 9 paper
A special issue of the journal Business History

FRANK CASS PUBLISHERS
Crown House, 47 Chase Side, Southgate, London N14 5BP
Tel: +44 (0)20 8920 2100 Fax: +44 (0)20 8447 8548 E-mail: info@frankcass.com
NORTH AMERICA
5824 NE Hassalo Street, Portland, OR 97213 3644, USA
Tel: 800 944 6190 Fax: 503 280 8832 E-mail: cass@isbs.com
Website: www.frankcass.com

The Emergence of Modern Retailing 1750–1950

Nicholas Alexander, *Bournemouth University* and
Gary Akehurst, *Portsmouth University* (Eds)

This volume considers the emergence and development of modern retailing
from an historical and management perspective in the period 1750–1950.
The history of retail business development is an under-researched area and
these studies address the need for further research and provide examples of
current research activity. The book considers the early emergence of retail
forms in the late eighteenth century, the evolution of retail forms in the
nineteenth century and the late adaptation of retail innovation in the early
twentieth century.

This book brings together the literature from retail management as well as
history. In this, it bridges the gap between the two disciplines. This gap in
the understanding of the historical dimension within retail management
studies and the understanding of retail management issues in history has
hindered the development of valuable research in this area.

184 pages 1999
0 7146 4922 8 cloth
0 7146 4481 1 paper
A special issue of the journal Business History

FRANK CASS PUBLISHERS
Crown House, 47 Chase Side, Southgate, London N14 5BP
Tel: +44 (0)20 8920 2100 Fax: +44 (0)20 8447 8548 E-mail: info@frankcass.com
NORTH AMERICA
5824 NE Hassalo Street, Portland, OR 97213 3644, USA
Tel: 800 944 6190 Fax: 503 280 8832 E-mail: cass@isbs.com
Website: www.frankcass.com